...the best of Oklahoma

The Junior League of Oklahoma City, Inc.
Oklahoma City, Oklahoma

*The purpose of the Junior League is exclusively educational
and charitable and is to promote voluntarism;
to develop the potential of its members for voluntary participation
in community affairs; and to demonstrate the effectiveness
of trained volunteers.*

The proceeds from the sale of this book will be returned
to the community through projects sponsored by the
Junior League of Oklahoma City, Inc.

Additional copies may be obtained by writing to:
Superlatives
The Junior League of Oklahoma City, Inc.
6300 N. Western
Oklahoma City, Oklahoma 73118
or by filling out the order blank in the back of this book.
Superlatives may be obtained by organizations for
fundraising projects or by retail outlets at special rates.
Write to the above address for further information.

International Standard Book Number: 0-9613374-0-0
Library of Congress Number 84-80833

Junior League of Oklahoma City, Inc.
Oklahoma City, Oklahoma

First Edition

First Printing   October 1984   20,000 copies

Printed by S. C. Toof and Company
Memphis, Tennessee

Table of Contents

Cookbook Committee

General Chairman
Marilyn Novak Sullivan

**Editor—Design &
Format Chairman**
Ranell Bules Brown

Recipe Chairman
Franci King Hart

Executive Liaisons
Susan Samis Hoffman
Evalie Hawes Horner

**Assistant Design
& Format**
Adonna Morgan Meyer

Public Relations
Lisa Elder

Etcetera Editor
Berta Faye Curtis Rex

Section Chairmen
Sandy Simon Childress
Joann Davies Graham
Becky Brown Johnston
Marty Johnson Margo
Patty Hadlock Ramsey
Carol Rowsey Solomon
Carol Sue Jennerjahn Taylor

Marketing Chairman
Mary Tolle Walsh

Testing Chairman
Marty Clay Conkle

Sustaining Advisors
Margaret Fisher Eskridge
Karel Frank Love

Copywriter
Patsy King Hosman

Index
Judy Monroe Pitts

Resource Information
Susan Swan Currie
Gennie LeForce Johnson

Professional Advisor
Jane Carey Wheeler

Proof Readers
Gretchen Bennett
Grenda Penhollow Moss
Sally Morrison Stringer
Cynthia Caldwell Weglicki

Superlatives is filled with more than 450 recipes submitted by active and sustaining members of our League. All recipes received excellent or superlative ratings after being tested twice. We hope that you will enjoy the sampling of the best of Oklahoma we bring to you in our cookbook.

Introduction

Superlatives, by definition, describes those things of the highest quality, the highest possible excellence. To us, it is synonymous with our city, our Junior League and our cookbook.

Our cookbook has been superlative from the very beginning. With over 2000 recipes from which to choose, we are able to offer a blend of diverse recipes to satisfy any cook. Each section has a combination of gourmet, homestyle, entertainment, and quick and easy recipes. We have included recipes passed from generation to generation, as well as updated recipes which call for the conveniences of a contemporary kitchen.

Some of the recipes in **Superlatives** accompanied the early settlers in their move to Oklahoma. By presidential proclamation, the 1889 Land Run opened the central part of Oklahoma to settlement. As a result, Oklahoma City grew from zero to 10,000 in a single afternoon. Today, Oklahoma City combines economic prosperity and sophistication with the relaxed and friendly atmosphere of its small town past. This is what makes our city unique.

Chartered in 1928, the Junior League's first project was to establish and operate the Walnut Grove Community Center and Clinic for school age children. Since then, the League has contributed to various areas of our city – from health to the arts, from education to criminal justice, and from children and families to advocacy. Many of our projects have become integral parts of our city from the Creative Playground at the zoo, to the Remarkable Shop (which has served the city for over 50 years both as a fund raiser for the League projects and as a resale clothing store for the community), to the Speech and Hearing Clinic and the Child Study Center. The Arts Council, Leadership OKC (a leadership conference for local businesses and organizations), WAVE Center (Witness and Victim Education) and the Infant Center fulfill needs of our community.

The Junior League has grown as Oklahoma City has grown. Today, with over 400 active members in various projects in the community, we feel we make a superlative impact on our city. Our projects have changed as the needs of the city have changed.

Basic ingredients of talent, dedication and time have contributed to make our city, our Junior League and our cookbook superlative. Our cookbook will serve as a tangible example of the superlatives we have to offer – the best of Oklahoma!

Superlative Acknowledgements

Our superlative appreciation goes to the members, husbands and friends who faithfully supported us as we brought this from an idea to a reality.

In addition to those listed elsewhere in **Superlatives** the following is a list of Oklahoma City Junior League members who spent hours submitting, testing, tasting and even advising us – without them we could never have made it.

Thanks to all our Superlative volunteers!

Beth Adams
Nancy Altman
Sidney Anderson
Patty Anthony
Virginia Austin
Madeline Baldwin
Lezlie Bales
Carolyn Barnes
Susan Bernardy
Becky Berry
Christy Berry
Nancy Berry
Marilyn Bethea
Bonnie Black
Libby Blankenship
Barbara Bolen
Dolores Boyle
Donna Bozalis
Priscilla Braun
Liz Brown
Virginia Brown
Karen Browne
Marie Brunner
Shari Buxton
Ann Byrd
Ann Cantrell
Jackie Carey
Kathy Carey
Patsy Carey
Julie Carr
Missy Carroll
Elizabeth Champion
Kitty Champlin
Dorothy Cheek
Helen Cleary
Mary Clements
Elizabeth Coe
Martha Coe
Patty Cohenour
Betty Collar
Betty Collier
Janie Cook
Kaye Cook
Allison Cotton
Barbara Covington
Ellen Covington
Lillian Cox
Kim Craft
Lorinda Crouch
Virginia Cruce
Dee Curtis
Mary Curtis

Linda Daxon
Mary Denman
Mary Ann Disser
Sydney Dobson
JoAnn Donovan
Susan Douglass
Janis Dozier
Carole Drake
Megan Drerup
Sylvia Dulaney
Terry Elkouri
Betty Ellis
Barbara Eskridge
Nancy Eskridge
Christy Everest
Betty Fallin
Ann Felton
Mary Ruth Ferguson
Jane Fixley
Joan Fleetwood
Dolly Foster
Aileen Frank
Susan Frank
Kristin Frankfurt
Louamma Franklin
Mex Frates
Patty Gardner
Linda Garrett
Virginia Giles
Meredith Glenn
Gladys Gockel
Connie Gore
Nancy Greer
Audrey Hagmann
Beth Hammack
Kirk Hammons
Megan Hahn
Mary Ann Haskins
Jayne Henline
Virginia Henry
Pamela Henthorn
June Heusel
Betty Hill
Cynthia Hoenig
Victoria Holland
Courtney Holliday
Joanie Holmboe
Mary Holmes
Sally Holmes
Cindy Howard
Pam Howard
Carolyn Howell

Lucinda Huffman
Eileen Hulsey
Katy Imel
Debbie Jennings
Christy Johnson
Glennie Jones
Laura Ann Jones
Jane Joyce
Bev Kanaly
Cindy Keithley
Marion Kiker
Nancy Kimberling
Evelyn King
Eleanor Kirkpatrick
Mona Lambird
Nancy Law
Patti Marshall
Patti Leeman
Karen Leonard
Ann Linn
Gladys London
Coe London
Margaret Long
Hayden Lowry
Linda Lucas
Peggy Lunde
Rosemary Luttrell
Deborah Magness
Mary Mahaffey
Mary Ann Malone
Ann Marshall
Janet Massad
Linda Massad
Valerie Massey
Debbie McCord
Eleanor McLean
Marilyn Meade
Marie Meisenbach
Sandy Meyers
Cynthia Meyerson
Ethlyn Mills
Nancy Nagle
Debbi Nevard
Nancy Olney
Donna Onan
Yvonne Parker
Miki Payne
Ashley Parrish
Colleen Pease
Ann Peetoom
Brooke Phillips
Kathryn Powell

Gudbjorg Price
Cynthia Rapp
Patricia Reynolds
Mildred Richard
Betty Ann Ridley
Margaret Ringwald
Linda Rosser
Nancy Rowntree
Caroline Rumsey
Billie Schafer
Sherry Schleider
Pat Schonwald
Madeline Schwartz
Jeary Seikel
Sharon Seminoff
Cynthia Shelby
Janell Shelley
Susan Sigmon
Mary Sims
Terry Sinclair
Myra Slusky
Betsy Smith
Jane Smith
Jeanne Smith
Kay Snipes
Graham Solomon
Suzanne Spradling
Jackie Stanford
Paula Stover
Lynn Sully
Cheryl Sweetser
Lois Swinford
Linda Tate
Marnie Taylor
Judy Thomas
Barbara H. Thompson
Barbara T. Thompson
Patsy Thompson
Dencie Thomson
Sue Timberlake
Barbara Tongue
Mary Truss
Jane H. Van Cleef
Patricia Van Meter
Kanela Voegeli
Gingie Watson
Harriet Weirich
Karen Whitaker
Judi Wilkinson
Anna Williams
Stephania Williams
Dorothy Yoakam
Carol Zavislan

Beginnings

Appetizers
Soups
Beverages

Judy's Bacon-Wrapped Bread Sticks

Serves 6 to 8

1 pound bacon
1 package Angonoa's sesame
  bread sticks

Parmesan cheese

Cut bacon slices in half lengthwise. Take one half and wrap around bread stick like a barber pole. Place on bacon rack for microwave, tucking under end. Continue until rack is filled. Lay paper towel over. Microwave on high for 3 to 4 minutes and then turn pan. Microwave on high for another 3 to 4 minutes (time may vary according to microwave oven). When done, roll in Parmesan cheese. Store in an airtight container or freeze.

Ranell Bules Brown (Mrs. Steve M.)

Empanadas

Yields 6 to 7 dozen

Pastry
1 8-ounce package cream
  cheese

1 cup butter or margarine
2 cups flour

Filling
2 pounds lean ground beef
1/2 cup grated onion
2 teaspoons salt
1 egg, beaten

1/2 teaspoon pepper
2 tablespoons chili powder
1 12-ounce can tomato paste

To prepare pastry, let cream cheese and butter or margarine soften and cream together. Add flour and mix well. Wrap in wax paper and foil and refrigerate at least overnight.

To prepare filling, brown ground beef and onion, then drain. Add remaining ingredients except egg and simmer 5 minutes. Refrigerate overnight.

To assemble, let pastry sit out about 20 minutes before rolling. Do small amounts at a time. Take a section about the size of a softball and roll about 1/8-inch thick. Be sure to use plenty of flour and turn often, as this will stick. Cut into circles 3-inches in diameter. Put a rounded teaspoon of filling in the center of each circle. Brush around circle edges with beaten egg, fold over and press edges together. Prick top with a fork and put on tray in freezer. After about 20 to 30 minutes they can be put into freezer bags. This pre-freeze keeps them from sticking to each other. Bake at 350 degrees for 20 minutes.

Leslie Hood Diggs (Mrs. James Barnes, IV)

Chafing Dish Meatballs
Yields 42 meatballs

1 pound ground beef
1 teaspoon salt
1/4 teaspoon pepper
1/4 teaspoon ketchup
1 tablespoon Worcestershire
   sauce

1/4 cup cup chopped onion
1/2 cup corn flakes
1/2 cup evaporated milk
1/2 18-ounce bottle barbeque
   sauce

Mix together all ingredients except barbeque sauce, and shape into 42 tiny balls. Place in shallow pan and bake at 400 degrees for 15 minutes or until brown. Heat barbeque sauce in chafing dish. Add meatballs and serve. Meatballs can be prepared and refrigerated a day ahead. Heat with sauce when ready to serve.
Millie Farmer Hightower (Mrs. Johnson)

Toasted Mushroom Rolls
Yields 3 1/2 dozen

1/2 pound mushrooms, finely
   chopped
1 pound lobster meat, minced
   (optional)
1/2 cup butter
3 tablespoons flour
3/4 teaspoon salt

1/2 teaspoon monosodium
   glutamate
1 cup half and half
2 teaspoons minced chives
1 teaspoon lemon juice
1 loaf sliced bread, crust
   removed
1/4 cup butter, melted

Clean and chop mushrooms in food processor or blender. Add lobster, if desired. Saute for 5 minutes in 1/2 cup butter. Blend in flour, salt and monosodium glutamate. Stir in cream and cook until thick. Add minced chives and lemon juice. Cool. Remove crust from bread and roll each slice thin. Spread with mixture, roll up. Can freeze at this time. When ready to serve, defrost (if frozen), cut in half, brush with the 1/4 cup melted butter and toast in 400 degree oven until lightly browned.
Sandy Simon Childress (Mrs. Bob)

Roz's Cheese Tidbits
Yields 30

1 loaf regular Pepperidge
Farm bread
1¼ pounds butter

1 10-ounce cube Coon cheese,
grated
3 egg whites, beaten stiff

Trim crusts from bread, 3 slices at a time and then cut the stack of 3 into quarters. Melt butter, add Coon cheese and stir until well blended. Beat. Fold egg whites into cheese mixture. Dip each bread piece into cheese and egg mixture and form three layer sandwiches. Place on cookie sheet covered with waxed paper. Immediately place in freezer until frozen. Remove from waxed paper when frozen and store in plastic bags until ready to use. Bake at 350 degrees for 15 minutes until golden brown. May be cut in half before baking or served whole.

Chelin Hancock Satherlie (Mrs. Gregg)

Artichoke Squares
Serves 8

3 cups grated sharp Cheddar
cheese
2 6-ounce jars marinated
artichoke hearts, drained
and chopped
6 soda crackers, crushed

4 eggs, beaten
1 bunch green onions,
chopped
Tabasco
Salt
Pepper

Grease an 8-inch square baking dish. Mix all ingredients together and pour into dish. Bake at 325 degrees for 50 minutes to 1 hour. Cut into squares. Serve warm.

Linda Gist Kerran (Mrs. Michael L.)

Little Pizzas
Yields 10 to 12

1 cup chopped black olives
½ cup chopped green onions
1½ cups grated Cheddar
  cheese
½ to ¾ cup mayonnaise

½ teaspoon curry powder
½ teaspoon salt
1 package split English
  muffins

Mix first 6 ingredients together. Spread on English muffin halves. Broil until cheese is melted and slightly browned. Cut into quarters and serve while hot.
Carla Chenoweth Splaingard (Mrs. Randy)

Marinated Cauliflower
Serves 4 to 6

2 tablespoons vegetable oil
1 tablespoon seasoned salt
2 tablespoons white vinegar

1 teaspoon parsley flakes
¼ teaspoon garlic salt
1 large head cauliflower

Mix first 5 ingredients together in a large bowl with tightly fitting lid. Cut cauliflower into small bite size pieces. Add cauliflower to the mixed ingredients above. Marinate overnight. Shake bowl several times. Serve cold.
Christi McGrew

Cecie's Hot Pepper Jelly
Yields 6 ½ pints

¼ cup fresh finely chopped
  Jalapeno peppers
¾ cup finely chopped green
  bell peppers
1½ cups apple cider vinegar

6½ cups sugar
1 6-ounce bottle liquid
  fruit pectin
Green or red food coloring

Mix peppers, vinegar and sugar in a 2-quart saucepan and bring to a boil, boiling hard for 1 minute. Remove from heat and add the fruit pectin. Mix in enough food coloring to suit. Pour into prepared jelly jars and seal. This is great to serve over cream cheese with crackers.
Nita Forrest Folger (Mrs. Doug)

11

Pimento Cheese Spread
Serves 8

1 pound sharp Cheddar cheese
2 7-ounce jars diced pimentos, rinsed in cold water
1 tablespoon chopped fresh parsley
1 tablespoon chopped fresh chives
1 rounded teaspoon celery seed
Garlic powder
Black pepper
Mayonnaise
Tabasco

Grate Cheddar cheese and add diced pimentos. Add remaining ingredients, using enough mayonnaise to hold mixture together.
Gwen Selecman Donnell (Mrs. Tom)

Quickie Ham Dip or Spread
Yields 1½ cups

½ cup mayonnaise
1 tablespoon lemon juice
2 teaspoons chili sauce
1 tablespoon chopped chives
1 teaspoon vinegar
⅓ cup minced onion
1 4½-ounce can deviled ham
1 teaspoon onion salt
Evaporated milk

Combine all ingredients except evaporated milk and mix well. Chill until ready to serve. If using as a dip, thin to dipping consistency with evaporated milk. Serve with raw vegetables or crackers.
Anita Dow Johnson (Mrs. Milo Mike)

Ripe Olive Spread
Serves 8 to 10

1 cup mayonnaise
1 cup grated sharp Cheddar cheese
1 teaspoon curry powder
2 2¼-ounce cans sliced black olives
½ cup chopped green onions

Mix ingredients together. Spread on whole wheat English muffin halves. Broil until bubbly. Cut in quarters and serve.
Darlene Trammell Parman (Mrs. Larry V.)

Cheddar Cheese Spread
Yields 3 cups

1 pound sharp Cheddar
cheese, grated
1 cup chopped onion
1 clove garlic, minced
1 4-ounce can chopped green
chilies

1 4-ounce can stuffed green
olives, sliced
2 tablespoons vinegar
1 8-ounce can tomato sauce
1 teaspoon Worcestershire
sauce
2 tablespoons salad oil

Mix above ingredients in food processor or blender. Spread on sliced French bread or crackers and broil until brown and bubbly. Spread keeps well in refrigerator for weeks and may be frozen. Also good with soup and salad.

Kristen Van der Hoof Freeland (Mrs. Royden R.)

Crab Meat Cocktail Spread
Serves 12

1 8-ounce and 1 3-ounce
package cream cheese
1 tablespoon Worcestershire
sauce
1/4 cup chopped green onion
1/4 teaspoon garlic powder
2 tablespoons lemon juice

2 tablespoons mayonnaise
1/2 pound crab meat, fresh,
frozen or canned
1 12-ounce jar cocktail sauce
1/4 teaspoon parsley, dried
or fresh

Whip cream cheese with Worcestershire, onion, garlic powder, lemon juice and mayonnaise. Spread evenly in a shallow glass serving dish. Sprinkle with crab meat which has been drained. Cover with cocktail sauce and sprinkle with parsley for garnish. Cover with plastic wrap. Refrigerate 24 hours. Serve with crackers.

Gail Price Fine (Mrs. Douglas P.)

Mock Boursin au Poivre
(Herb Cheese Spread)
Serves 8

1 8-ounce package cream
  cheese
1 clove garlic, crushed
1 teaspoon caraway seed
1 teaspoon basil

1 teaspoon dill weed
1 teaspoon chopped chives
3 or 4 drops of lemon juice
Cracked black pepper

Blend all ingredients except pepper. Form into round flat shape. Roll in cracked pepper. Chill. Best if made a day ahead. Serve with crackers.
Nancy Frantz Davies (Mrs. Frank L., Jr.)

Shrimp Butter
Yields 2 cups

1 8-ounce package cream
  cheese
2 4½-ounce cans shrimp,
  drained
¾ cup margarine, softened

1 tablespoon minced onion
Juice of 1 lemon
4 tablespoons mayonnaise
Salt to taste

Combine all ingredients with a fork in a bowl. Serve on crackers.
Ann Whiting Hargis (Mrs. V. Burns)

Stuffed Edam Cheese
Serves 8

1 small Edam or Gouda cheese
Mayonnaise
Worcestershire sauce

Tabasco
Chopped walnuts

Hollow out cheese, leaving shell ⅛-inch thick. Grate cheese which was hollowed out and mix with enough mayonnaise to moisten. Season with Worcestershire and Tabasco to taste. Add chopped walnuts. Mix and refill shell. Chill. Let stand at room temperature before serving. Serve on crackers.
Sally Morrison Stringer (Mrs. Edward H., Jr.)

Cheese Ball
Serves 10 to 20 – 1 large ball or 2 medium

1 5-ounce jar Kraft Roka
  cheese
1 5-ounce jar Kraft bleu cheese
1 5-ounce jar Kraft sharp
  cheese
1 5-ounce jar Kraft mild
  cheese
1 5-ounce jar Kraft bacon
  cheese

1 8-ounce package cream
  cheese
Lemon juice
Garlic juice
Worcestershire sauce
Cayenne pepper
Dijon or other mustard
Paprika
Parsley
Chopped nuts

Soften Kraft cheeses and mix with cream cheese. Add lemon juice, garlic juice, a generous amount of Worcestershire, cayenne pepper, mustard and paprika to taste. Roll into a ball. Chill and roll in parsley and nuts or set aside some cream cheese before adding to mixture and blend with bleu cheese crumbles, then ice top of cheese ball.
Marion Louise Joullian

Caviar Pie
Serves 6 to 8

3 to 4 hard-boiled eggs,
  chopped
¼ cup mayonnaise
5 to 6 green onions, chopped
Tabasco

1 8-ounce carton sour cream
1 8-ounce package cream
  cheese, softened
1 3½-ounce jar caviar
Lemon wedges

Mix eggs, mayonnaise, one of the chopped green onions and 1 or 2 drops Tabasco to smooth consistency. Spread in bottom of pie plate. Mix remaining green onions with sour cream and cream cheese. Layer over egg mixture. Top with caviar. Garnish with lemon wedges. Serve with toasted, buttered French bread slices.
Carol Rowsey Solomon (Mrs. Steven G.)

Ethel Matthews' Caviar Supreme

Serves 12 to 16

1 package unflavored gelatin
1/2 cup cold water
4 hard-boiled eggs, chopped
1/2 cup mayonnaise
1/2 cup minced parsley
1 green onion, minced
Tabasco
White pepper
Salt
1 medium avocado, peeled
  and pureed
1 medium avocado, peeled
  and diced

2 tablespoons lemon juice
1 shallot, minced
2 tablespoons mayonnaise
1/2 teaspoon salt
Black pepper
1 cup sour cream
1/2 cup minced onion
1 4-ounce jar black caviar
Fresh lemon juice
Pumpernickel bread, thinly
  sliced

Line the bottom of a 1-quart souffle dish with a piece of aluminum foil large enough to extend 8 inches beyond the rim of the dish on all sides after you have pressed the foil into the dish. Double the foil overhang to make a sturdy rim standing 4 inches above the top of the dish. Oil lightly. Soften the gelatin in cold water and liquefy by setting cup in hot water or microwaving 20 seconds at lowest setting. Combine 1 tablespoon of this gelatin mixture with the eggs, 1/2 cup mayonnaise, parsley, green onion, dash of Tabasco, white pepper and salt. Spread on bottom of lined souffle dish. Combine the avocado, lemon juice, shallot, mayonnaise, salt, pepper and dash of Tabasco with another tablespoon of the gelatin mixture and spread evenly on top of the egg layer. Mix the sour cream, onions and remaining gelatin. Spread evenly over the avocado layer. Cover tightly with plastic wrap and refrigerate for 12 hours or more. Just before serving, place the caviar in a fine sieve and rinse gently under cold running water to remove excess salt. Sprinkle with lemon juice. Lift the mold out of the souffle dish and gently tear away the foil after centering the mold on your serving dish. Sprinkle the caviar on top of the sour cream layer. Serve with pumpernickel bread.

Beth Matthews McMullan (Mrs. Harry)

Poor Man's Caviar
Serves 12

3 hard-boiled eggs
1 2.2-ounce can black pitted
  olives
1 medium red onion

1 cup pecans
2 cups mayonnaise
Salt
Pepper

Chop eggs, olives, onion and pecans in food processor or blender. Add mayonnaise. Add salt and pepper to taste. Chill and serve with crackers.
Carol Walton Cordell

Savita Sauce
Yields 1 quart

1 8-ounce package cream
  cheese
1 4-ounce package bleu cheese

2 teaspoons B-V Broth and
  Sauce Concentrate
2 cups mayonnaise
1 medium onion, finely grated

Mix ingredients in order listed in mixer, food processor or blender until smooth. Refrigerate. Serve as spread or with vegetables.
Barbara Pannage Stanfield (Mrs. Neil)

Hearty Clam Delight
Yields 1½ cups

2 3-ounce packages cream
  cheese
2 teaspoons lemon juice
2 teaspoons grated onion
1 teaspoon Worcestershire
  sauce

3 to 4 drops Tabasco
¼ teaspoon salt
1 can minced clams
1 teaspoon minced parsley

Stir cream cheese to soften. Blend in lemon juice, onion, Worcestershire, Tabasco and salt. Add clams and parsley. Serve with crackers.
Carole Sue Sutton Carlin

Marinated Shrimp
Serves 6

1½ to 2 pounds raw shrimp
 with tails, cleaned
2 tablespoons lemon juice
½ cup olive oil
½ cup finely chopped onion

1 to 2 cloves garlic, minced
3 shallots, minced
¼ cup minced parsley
¼ cup butter, melted
Juice of 1 lemon

Combine first 7 ingredients and let marinate all day in refrigerator in a 9 x 13-inch ovenproof dish. Add melted butter and bake at 400 degrees for 15 minutes. Top with the juice of 1 lemon before serving.
Katherine Walbert Walker (Mrs. Russell)

Laura's Marinated Sirloin
Serves 4

1 large sirloin steak
1 8-ounce bottle Kraft Zesty
 Italian Salad Dressing

1 4-ounce can Jalapeno
 peppers
Sour cream

Charcoal steak until medium rare. Slice into strips (finger length), cutting off any fat. Marinate overnight with Italian dressing and Jalapenos, covered with foil. Before serving, drain and discard marinade. Toss meat with sour cream. Serve cold alone or with warm homemade rolls.
Stephanie Irwin Neville (Mrs. Drew)

Oklahoma Prairie Fire
Serves 6

1 15-ounce can Wolf Brand
 chili (no beans)
1 4-ounce can chopped
 green chiles

1 bunch green onions,
 chopped
1 pound Velveeta, sliced

Mix first 3 ingredients in 1½-quart casserole. Top with sliced cheese. Bake at 275 degrees for 30 to 40 minutes. Serve in chafing dish, fondue pot or on warming tray with Doritos.
Olive Kees Austin (Mrs. Gerald G.)   *Christa Schwab Chain (Mrs. John W.)*

Artichoke Dip
Serves 8

1 14-ounce can artichoke
  hearts, drained and
  quartered
1 cup mayonnaise
1 cup grated Parmesan cheese

2 tablespoons minced onion
1 tablespoon lemon juice
Garlic salt
Salt
Pepper

Combine the above ingredients. If smoother consistency is desired, a food processor or blender may be used. Pour into an ovenproof dish and bake at 350 degrees for 20 to 30 minutes. Serve with Fritos or melba toast rounds.

Ranell Bules Brown (Mrs. Steve M.)   *Kelsey Price Walters (Mrs. Roland)*

Hot Shrimp-Spinach Dip
Serves 10 to 12

½ bunch green onions,
  chopped
1 clove garlic, minced
¼ cup butter
½ pound shrimp, cooked
  and diced
1 10½-ounce package frozen
  chopped spinach, thawed
  and drained
1 10¾-ounce can Golden
  Mushroom soup
1 package Green Onion
  Dip mix

1 tablespoon grated Parmesan
  cheese
1 3-ounce can mushroom
  stems and pieces, drained
½ 5-ounce can water
  chestnuts, drained
  and sliced
1 tablespoon Worcestershire
  sauce
Tabasco
Salt
Pepper

Saute onions and garlic in butter until the onions are soft. Combine remaining ingredients and mix well. Add to the onion mixture and heat slowly, stirring frequently, until mixture is hot. Season to taste. Pour into a chafing dish and serve with assorted crackers.

Mary Hazel Mitchell Miles (Mrs. W. Howard)

Curry Shrimp Dip
Yields 1 cup

1 8-ounce package cream
cheese
1 tablespoon curry powder
1/4 teaspoon garlic powder
1/4 cup chutney, finely cut

1 cup diced fresh cooked
shrimp
1/2 cup sour cream
2 tablespoons milk or
half and half

Cream together cream cheese, curry powder, garlic powder and chutney. Add shrimp, sour cream and milk. Mix thoroughly. Refrigerate. Serve with chips.

Betty Lou Morgan Stewart (Mrs. Michael M.)

Curry Dip for Fresh Vegetables
Serves 10 to 12

2 cups mayonnaise
1/4 cup chili sauce
2 tablespoons white vinegar
1 1/2 teaspoons curry powder

1 teaspoon paprika
1/2 teaspoon salt
1/4 teaspoon pepper

Combine all ingredients thoroughly and chill for 3 hours. Serve with raw vegetables.

Olive Kees Austin (Mrs. Gerald G.)

Spinach Dip
Yields 5 to 6 cups

2 10 1/2-ounce packages frozen
chopped spinach, thawed
and squeezed dry
(uncooked)
1 cup fresh parsley, finely
chopped
2 teaspoons salt

2 teaspoons pepper
1 cup chopped green onions
3 cups Hellmann's
mayonnaise
1/2 teaspoon dill weed
Juice of 1 lemon

Mix ingredients well and chill 4 hours before serving. Serve with Wheat Thins.

Patricia Hadlock Ramsey (Mrs. Christian, Jr.)

Bean Dip
Yields 1 1/2 quarts

1 10 1/2-ounce can Frito
  Bean Dip
1 8-ounce carton sour cream
1 8-ounce package cream
  cheese
1 to 2 tablespoons chili
  powder, to taste
2 tablespoons dried parsley
  flakes

12 drops Tabasco
1/2 cup chopped green onion
  tops
5 ounces Cheddar cheese,
  grated
5 ounces Monterey Jack
  cheese, grated

Mix all ingredients except cheese and put in 2-quart ovenproof baking dish. Put cheese on top. Bake 10 to 20 minutes at 375 degrees until hot and bubbly. Serve with Doritos.
Suzanne Wells Blinn (Mrs. Robert D.)

Southern Beef and Cheese Dip
Yields 4 cups

1/3 cup chopped pecans
1 1/2 tablespoons butter
1 2 1/2-ounce jar dried beef
1 8-ounce package cream
  cheese
2 tablespoons milk

1/4 cup finely chopped
  green pepper
1/4 cup finely chopped green
  onion
1 clove garlic, pressed
1/4 teaspoon white pepper
1/2 cup sour cream

Saute pecans in butter 3 to 5 minutes. Drain and set aside. Place beef in blender or food processor, chop finely and set aside. Combine cream cheese and milk and beat until smooth. Stir in beef, green pepper, onion and spices. Mix well. Stir in sour cream. Spoon into greased 1-quart casserole. Sprinkle pecans on top. Bake at 350 degrees for 25 minutes. Serve hot with assorted crackers.
Cookbook Committee

Sombrero Dip
Serves 10 to 12

1 pound ground beef
1/2 cup chopped onion
1 clove garlic, minced
2 7-ounce cans or 2 cups
   Ortega Green Chili Salsa
1 17-ounce can Ortega Lightly
   Spicy Refried Beans

1 teaspoon salt
1/2 cup grated Longhorn
   cheese
1/4 cup sliced black olives
Tortilla chips

In a 10-inch skillet, brown beef until crumbly. Drain. Add 1/4 cup onion and garlic. Cook until onion is soft. Add chili salsa, refried beans and salt. Cook until hot and bubbly. Spoon into chafing dish. Garnish with cheese, olives and remaining onion. Serve with tortilla chips.
Linda Wright Elliott (Mrs. Earl)

California Guacamole
Serves 20

8 avocados
1/2 teaspoon oregano
1/2 teaspoon cumin
Dash of chili powder

Juice of 1 lemon
3 tomatoes
1 tablespoon salt
1/4 onion, grated

Peel and place avocados in large bowl. Add oregano, cumin, chili powder and lemon juice. Mash with a potato masher. Cube tomatoes. Add tomatoes, salt and onion to mixture. Stir to blend. Cover with plastic wrap (place wrap directly on guacamole – allow for no air). Refrigerate until ready for use. Cover with grated Monterey Jack cheese. Decorate with parsley. Serve with Doritos.
Kay Davies Oliver (Mrs. Gates E.)

A B C Dip (Almonds, Bacon, Cheese)
Serves 8

1/3 cup toasted almonds, chopped
3 strips cooked bacon, crumbled
3/4 cup mayonnaise

1 1/2 cups grated sharp Cheddar cheese
1 tablespoon onion, finely minced
1/4 teaspoon salt

Combine all ingredients and mix lightly. Serve with shredded wheat crackers.

Margaret Patzer Holdridge (Mrs. Curtis)

Mexican Bean Dip
Serves 20

1 16-ounce can refried beans
1 cup shredded Cheddar cheese
5 or 6 green onions, chopped

1/4 teaspoon salt
1/2 cup or more Picante sauce (hot)
1/2 cup sour cream

Combine all ingredients and chill. Serve with Doritos.

Ranell Bules Brown (Mrs. Steve M.)

Shrimp Dip
Serves 6

1/2 cup chopped celery
1 4-ounce can shrimp, drained and mashed
1/2 cup mayonnaise

1 3-ounce package cream cheese, softened
1/2 cup chopped green onions
1 1/2 tablespoons lemon juice

Mix ingredients together and chill. Serve with crackers.

Linda Samis James (Mrs. Ronald)   *Linda Gist Kerran (Mrs. Michael L.)*

23

Hot Crab Dip
Serves 4 to 8

12 ounces cream cheese
⅓ cup mayonnaise
½ teaspoon dried onion flakes
  (optional)

1 8-ounce package frozen
  crab meat, drained
Paprika
Dill seed

Mix cream cheese, mayonnaise and onion. Add crab meat. Put in a quiche dish. Sprinkle with paprika and dill seed. Bake at 350 degrees for 35 to 45 minutes. Serve with crackers.

Jamie Lewinon Davis   *Kay Royalty Salyer (Mrs. Jerry)*

Smoked Beef Dip
Serves 10

2 cups sour cream
2 teaspoons Beau Monde
  seasoning
2 teaspoons dill weed
2 teaspoons chopped onion
2 tablespoons parsley flakes

2½-ounce jar dried smoked
  beef, chopped
1 cup mayonnaise (not salad
  dressing)
1 large loaf unsliced bread
  which can be scooped out

Mix all ingredients except bread together. Scoop out inside of bread. Place dip in bread shell and use bread torn from center for dipping.

Janet Kamber Price (Mrs. Mark H.)

Cream Cheese Olives
Yields 48

1 5-ounce jar jumbo green
  olives

1 8-ounce package cream
  cheese
½ box sesame seeds, toasted

Drain olives and dry with a paper towel. Roll olives in cold cream cheese. Roll in toasted sesame seeds. Refrigerate overnight and cut in half.

Dee Lane Colley (Mrs. W. Tyler)

Curried Chicken Pate
Serves 8

Chopped parsley or toasted
  coconut
1 whole chicken breast,
  cooked
1 shallot or 2 green onions
¼ apple, peeled and cored

½ teaspoon salt
½ teaspoon pepper
1 teaspoon lemon juice
1 teaspoon curry powder
¼ cup prepared buttermilk
  dressing with herbs

Chop parsley or toasted coconut in food processor. Remove from food processor and set aside. Put chicken, shallot and apple into food processor with metal blade. Turn on and off until mixture is finely chopped. Add remaining ingredients except parsley or coconut. Turn on and off several times until mixture is smooth. Roll mixture in either parsley or toasted coconut to form a ball.
Marian Briscoe DeVore (Mrs. John)

Rusty's Pate
Yields 2 cups

Bacon fat
2 tablespoons butter
1½ pounds chicken livers
½ pound unsalted pork fat,
  ground
2 tablespoons dry sherry

2 tablespoons brandy
½ teaspoon ground pepper
3 green onions, chopped
1 clove garlic, minced
1½ teaspoons salt
Green olive slices

Coat 7-inch souffle mold with cold bacon fat. Melt butter in skillet. Saute livers until pink has disappeared. Combine livers, pork fat, sherry, brandy, pepper, onions, garlic and salt. Mix well. Place in blender and puree. Spoon into prepared mold. Cover with foil. Put mold in a baking dish. Pour hot water half way up. Bake at 350 degrees for 1 hour. Let cool. Refrigerate before serving. Garnish with green olive slices.
Lisa King Brashear (Mrs. Herb)

Liver Pate in Port Aspic
Serves 15 to 20

Port Aspic
2 teaspoons unflavored
  gelatin
1 cup port wine
2 tablespoons sugar

1 tablespoon water
3 tablespoons red wine
  vinegar
½ teaspoon dried tarragon

Pate
1 pound chicken livers
1 cup milk
¼ cup cognac
1¼ cups butter, room
  temperature
1 cup sliced onion

1 small green apple, peeled
  and sliced
¼ cup sherry
¼ cup whipping cream
1¼ teaspoon salt
1 teaspoon lemon juice

To prepare aspic, butter an 8 x 4-inch loaf pan. Dissolve gelatin in small bowl with ¼ cup port. Set aside. Combine sugar and water in pan and cook until dissolved. Cook until mixture is dark caramel color, 8 to 10 minutes. Whisk in vinegar, remaining port and tarragon. Reduce heat and simmer 2 minutes. Add gelatin and stir until dissolved. Pour into prepared loaf pan and chill until set.

To prepare pate, soak livers, milk and cognac for 1 hour. Melt ½ cup butter in a large skillet, add onion and saute until browned. Add apple and cook until soft. Put in blender with slotted spoon. Drain livers. Saute until pink has disappeared, about 10 minutes. Add to onion mixture in blender. Add sherry to skillet and heat to clean skillet, then add with whipping cream to liver mixture and puree until smooth. Let stand until lukewarm. Beat remaining butter until creamy, add to liver mixture while blender is running. Mix in salt and lemon juice. Pour over chilled aspic, smoothing top. Refrigerate. To serve, run sharp knife around edge of mold, dip mold briefly into hot water and invert pate onto serving platter.
Martha Vose Williams (Mrs. G. Rainey)

New Year's Day Good Luck Bean Soup
Yields 16 pint jars

1 pound dried split peas
1 pound dried lentils
1 pound dried navy beans
1 pound dried northern beans
1 pound dried black beans
1 pound dried pinto beans
1 pound dried red beans
1 pound dried garbanzo beans

1 pound dried black-eyed peas
1 pound dried kidney beans
1 pound dried small lima beans
1 pound dried large lima beans
1 pound dried barley

Mix together and put into 16 pint jars. To give as gifts, attach a card with the following recipe:

New Year's Day Good Luck Bean Soup
Yields 3 quarts

3 quarts water
2 tablespoons salt
2 quarts water
Ham or ham hock
1 onion, chopped
1 16-ounce can Rotel tomatoes

1 16-ounce can whole tomatoes
1 clove garlic, minced
Juice of 1 lemon
Salt
Pepper

Wash bean mixture. Cover with 3 quarts water. Add salt and soak overnight. Drain, wash, and put in 2 quarts water. Add ham and other ingredients, except lemon juice. Simmer slowly 2½ to 3 hours or longer. Add lemon juice the last 15 minutes of cooking.
Sandy Simon Childress (Mrs. Bob)

Garden Zucchini Soup
Serves 4

1 zucchini, sliced
1 onion, chopped
1 teaspoon curry powder
2½ cups chicken broth

1 cup sour cream
Salt
Pepper

In a saucepan gently boil zucchini, onion and curry powder in chicken broth until soft. Add sour cream and puree in food processor or blender until smooth. Season and serve either hot or cold.
Karel Frank Love (Mrs. Joe R.)

Broccoli Mushroom Soup
Yields 4 quarts

1/2 cup butter
1 large red onion, finely chopped
1 stalk celery, finely chopped
1 carrot, finely chopped
1 pound fresh mushrooms, finely chopped
1 10-ounce package frozen broccoli, cooked and drained

3 to 4 cups chicken broth, homemade if possible
1/4 cup sherry or white wine
Salt
1 bunch fresh parsley
2 teaspoons thyme (optional)
1 cup whipping cream

In a large pot or Dutch oven saute onions in butter on medium low heat. Add celery, carrot and mushrooms and saute for about 15 minutes or until tender. Add broccoli and heat through along with 3 tablespoons of chicken stock. Transfer to food processor or blender and puree. Return to Dutch oven and add remaining 3 to 4 cups of chicken broth, sherry, salt, fresh parsley and thyme (optional). Simmer 1 hour or more. The soup may be served at this point, or for a richer taste, add 1 cup whipping cream, which has been warmed, and serve.

Sharon Fitkin Boecking (Mrs. H. E., III)

Beef Steak Soup
Serves 8 to 10

1/2 cup butter or margarine
1 cup flour
3 quarts water
2 pounds ground beef, browned and drained
1 cup chopped onion
1 cup chopped potato

1 20-ounce package frozen mixed vegetables
1 14 1/2-ounce can tomatoes
1 tablespoon monosodium glutamate
2 tablespoons Shilling Beef Flavor Base
1 teaspoon black pepper

Melt margarine and whip in flour. Stir in water. Add ground beef. Add the onions and potatoes, which have been parboiled in enough water to cover. Add frozen mixed vegetables, tomatoes, monosodium glutamate, beef concentrate and pepper. Bring to a boil. Reduce to simmer and cook until the vegetables are done, usually 1 1/2 to 2 hours.

Ranell Bules Brown (Mrs. Steve M.)

Eggplant Supper Soup
Serves 6 to 8

2 tablespoons salad oil
2 tablespoons butter
1 medium onion, chopped
1 pound lean ground beef
1 medium eggplant, diced
1 clove garlic, minced
1/2 cup chopped carrot
1/2 cup chopped celery
1 1-pound 12-ounce can
  Italian tomatoes

2 14-ounce cans beef broth
1 teaspoon salt
1 teaspoon sugar
1/2 teaspoon pepper
1/2 teaspoon nutmeg
1/2 cup elbow macaroni
2 tablespoons parsley
Parmesan cheese

In a Dutch oven heat oil and butter. Add onion and saute until limp. Add meat and stir until meat is no longer pink. Add eggplant, garlic, carrot, celery, tomatoes (which have been broken up), beef broth, salt, sugar, pepper and nutmeg. Cover and simmer for 30 minutes. Add macaroni and parsley and simmer 10 more minutes or until macaroni is tender. Pass Parmesan cheese as topping.

Marjory Pielsticker Feighny (Mrs. James A.)

Shrimp Bisque
Serves 6

1 pound raw shrimp
1/2 cup chopped onion
1/2 cup chopped celery
1 medium carrot, sliced
2 cups water

1/4 cup brandy
1/2 cup dry white wine
2 cups light cream
1 tablespoon butter
1 teaspoon salt

Wash shrimp and put in saucepan with onion, celery, carrot and water. Bring to a boil and simmer for 30 minutes. Drain, reserving the stock. Peel and devein shrimp and cut into pieces. Combine vegetables and stock in food processor or blender and blend until smooth. Return to saucepan and add brandy and wine. Gradually stir in cream. Add butter a little at a time and salt to taste.

Mary Slattery Price (Mrs. William S.)

Hamburger Vegetable Chowder
Serves 6

1 pound ground beef
3 tablespoons fat
2 cups canned tomatoes
2 medium carrots, diced
1/2 cup diced celery
1 medium onion, chopped

2 teaspoons salt
1/4 cup rice or barley
1/8 teaspoon pepper
1 1/2 quarts water
2 cups coarsely cubed
potatoes

Brown meat in fat. Put in all ingredients except potatoes, and simmer slowly for 1 hour. Add potatoes, and simmer an additional hour.
Mary Sue Dunlevy Shelley (Mrs. John A.)

Mexican Pepper Soup
Serves 4

2 1/2 cups water
1 medium tomato, peeled and
chopped
1 4-ounce can chopped green
chile peppers
1/2 teaspoon garlic salt
1/4 teaspoon pepper

1 13-ounce can evaporated
milk
1 10 3/4-ounce can cream of
potato soup
1 10 3/4-ounce can cream of
onion soup
8 ounces Monterey Jack
cheese, cubed

Combine first 5 ingredients and bring to a boil. Lower heat. Cover and simmer for 5 minutes. Blend in milk and soups and heat thoroughly. Divide cheese into bowls and pour hot soup over cheese.
Susan Holt Ingham (Mrs. Richard)

Four Minute Tomato Bisque
Serves 4

1 10 3/4-ounce can tomato soup
1 pint half and half
1/2 teaspoon crumbled dried
basil

1 teaspoon instant minced
onion
1 teaspoon sugar
Croutons
1 tablespoon chopped chives

In a 1 1/2-quart saucepan combine soup, half and half, basil, onion and sugar. Gradually bring just to boiling. Simmer 2 minutes, stirring constantly. Top with croutons and chives.
Sally Morrison Stringer (Mrs. Edward H., Jr.)

Clam Chowder
Serves 6

6 ounces lean pork, diced
Butter, melted
2 cups diced onion
6 tablespoons flour
3 3-ounce cans minced clams
    with juice
2 cups water

3 1/2 cups diced potatoes
1 teaspoon thyme
2 cups whipping cream or
    half and half
Salt
Pepper
Tabasco or cayenne (optional)

Saute pork in a 10-quart pan with tight fitting lid. Add enough butter to clam juice to make 1/2 cup. Stir flour into liquid and add diced onions. Cook 3 to 6 minutes. Watch carefully as it will burn easily. Add clams which have been spooned from the can, water, potatoes and thyme. Cover and simmer until potatoes are tender, about 20 to 30 minutes. Add heavy cream and simmer until well blended. Add salt and pepper to taste. A dash of Tabasco or cayenne may be added for a hotter taste.
Marcia Hopping Powell (Mrs. John L.)

Corn Chowder
Serves 4 to 6

10 slices good quality bacon,
    diced
1 small onion, finely chopped
3 cups diced raw potatoes
2 cups water
1 1/2 teaspoons salt
1/4 teaspoon pepper

1 16 1/2-ounce can cream style
    corn
3 tablespoons unsalted butter
3 tablespoons flour
3 cups milk
Fresh parsley, minced

Fry diced bacon until it is crisp. Drain. Pour off all but 2 tablespoons drippings from pan. Saute onion until clear; do not brown. Set aside. Cook potatoes in salted water with onion and bacon. Cover pan and simmer gently until potatoes feel fork tender, about 20 minutes. Add pepper and cream style corn. Melt butter in separate saucepan and whisk in flour. Stir in milk slowly, whisking constantly until all milk is added. Cook until slightly thickened, then add to potato and corn mixture. Sprinkle with fresh finely minced parsley after soup is ladled into bowls ready for serving.
Carol Sue Jennerjahn Taylor (Mrs. Jerry A.)

Cream of Artichoke Soup
Serves 8

½ cup chopped shallots or
  green onions
1 stalk celery, chopped
1 bay leaf
Pinch of thyme
¼ cup butter
1 quart chicken consomme

1 14-ounce can artichoke
  hearts, sliced
2 egg yolks, slightly beaten
1 cup whipping cream
Salt
Pepper

Saute first 4 ingredients in butter. Add consomme and cook on medium heat 20 to 30 minutes. Add artichoke hearts and simmer 5 to 10 minutes more. Add a few tablespoons warm broth to beaten egg yolks. Return to broth and add cream. Season and heat to boiling.
Sandy Simon Childress (Mrs. Bob)

Lobster Bisque
Serves 6 to 8

⅔ cup butter, divided
1 pound small frozen lobster
  tails, defrosted and cut into
  2 to 3 pieces each with
  shells on
2 carrots, diced
2 cups diced onion
3 sprigs parsley
1 bay leaf
⅛ teaspoon thyme

4 tablespoons brandy
½ cup white wine
2 14½-ounce cans chicken
  broth
¼ cup tomato paste
¾ cup flour
2 cups light cream
1 quart milk
1 teaspoon salt
¼ teaspoon pepper

In a large heavy saucepan melt 2 tablespoons butter. Add lobster and saute 5 minutes or until shells turn red. Add vegetables and herbs and cook until tender. Add 2 tablespoons brandy and wine and cook 1 minute. Add broth and tomato paste and bring to boiling. Simmer 8 to 10 minutes. Remove lobster with slotted spoon. Cool and remove meat from shells. Dice meat and reserve. Return shells to saucepan for added flavor. Melt remaining butter in another saucepan over medium heat. Stir in flour and cook 1 minute, stirring. Add cream, milk, salt and pepper. Simmer 5 minutes. Mix with broth mixture. Simmer 30 minutes. Strain everything. Add lobster and 2 remaining tablespoons brandy.
Barbara Pannage Stanfield (Mrs. Neil)

French Onion Soup
Serves 8 to 10

2 onions, sliced
3 tablespoons butter or
  margarine
1 tablespoon flour
3 14½-ounce cans Swanson
  Beef Broth
Salt

Pepper
1 slice French bread per
  serving
1 tablespoon grated Parmesan
  cheese per serving
1 slice Swiss cheese per
  serving

Saute onions in butter until brown. Sprinkle 1 tablespoon flour and cook for 1 minute. Add 3 cans beef broth, salt and pepper. Bring to a boil, reduce heat and simmer 30 minutes. Toast French bread slices in oven on broil, toasting both sides of bread. Place bread in soup bowls. Add 1 tablespoon of Parmesan cheese and ladle soup into bowls. Place one slice of Swiss cheese on top of each bowl and place under broiler until cheese is melted. Grated Monterey Jack cheese may be substituted for Swiss.

Nancy Morehouse Giasson   *Alison Evans Taylor*
(Mrs. Wallace)   *(Mrs. Zach D., Jr.)*

Leek and Potato Soup
Yields 2 quarts

8 leeks, white and light green
  parts only
½ cup butter
4 medium potatoes, peeled
  and diced
1 carrot, sliced

4 cups chicken broth, heated
1 quart water, heated
1 cup milk
Salt
White pepper

Cut leeks in half lengthwise and then crosswise into 1-inch pieces. Simmer leeks in butter for 10 minutes. Add potatoes, carrot, chicken broth and water. Cover and simmer for 40 minutes. Let cool and blend in food processor or blender. Return to pot and add milk. Season with salt and pepper.

Stephanie Irwin Neville (Mrs. Drew)

Hungarian Goulash Soup with Spaetzle
Serves 6

1 onion, chopped
1 clove garlic, minced
2 tablespoons lard or oil
1 teaspoon sweet Hungarian
  paprika
1 teaspoon hot Hungarian
  paprika
2 pounds chuck steak, cut into
  ½-inch cubes
¾ cup water, divided

1 tablespoon caraway seed
Salt
Pepper
10 cups water
3 potatoes, diced
1 carrot, diced
1 parsnip, diced
1 tomato, seeded and chopped
½ green pepper, minced
¼ cup minced parsley

Spaetzle
½ cup flour
1 egg

2 tablespoons water
⅛ teaspoon salt

In a Dutch oven saute onion and garlic in fat until soft. Stir in paprika and then cubed beef. Add ½ cup of the water. Bring to a boil over moderate heat and cook 5 minutes. Stir in the remaining ¼ cup of water mixed with caraway seed and cook mixture until liquid has evaporated. Stir in 9½ cups of water, salt and pepper and bring to a boil again. Reduce heat and simmer 1½ hours until meat is almost tender. To prepare spaetzle dough, mix ingredients. Cover and set aside for 30 minutes. Add diced vegetables to soup and simmer another 30 minutes. Pinch spaetzle dough into pieces the size of peas and drop in simmering soup, lifting spaetzle from the bottom of the pan. Add parsley and simmer 5 minutes longer, or until spaetzle is cooked. Add salt and pepper to taste.

Patti Jo Jeter Elder (Mrs. John B.)

Black Bean Soup
Serves 4 to 6

1½ cups dried black beans,
  rinsed in cold water
5 cups cold water
1 ham hock or 1 thick ham
  slice, cut in cubes
4 cloves
2 tablespoons olive oil
½ cup finely chopped green
  pepper

2 tablespoons finely chopped
  onion
½ teaspoon finely chopped
  garlic
3 fresh coriander sprigs or
  ½ teaspoon dried
¼ cup sherry

Toppings
1 cup shredded Cheddar
  cheese
1 cup chopped onion

1 cup sour cream
Tabasco

In a heavy 4 to 5-quart flameproof casserole, combine the black beans and cold water. Bring to a boil over high heat. Add ham hock or ham cubes and cloves. Reduce the heat to its lowest point and simmer uncovered for 2 hours, adding additional water as needed. In a heavy 8 to 10-inch skillet heat 2 tablespoons of oil over moderate heat. Add green pepper, onion and garlic. Cook until transparent, stirring constantly. With rubber spatula scrape mixture into simmering beans. Add coriander and cook on very low heat until beans are tender. Add water as needed. When beans are done, remove and mash 1 cup of beans into a paste using a potato masher. Place paste back into beans to thicken soup. Add sherry. Top with any combination of cheese, onions, sour cream and Tabasco.
Sue Ann White Hyde (Mrs. James Dudley)

Cold Blueberry Soup
Serves 6

1 pint blueberries, rinsed
and stems removed
1½ cups water
¼ cup sugar

1 3-inch strip lemon peel
1 2-inch piece cinnamon stick
¾ cup sour cream

In a medium saucepan combine all ingredients except sour cream. Bring to a boil, lower heat and simmer 15 minutes. Cool 10 minutes. Remove lemon peel and cinnamon stick. Puree in food processor or blender. Chill at least 4 hours, or overnight. Stir in sour cream just before serving.

Margo Maidt Winfrey (Mrs. Ron)

Potage d'Abricotine (Apricot Soup)
Yields 1 quart

5 ripe apricots
1 16-ounce carton plain
yogurt
1 cup milk
½ cup fresh orange juice

2 teaspoons Abricotine
Liqueur or Apricot Brandy
(optional)
6 sprigs mint
6 thin slices of orange, peeled
and quartered

Wash and pit unpeeled apricots and cut them up coarsely. Combine the yogurt, apricots, milk and orange juice in a blender and blend at medium speed 1 minute. Stir in liqueur, if desired. Refrigerate until well chilled, 2 hours or more. Float orange sections and mint in soup when ready to serve.

Susan Esco Crain (Mrs. R. Dean)

Garden Fresh Gazpacho
Serves 4

1 medium clove garlic
1 medium onion, chopped
5 large tomatoes, peeled
   and seeded
1 cup beef stock
3 tablespoons olive oil
2 tablespoons wine vinegar

2 tablespoons chopped
   parsley
½ tablespoon Worcestershire
   sauce
¼ to ½ teaspoon paprika
Salt
Pepper

Garnishes
Tomato, chopped
Cucumber, chopped
Green pepper, chopped

Green onions, chopped
Croutons

   Place all ingredients except garnishes in food processor or blender
and blend for 2 minutes. Chill for at least 4 hours. Stir well and serve
with bowls of garnishes. This is even better if made a day ahead.
Suzie Chandler Sargent (Mrs. John, Jr.)

Cold Cucumber Soup
Yields 1 quart

2 tablespoons butter
¼ onion, chopped
2 cups unpeeled and diced
   cucumbers
1 cup watercress or spinach
   leaves
½ cup finely diced raw potato

2 cups chicken broth
2 sprigs parsley
½ teaspoon salt
¼ teaspoon ground pepper
¼ teaspoon dry mustard
1 cup heavy cream

Garnishes
Radishes, sliced

Scallions, sliced

   In a saucepan melt butter and add onion. Cook until onion is transparent. Add the remaining ingredients, except heavy cream and garnishes, and bring to a boil. Simmer for 15 minutes. Puree in food processor or blender. Whip the cream until slightly thickened. Add to soup,
correct seasonings and garnish with sliced vegetables. Chill the bowls
prior to serving the soup.
Elizabeth White Hoffman (Mrs. Kent)

Mushroom and Chive Bisque
Serves 6

½ cup butter
2 cups finely chopped
  mushrooms, including stems
4 tablespoons flour
¼ teaspoon dry mustard
1 teaspoon salt

2 cups chicken broth
2 cups half and half
¼ cup sherry
¼ cup finely chopped chives
¼ cup whipping cream

In a Dutch oven melt butter and add mushrooms. Saute until soft. Add flour, mustard and salt and cook 1 minute. Pour in chicken broth and cook until thickened. Add half and half, sherry and chives. Heat thoroughly but not to boiling. Place Dutch oven over hot water until ready to serve. Whip the cream and float on top of the soup. This soup may also be served cold. If so, place everything but the whipping cream in food processor or blender and blend. Then chill before serving.
Victoria Caudill Moran (Mrs. Henry Thomas)

Vichyssoise
Serves 12

4 tablespoons butter
2 yellow onions, sliced
4 leeks, sliced
6 large Idaho potatoes,
  peeled and cut into pieces
2 tablespoons salt
1 teaspoon white pepper

6 to 8 cups chicken broth
6 tablespoons butter
1 bunch watercress
⅛ teaspoon nutmeg
2 cups half and half, warmed
2 cups milk, warmed
1 cup whipping cream

In a large saucepan saute onion and leeks in 4 tablespoons butter. Add potatoes, salt, pepper and enough broth to cover. Place 6 tablespoons butter on top. Cover pan and gently boil until potatoes are soft, about 35 minutes. After butter melts, stir occasionally. Wash watercress, reserving a few large leaves for garnish. When potatoes are soft, add watercress leaves. Remove from heat. Blend vegetables and liquid in food processor or blender until smooth. Return to saucepan and add nutmeg. Add warmed half and half and milk to soup, stirring. Reheat without boiling. Chill soup. Before serving, blend in whipping cream and garnish with watercress.
Gennie LeForce Johnson (Mrs. Robert M.)

Annie's Downfall
Serves 1

4 ounces coffee ice cream
2 ounces whipped cream
2 ounces Kahlua

Extra whipped cream for
  garnish
Cherries (optional)
Shaved chocolate bits

Mix first 3 ingredients together in blender. Pour into parfait glass. Add dollop of whipped cream to top. Then add cherries. Cover with chocolate shavings.
Lisa Elder

Southern Comfort Punch
Serves 32

1 fifth Southern Comfort
  bourbon (or other bourbon)
1 6-ounce can frozen
  lemonade concentrate,
  thawed

Red food coloring
6 ounces fresh lemon juice
1 6-ounce can frozen orange
  juice concentrate, thawed
3 quarts 7-Up

Mix all ingredients except 7-Up in advance. Add 7-Up and ice when ready to serve.
Marty Johnson Margo (Mrs. Robert C.)

Bloody Marys
Serves 6 to 8

1 46-ounce can tomato juice
¼ cup Worcestershire sauce
⅛ teaspoon basil
⅛ teaspoon oregano
⅛ teaspoon celery salt

2 teaspoons salt
2 teaspoons pepper
¾ to 1 cup lemon juice
6 to 8 ounces vodka
Celery sticks

Mix all ingredients together. Chill at least 2 hours to blend flavors. Serve in tall glasses with a celery stick as a stirrer.
Andrea Samara Jones (Mrs. Johnny H., Jr.)

Daiquiri Punch
Yields 30 5-ounce servings

2 6-ounce cans frozen limeade
concentrate, thawed
1 6-ounce can frozen
lemonade concentrate,
thawed

1 6-ounce can frozen orange
juice concentrate, thawed
2 quarts water
1 fifth rum
1 quart soda, chilled

Ice Ring
Canned pineapple slices

Green maraschino cherries

Combine fruit concentrates with water. Chill. To prepare ice ring, alternate canned pineapple slices (halved) and green maraschino cherries in bottom of ring mold. Fill with water and freeze. To serve, combine with rum in a punch bowl. Carefully pour soda over ice ring.
Catherine Coburn Langford (Mrs. Dennis)

Frozen Margaritas
Serves 4

4 ounces tequila
3 ounces Mr. and Mrs. T. Sweet
and Sour Mix
3 ounces triple sec

1 6-ounce can frozen limeade
Ice cubes
Margarita salt (optional)

Mix all liquids in blender with ice cubes until desired consistency. It is best to add a few ice cubes at a time and start and stop the blender often. Dip each glass in blender mixture, then in salt, if desired, before filling.
Marty Clay Conkle (Mrs. Cliff)

Society Slush

White port wine
Pineapple juice

Pink grapefruit juice
Fresh strawberries

Use equal parts of ingredients. Mix and freeze in a plastic container. Thaw 30 minutes before serving. Garnish with fresh strawberries.
Sarah Powell Newcomb (Mrs. Ralph S.)

Suzann's Bourbon Slush
Serves 24

1 12-ounce can frozen
   lemonade concentrate
1 6-ounce can frozen orange
   juice concentrate

1 cup sugar
2 cups strong tea
7 cups water
1½ cups bourbon

Mix all ingredients and freeze. Remove from freezer 30 minutes to 1 hour before serving. Can be served in a punch bowl.
Ranell Bules Brown (Mrs. Steve M.)

Spearmint Cooler
Serves 8

2 cups sugar
2½ cups water
Juice of 4 oranges
Juice of 6 lemons

Handful of mint leaves
Vodka
7-Up or Fresca or soda

Combine sugar and water and boil 10 minutes. Pour this mixture over juices and mint and steep for 1 hour. Strain. Refrigerate or freeze in small container. To serve, fill glass with ice and add ½ to 1 jigger vodka and equal parts of juice mixture and soda.
Barbara Workman Vose (Mrs. Charles, Jr.)

Campers Ramos Gin Fizz
Serves 4

Ice cubes
1 6-ounce can frozen
   lemonade concentrate
1 6-ounce lemonade can of gin
2 pints half and half

2 egg whites
¼ teaspoon orange flower
   water
1 tablespoon orange juice
2 tablespoons sugar

Using blender, fill half full of ice cubes. Then pour in all ingredients and blend.
Marjory Pielsticker Feighny (Mrs. James A.)

Coffee Liqueur
Yields 2 quarts

4 cups water
4 cups sugar
2 ounces instant coffee
2 tablespoons water

1 vanilla bean
1 quart 100 proof vodka
1 teaspoon vanilla

Bring water and sugar to boil in a large pot. Mix instant coffee with 2 tablespoons water. Add to boiling mixture. Remove from heat and let cool 5 minutes. Add vanilla bean that has been split in half lengthwise. Put lid on pan and let cool completely. Remove vanilla bean. Add vodka and vanilla. Pour into bottles, seal and let age a minimum of 2 weeks. The longer it ages, the better.
Andrea Samara Jones (Mrs. Johnny H., Jr.)

Jessie's Apricot Liqueur
Yields 1 fifth

2 packages dried apricots
1 fifth gin

16 to 20 ounces rock candy

Put 2 packages apricots in large jar. Add gin and rock candy. Soak in jar for 1 month. Pour liqueur into a fancy decanter and – "Voila"!
Karel Frank Love (Mrs. Joe R.)

Wassail
Serves 20

1 cup sugar
4 cinnamon sticks
Lemon slices
½ cup water
2 cups pineapple juice

2 cups orange juice
6 cups claret
½ cup lemon juice
1 cup dry sherry

Boil sugar, cinnamon sticks and 3 lemon slices in ½ cup water for 5 minutes to make a syrup. Strain. Heat, but do not boil, the remaining ingredients. Combine with syrup, garnish with lemon slices and serve hot.
Sally Morrison Stringer (Mrs. Edward H., Jr.)

Hot Spiced Wine
Yields 2 quarts

Juice from 3 lemons
Juice from 3 oranges
Grated peel of 1 orange
Grated peel of 1 lemon
2 cups sugar

2 cups water
3 cinnamon sticks
10 whole cloves
2 pinches allspice
1 quart Burgundy wine

In a saucepan simmer all ingredients, except wine, for 20 minutes until well mixed. Remove from heat and strain. Add 1 quart Burgundy wine and stir well. Enjoy the aroma and flavor. Serve hot.
Midge Wasson Lindsey (Mrs. Paul B.)

Hot Buttered Rum Mix
Yields 5 cups frozen mix

1 pint French vanilla ice cream
½ pound butter
½ pound brown sugar
½ pound powdered sugar
1 teaspoon nutmeg

1 teaspoon cinnamon
Rum
Boiling water
Cinnamon sticks

Soften ice cream and butter. Add sugars and spices. Stir until smooth. Freeze. Place 3 tablespoons of ice cream mix into a mug. Add 3 tablespoons rum and fill with boiling water. Stir with a cinnamon stick.
Ann Whiting Hargis (Mrs. V. Burns)

Instant Cocoa Mix

1 14-quart box dry milk
1 16-ounce jar Coffeemate
1 pound Quik cocoa mix

1 16-ounce box powdered
  sugar
2 cups sugar
1 cup cocoa

Mix together in large container. Add ⅓ cup mix to a cup of hot water.
Marty Johnson Margo (Mrs. Robert C.)

Percolator Punch
Yield 30 cups

9 cups unsweetened
   pineapple juice
9 cups cranberry juice cocktail
4¼ cups water

1 cup brown sugar
4½ teaspoons whole cloves
4 cinnamon sticks
¼ teaspoon salt

Combine pineapple juice, cranberry juice, water and brown sugar in a 30-cup percolator. Place cloves, cinnamon sticks (broken in pieces) and salt in basket. Assemble, plug in and perk. Serve piping hot.
Becky Brown Johnston (Mrs. Brad)

Spiced Tea Mix
Yields 5 cups mix

3 ounces lemonade mix
2 cups Tang
2 cups sugar

¾ cup instant tea
½ teaspoon cloves
½ teaspoon cinnamon

Mix all ingredients together. Place in container for storage. To serve, mix 3 to 4 heaping teaspoons of spiced tea mixture with 1 cup boiling water. Serve.
Diane Blinn Kenney (Mrs. Herbert K.)

Spiced Tea
Yields 30 cups

1 teaspoon cinnamon
½ teaspoon nutmeg
1 teaspoon whole cloves
½ cup loose orange pekoe tea
1 quart boiling water

3 oranges, juiced
3 lemons, juiced
3 cups sugar
3 quarts boiling water

Put spices in a spice bag and moisten with cold water. Pour the quart of boiling water over tea and spice bag. Let stand until cold. Remove spice bag and strain tea. Add juice of oranges, lemons, sugar and the 3 quarts of boiling water. Let stand at least 3 hours. Reheat to serve.
Mary Hazel Mitchell Miles (Mrs. W. Howard)

Cranberry Fruit Punch
Serves 30

2 cups water
1 cup sugar
4 cups cranberry juice
4 cinnamon sticks
12 whole cloves
1½ cups lemon juice, fresh
   or frozen

2 cups orange juice, fresh
   or frozen
2 cups unsweetened
   pineapple juice, canned
   or frozen
1 quart ginger ale

Boil water and sugar until sugar dissolves. Add cranberry juice, cinnamon sticks and cloves to water and sugar mixture. Heat on low. Strain into a bowl. Add lemon juice, orange juice and pineapple juice and chill. Add cold ginger ale right before serving. Serve with large ice cubes in center of punch bowl.

Ginger Smith Shaw (Mrs. James Crawford)

Pi Phi Mocha Punch
Yields 2 quarts syrup

1 cup cocoa
1½ cups cold water
2½ cups boiling water
2¾ cups sugar
Pinch salt

1 teaspoon vanilla
Coffee, double strength
Milk
Vanilla ice cream

Mix cocoa and cold water into a paste. Add boiling water, sugar and salt to the paste mixture. Simmer slowly for 1 hour, stirring often. Cool syrup mixture and add vanilla. Refrigerate. Make double strength coffee and set aside.

To make 3 or 4 servings of punch, mix 8 ounces cold coffee, 8 ounces cold milk and 2 tablespoons of chocolate syrup mixture. For larger amounts, use 1 64-ounce pot of coffee, ½ gallon milk and 1 cup syrup. Serve very cold over ½ to 1 gallon vanilla ice cream in punch bowl. Proportions can vary according to taste preference. Syrup will keep in refrigerator up to 2 months.

Diane Blinn Kenney (Mrs. Herbert K.)

Orange Mint Drink
Serves 8

2½ cups water
2 cups sugar
2 oranges, juiced
1 orange rind, grated

6 lemons
2 lemon rinds, grated
2 large handfuls fresh mint

Dissolve sugar in water and boil 10 minutes. While hot, pour over all other ingredients mixed together in large bowl. Cover and let stand all afternoon. Strain and put in a jar. To serve, fill glass ⅔ full of ice, add 8 tablespoons juice mixture and fill remainder of glass with water or ginger ale.

Carole Sue Sutton Carlin

Ibbie's Banana Punch
Serves 18 to 28 or Yields 1¾ gallons

4 cups sugar
6 cups water
1 46-ounce can pineapple
juice

16 ounces orange juice
2 lemons, juiced
5 large ripe bananas, mashed
Ginger ale

Mix sugar and water in saucepan. Heat to boiling. Boil 3 minutes and cool. Add pineapple juice, orange juice, lemon juice and bananas. Blend well. Pour into 2 clean half gallon milk cartons. Freeze. To serve, partially thaw frozen punch in punch bowl and add 1½ quarts ginger ale per half gallon of punch.

Suzanne Peterson Pardue (Mrs. W. Dave)

Lou's Flips
Serves 4 to 6

3 ounces frozen orange juice
concentrate
1 whole banana
¼ cup powdered dry milk or
½ cup plain yogurt

1 raw egg
¼ cup water
1½ cups ice cubes

Combine ingredients in blender or food processor in order given. Blend until smooth. Serve immediately or frozen.

Karen Hulsey Samis (Mrs. Michael S.)

Essentials

Meat
Seafood
Poultry
Casseroles

Veal Chops in Cream
Serves 6

6 thick veal loin chops
6 tablespoons butter
3 tablespoons brandy
¾ cup mushrooms, sliced
4 tablespoons flour
1½ cups light beef stock
1 teaspoon glace de viande or
   meat extract

½ cup whipping cream
Salt
Pepper
1 bay leaf
Thyme
Grated Parmesan cheese
Butter

Brown chops quickly in butter and flame them with heated brandy. Transfer the chops to a flameproof serving dish and keep them warm. In the remaining butter, cook sliced mushrooms for 2 to 3 minutes. Sprinkle the mushrooms with flour and stir in light beef stock and glace de viande. Cook the sauce, stirring constantly, until it comes to a boil. Stir in whipping cream and pour the sauce over the chops in the casserole. Add salt and pepper to taste, bay leaf and thyme. Cover the dish and simmer the chops for about 45 minutes or until they are very tender. Just before serving, sprinkle chops with Parmesan cheese, dot them with butter and brown them briefly under the broiler.
Anne Wileman Schafer

Veal Piccata
Serves 3 to 4

1½ pounds veal, cut into very
   thin slices
Flour
Salt
Pepper

Parmesan cheese
2 tablespoons butter
2 tablespoons olive oil
1½ lemons
Parsley

Lightly pound veal slices between 2 sheets of waxed paper until they are ⅛ to 1/16-inch thick. Dip veal slices in a mixture of flour, salt, pepper and Parmesan cheese. Melt butter and oil in a large skillet. Saute veal about 2 minutes on each side. Remove to platter and keep warm. Deglaze the pan with juice of 1 lemon. Pour over the veal. Garnish with parsley and lemon wedges.
Carol Rowsey Solomon (Mrs. Stephen G.)

Pam's Lasagne
Serves 8 to 12

1 pound ground round
2 cloves garlic, chopped
Salt
Pepper
1/2 cup Contadina tomato
  paste
1/2 cup water
1/2 cup Rotel tomatoes
2 teaspoons leaf oregano
1/4 teaspoon sweet basil

1/4 teaspoon rosemary leaves
Thyme
Lasagne noodles
Garlic salt
2 cups grated Parmesan
  cheese
1 24-ounce container small
  curd cottage cheese
4 cups shredded Mozzarella
  cheese

Brown meat with garlic. Salt and pepper meat to taste. Add tomato paste, water, Rotel, oregano, basil, rosemary and a pinch of thyme. Let simmer 20 minutes. Cook lasagne noodles according to package directions and drain. Butter lasagne pan and sprinkle bottom with garlic salt. Layer noodles and sprinkle with Parmesan cheese. Cover with half of cottage cheese, then half meat sauce, top with half of Mozzarella cheese. Start over by sprinkling with garlic salt, repeat layers ending with Mozzarella cheese. Refrigerate for 1 day. Bake at 350 degrees for 40 minutes.
Christa Schwab Chain (Mrs. John W.)

Meatballs
Yields 48

2 pounds lean ground round
  or sirloin
1 teaspoon salt
Pepper
1/2 cup bread crumbs
1 small onion, chopped

1 clove garlic, minced
2 eggs, beaten
1 10-ounce jar Welch's grape
  jelly
1 12-ounce bottle chili sauce
Juice of 1 lemon

Combine ground beef, salt, pepper, bread crumbs, onion, garlic and eggs and form into balls about the size of walnuts. Arrange balls side by side touching in an oblong pan. Mix together jelly, chili sauce and lemon juice and simmer for 5 minutes. Pour sauce over meatballs and bake at 325 degrees for 1 hour, basting 3 times during baking. Serve over rice.
Marian Whitten Cathcart (Mrs. William R.)

Swedish Meatballs
Yields 2 dozen

1/2 to 3/4 cup whipping cream,
  heated
2 eggs
1 onion, chopped
2 1/2 teaspoons salt
1/2 teaspoon pepper

1/4 teaspoon nutmeg
Sprig of parsley
2 pounds ground beef
1/2 pound ground pork
1 cup bread crumbs
2 cups sour cream

Mix the cream, eggs, onion, salt, pepper, nutmeg and parsley in a blender or food processor. Mix in beef, pork and bread crumbs. Shape into balls and fry until brown. Pour sour cream over. Simmer until fully cooked.

Linda Meining Zahn (Mrs. Richard L.)

Spicy Chili
Serves 12 to 16

Oil
3 to 4 onions, finely chopped
3 green peppers, finely
  chopped
3 celery stalks, finely chopped
8 pounds lean beef, coarsely
  chopped
1 6-ounce can tomato paste
2 14 1/2-ounce cans stewed
  tomatoes
2 14 1/2-ounce cans tomato
  sauce
2 14 1/2-ounce cans water

3 small cloves garlic, chopped
1 1/2 to 2 3-ounce bottles chili
  powder
3 tablespoons salt
Oregano
2 teaspoons cumin powder
1/4 cup Worcestershire sauce
1/3 cup picante sauce, or more
1 medium hot chili pepper,
  seeded
2 tablespoons yellow
  cornmeal

Rub large stock pot with cooking oil. Add onions, green peppers and celery. Cook gently, stirring often. Brown the meat in another skillet a little at a time. Pour browned meat into pot with vegetables and increase heat slightly. Add remaining ingredients and simmer uncovered for 2 1/2 hours, stirring occasionally.

Janell Law Everest (Mrs. Jean I.)

Double Cheese Spaghetti
Serves 6 to 8

1 12-ounce package thin
  spaghetti
1/4 pound bacon, cut in small
  pieces
1 medium onion, chopped
1 pound ground beef
2 8-ounce cans tomato sauce

1 4-ounce can sliced
  mushrooms, drained
1 1/2 teaspoons salt
1/2 teaspoon oregano
1/2 teaspoon garlic salt
1 cup grated Cheddar cheese
1 cup grated Provolone cheese

Cook spaghetti according to package directions. Drain and set aside.
Meanwhile, fry bacon until browned. Drain off excess fat. Add onion and
beef and cook until meat is brown. Mix in tomato sauce, mushrooms,
and seasonings. Simmer 15 minutes. In a large bowl, combine sauce and
spaghetti. Place half of mixture in a buttered 2-quart casserole. Top with
half the Cheddar and half the Provolone cheese. Repeat layers. Bake at
375 degrees for 20 to 25 minutes.
Laurie Kennedy McCann (Mrs. James K.)

The T's Spaghetti Sauce

2 pounds ground beef
1/2 onion, chopped
2 cloves garlic, chopped
1 6-ounce can tomato paste
3 tablespoons Spice Islands
  spaghetti sauce seasoning
1 teaspoon cumin
1 teaspoon oregano
1 teaspoon thyme
1 teaspoon marjoram

Salt
Pepper
2 bay leaves, crushed
1 cup Mr. and Mrs. T's Bloody
  Mary Mix
1 3-ounce jar mushrooms,
  sliced
1/2 green pepper, chopped
3/4 cup water
Garlic salt

Brown meat, onion and garlic in pan. Add remaining ingredients and
simmer until all ingredients have blended together, at least 1 hour. More
Bloody Mary mix may be added for more liquid. Serve over spaghetti.
Linda Lee Rooker (Mrs. Barry)

Helen Caporal's Fabulous Spaghetti Sauce
Serves 12

Meatballs

2 pounds ground beef
2 eggs
1/2 to 1 onion, chopped
3 cloves garlic, minced
1 teaspoon oregano
2 pounds Italian sausage

1/4 pound Romano or
  Parmesan cheese, grated
Salt
Pepper
2 pieces bread
1 foot long pepperoni, sliced

Spaghetti Sauce

8 8-ounce cans tomato sauce
2 teaspoons oregano
1/2 pound fresh mushrooms,
  sliced and sauteed, or
  1 8-ounce can sliced
  mushrooms

1/4 teaspoon red pepper
1/2 gallon red dry wine (Gallo
  Chianti)
Romano cheese, cut into small
  chunks

Start this recipe early in the day. To prepare meatballs, combine ground beef, eggs, chopped onion, garlic, oregano, Romano cheese, salt and pepper to taste. Moisten 2 pieces of bread with a small amount of the red wine. Mix well and add to meat mixture. Shape into small meatballs and fry in oil. Then fry Italian sausage, which has been cut into bite size pieces. Set aside. (Meatballs and sausage can be fried a day ahead and refrigerated.) To prepare spaghetti sauce, add 8 cans of tomato sauce, oregano, red pepper and half of the red wine. Add meatballs, sausage and pepperoni pieces to the spaghetti sauce and simmer. Continue adding the red wine throughout the day until sauce is very dark red in color. The sauce will have lost some of its tomato flavor. About 15 minutes before serving, add mushrooms and small chunks of Romano cheese. (Two large pans may be needed to accommodate sauce.) Serve over hot spaghetti.

Marty Johnson Margo (Mrs. Robert C.)

Indian Beef Curry
Serves 8

2 to 3 pounds beef, cut into
  1-inch cubes
1/2 pound ground beef
1/2 cup flour
1/2 cup margarine or oil
3 onions, chopped
1 teaspoon salt
1/4 teaspoon pepper
1 8-ounce can tomato sauce

1/2 teaspoon cayenne pepper
1/2 teaspoon curry
1/2 teaspoon ginger
1/2 teaspoon turmeric
1/4 teaspoon cinnamon
1 teaspoon coriander
1 teaspoon cumin
1 teaspoon chili powder

Dust meat with flour and brown in oil. Add onions and spices. Simmer 2 hours. Serve with rice and usual curry accompaniments such as chutney, coconut and peanuts.
Ann Whiting Hargis (Mrs. V. Burns)

Italian Meat Loaf
Serves 8

1 1/2 pounds lean ground beef
1 egg, beaten
3/4 cup cracker crumbs
1/2 cup chopped onion
1/3 cup ketchup
1 8-ounce can tomato sauce
2 tablespoons grated
  Parmesan cheese

1 teaspoon salt
1 teaspoon Italian seasoning
1/2 teaspoon sweet basil
1/8 teaspoon pepper
1/2 teaspoon sugar
2 cups grated Mozzarella
  cheese

Combine ground beef, egg, cracker crumbs, onion, ketchup, half of the tomato sauce, Parmesan cheese, seasonings and sugar. Mix well. Shape into a flat 10 x 12-inch rectangle on waxed paper sprayed with nonstick spray. Sprinkle Mozzarella cheese evenly over meat mixture. Roll up jelly roll fashion, lifting one end of the waxed paper as you go. Press ends and seam to seal. Place in a 9 x 13-inch baking dish that has been lined with heavy duty foil and sprayed with nonstick spray. Bake at 350 degrees for 1 hour. Drain off fat. Pour on remaining 1/2 can of tomato sauce and bake 15 minutes longer.
Sandra Davis Malone (Mrs. George D.)

Meat Loaf with its own Barbeque Sauce

Serves 4 to 6

1¼ pounds ground beef
1 onion, chopped
1 egg, beaten
1 teaspoon salt
¼ teaspoon pepper

½ green pepper, chopped
   (optional)
½ cup tomato sauce
Cracker crumbs

Barbeque Sauce
1½ cups tomato sauce
½ cup water
3 tablespoons vinegar

3 tablespoons brown sugar
2 tablespoons mustard
2 teaspoons Worcestershire
   sauce

Mix together ground beef, onion, egg, salt, pepper, green pepper and ½ cup tomato sauce. Add enough cracker crumbs to make mixture the consistency you like. Form into a loaf and put in shallow 7 x 10-inch baking dish. To prepare barbeque sauce combine ingredients and pour over loaf. Bake at 350 degrees for 1 hour and 15 minutes. Baste occasionally.

Berta Faye Curtis Rex (Mrs. John W.)

Shredded Beef

Serves 14 to 16

1 3-pound roast, chuck or arm
2 tablespoons fancy pickling
   spice in a bag
½ large onion
2 tablespoons dry mustard

2 tablespoons sugar
2 tablespoons vinegar
1 tablespoon salt
1 32-ounce bottle of ketchup

In a covered Dutch oven, cook meat, pickling spices and onion in enough water to cover for 4 hours or until tender. Take out of water and cool. Shred meat with a fork. Mix remaining ingredients, except ketchup, and pour over shredded meat. Pour some of the water over. Add ketchup and cook slowly for 1 hour until well blended. Serve on buns. This will freeze.

Ranell Bules Brown (Mrs. Steve M.)

Friends' Favorite Manicotti
Serves 6

1 8-ounce box manicotti

1 tablespoon olive oil

Sauce
1 pound or more ground beef
1 32-ounce jar Ragu sauce

1 tablespoon Italian seasoning

Stuffing
2 6-ounce packages
   Mozzarella cheese, grated
1 pound Ricotta cheese,
   crumbled

1 egg
1/2 cup chopped parsley
1/2 cup grated Parmesan
   cheese

Boil manicotti 10 minutes in salted water with olive oil. Remove from heat, add cold water in sink and let noodles soak. To prepare sauce, brown meat, add sauce and herbs and let simmer 15 to 20 minutes in large skillet, covered. Prepare stuffing while meat mixture is simmering. Mix Mozzarella cheese, Ricotta cheese, egg, parsley and Parmesan cheese in mixing bowl. Grease a 2-quart ovenproof dish and pour a little sauce mixture in the bottom to prevent noodles from sticking. Drain noodles, carefully, and stuff with cheese mixture and place in casserole. (It is easier to stuff with fingers.) Pour sauce mixture over the noodles. Bake uncovered for 30 minutes at 350 degrees.
Ann Munger Fleming (Mrs. Zane L.)

Easy Burgundy Beef Stew
Serves 4

1 pound chuck beef or stew
   meat, cut into 2-inch pieces
1/2 cup red wine
1 10 1/2-ounce can consomme
1 medium onion, sliced

Salt
Pepper
1/4 cup flour
1/4 cup dry bread crumbs
1/2 teaspoon Kitchen Bouquet

Combine beef, wine, consomme, onion, salt and pepper in a 2-quart baking dish. Mix flour with bread crumbs. Add Kitchen Bouquet, if desired. Stir in beef mixture and cover dish. Bake at 300 degrees for about 3 hours or until beef is tender. Serve over noodles.
Helen Holman Stuart (Mrs. Dan D.)

Meg's Forgotten Stew
Serves 6

2 pounds stew meat, cut into
  2-inch pieces
6 carrots, cut in half
6 red potatoes, cut in half
6 small onions
3 stalks celery, cut in 2-inch
  pieces
1 green pepper, cut in 1-inch
  pieces
1 8-ounce can tomato sauce

¼ cup red wine
3 tablespoons minute tapioca
1½ teaspoons instant beef
  bouillon
½ teaspoon ground pepper
1 teaspoon sugar
½ teaspoon garlic powder
3 tablespoons minced parsley
1 bay leaf

In a Dutch oven or large casserole with tight fitting lid, put unbrowned stew meat, vegetables and remaining ingredients. Mix together and put bay leaf on top. Bake for 4½ to 5 hours at 250 degrees. Do not lift lid.
Betsy Amis Daugherty (Mrs. Fred)

Charcoal Broiled Shish Kabobs
Serves 6

Marinade
1 cup Burgundy wine
2 tablespoons Worcestershire
  sauce
1 clove garlic
1 cup oil

2 to 3 tablespoons ketchup
2 tablespoons sugar
1 teaspoon salt
1 teaspoon monosodium
  glutamate

Shish Kabobs
1 pound mushrooms, cleaned
3 pounds sirloin, cut in
  1½-inch cubes
2 green peppers, seeded and
  cut into 1½-inch cubes

12 to 14 cherry tomatoes
2 onions, quartered and
  separated
1 large can pineapple cubes,
  drained

To prepare marinade, combine ingredients in a very large deep bowl and mix together thoroughly. Add remaining ingredients, each of which has been prepared in bite-size pieces. Cover and let stand in the refrigerator 4 to 5 hours or overnight. After well marinated, alternate meat, vegetables and fruit on skewers. Broil on outdoor grill for 4 to 5 minutes on each side, depending on taste.
Marca Downing Floyd (Mrs. Robert P.)

Island Teriyaki
Serves 4 to 6

1/2 cup soy sauce
1/4 cup brown sugar
2 tablespoons olive oil
1 teaspoon dry ginger
1/2 teaspoon monosodium
  glutamate

1/4 teaspoon cracked pepper
2 cloves garlic, minced
11/2 to 2 pounds sirloin steak,
  cut in 1/4 x 1-inch strips
Whole water chestnuts

Mix first 7 ingredients. Add meat and stir to coat. Let stand 2 hours or more at room temperature. Lace meat accordion-style on skewers and tip each end with a water chestnut. Broil meat skewers over hot coals 10 to 12 minutes. Turn often and baste with marinade.
Judy Weilert Savage (Mrs. Robert Leonard)

Beef Tenderloin Marinade

Beef tenderloin

Marinade
11/2 cups red wine
1 large onion, chopped
1 teaspoon dry mustard
1/2 teaspoon pepper
1 teaspoon soy sauce
1/2 cup vegetable oil

1 tablespoon Worcestershire
  sauce
1 tablespoon fines herbes
1 tablespoon garlic powder
Monosodium glutamate

Combine all ingredients and marinate tenderloin 24 hours. Drain liquid and save for basting. Bake tenderloin in a shallow pan for 35 to 45 minutes at 425 degrees. Baste occasionally. Meat thermometer will be 140 degrees at thick end for rare.
Karel Frank Love (Mrs. Joe R.)

Beef Stroganoff
Serves 6 to 8

2½ pounds round steak
2 to 4 tablespoons flour
1 teaspoon garlic salt
6 tablespoons butter or margarine
1 10½-ounce can consomme
1 tablespoon soy sauce

1 tablespoon Worcestershire sauce
½ tablespoon Tabasco
1 4-ounce can mushrooms, stems and pieces, drained
1 10¾-ounce can cream of mushroom soup
1 cup sour cream

Cut away fat and bone from steak. Pound flour into it with meat mallet. Sprinkle with garlic salt. Rub into meat. Cut into ½ x 2 x 4-inch strips. Saute slightly in butter until golden brown. Add consomme, soy sauce, Worcestershire and Tabasco. Simmer 1 to 1¼ hours, stirring occasionally. Add more liquid if necessary. When ready to serve, fold in mushrooms, cream of mushroom soup and sour cream. Heat thoroughly.
Mary D. Streich

Party Beef Stroganoff
Serves 10 to 12

4 pounds sirloin beef, cut into 2 x ½-inch strips
2 cups butter or margarine
2 medium onions, diced
2 cups fresh mushrooms, halved
Tabasco
2 tablespoons Worcestershire sauce

1 green pepper, seeded and diced
1 to 2 cloves garlic, minced
1 tablespoon garlic salt
2 cups sour cream
1 cup half and half
6 tablespoons wine vinegar
4 tablespoons flour

Saute sirloin strips in butter until brown. After meat begins to brown, add onions, mushrooms, Tabasco, Worcestershire, green pepper, minced garlic and garlic salt. When these ingredients begin to soften, add sour cream, half and half and wine vinegar. Add flour. Simmer and stir mixture until sauce thickens to desired consistency. Serve over rice or noodles.
Kelsey Price Walters (Mrs. Roland A., III)

Flank Steak Sandwich
Serves 6

2 pounds flank steak	4 cups sliced yellow onions
2/3 cup beer	1/2 teaspoon paprika
1/3 cup oil	12 slices French bread,
1 teaspoon salt	toasted
1/4 teaspoon garlic powder	1 1/2 cups sour cream, warm
1/4 teaspoon pepper	1 1/2 tablespoons horseradish
5 tablespoons butter	

Place flank steak in a long rectangular dish. Combine beer, oil, salt, garlic powder and pepper and pour over steak. Cover and marinate in the refrigerator overnight. Drain. Broil steak 3 inches from the heat for about 5 minutes on each side. In a saucepan, melt butter and saute onions until soft. Add paprika. Thinly slice the steak diagonally across the grain. For each serving, place meat slices over 2 pieces of toasted French bread. Spoon on onions. Top with a mixture of sour cream and horseradish.

Leslie Smith Wasson

Grilled Flank Steak with Wine and Shallot Sauce
Serves 4

1 pound flank steak	Freshly ground pepper
Soy sauce	1 teaspoon crumbled thyme
Salt	

Sauce

1 1/4 cups chopped shallots or	Salt
green onions	2 tablespoons chopped
1 1/4 cups red wine	parsley
1/2 cup butter	

Brush flank steak with soy sauce and sprinkle well with salt, pepper and thyme. Let stand 1 hour or more. Brush again with soy sauce and grill over a brisk fire 3 to 4 minutes on each side for rare steaks. Carve with sharp knife in thin slices on the diagonal. To prepare the sauce, combine shallots or green onions and red wine. Bring just to boiling. Add 1/2 cup butter and salt to taste. Stir until butter is melted. Add parsley and spoon over steak slices.

Patti Jo Jeter Elder (Mrs. John B.)

Marinated Flank Steak
Serves 4 to 6

2 1-pound flank steaks
1 cup salad oil
¾ cup soy sauce
½ cup lemon juice

¼ cup Worcestershire sauce
¼ cup mustard
1 tablespoon pepper
2 cloves garlic, minced

Place steaks in a large, flat baking dish. Mix together remaining ingredients and pour over steaks. Cover with aluminum foil and marinate overnight. Grill on a charcoal grill or in oven for 5 minutes per side or medium rare. Slice diagonally in thin slices. Serve immediately with pan juices.
Robin Thrift Mason (Mrs. Joe)

Barbeque Brisket
Serves 6 to 8

4 to 5 pound brisket
3 tablespoons Worcestershire sauce
½ bottle Liquid Smoke
1 teaspoon onion salt

1 teaspoon celery salt
1 teaspoon garlic salt
Salt
Pepper
1 cup barbeque sauce

Trim fat from brisket and place in pan deep enough that a foil covering will not touch brisket. Sprinkle with Worcestershire, Liquid Smoke and seasonings. Cover with aluminum foil and marinate overnight in refrigerator. To cook, sprinkle brisket with salt and pepper. Replace aluminum foil and bake at 275 degrees for 5 to 8 hours. Thirty minutes before the brisket is done, pour barbeque sauce over it and return to oven. Allow brisket to cool 30 minutes before serving in thin slices. Reheat pan drippings and serve as gravy.
Stacey Shannon Blake (Mrs. Joe)

Barbara Heinen Ryan (Mrs. Patrick M.)

Meme's Peppered Beef Brisket
Serves 6 to 8

1 4- to 5-pound brisket

Marinade
2/3 cup soy sauce
1/2 cup vinegar
1 tablespoon ketchup

1/4 cup coarsely ground black
pepper

1 teaspoon paprika
1/4 teaspoon garlic salt
Barbeque sauce

Trim all the fat from both sides of the brisket. Press the pepper into the meat with the palm of your hand. To prepare marinade, mix all ingredients. Put meat in plastic bag and pour marinade over. Seal and refrigerate 24 to 36 hours turning at least once. Drain meat and discard marinade. Seal in aluminum foil and bake at 300 degrees for 4½ to 5 hours. Slice and serve with barbeque sauce.
Ranell Bules Brown (Mrs. Steve M.)   *Becky Brown Johnston (Mrs. Brad)*

Barbeque Brisket Sandwich
Serves 8

1 7-pound beef brisket,
trimmed
1 4-ounce bottle liquid smoke

1 18-ounce bottle Heinz
Hickory barbeque sauce

The night before put whole brisket in medium roasting pan. Pour whole bottle of liquid smoke over it. Marinate overnight. The next morning pour off liquid smoke. Pour barbeque sauce over brisket. Cover and cook at 250 degrees for 5 to 6 hours. While warm, shred and chop. Add the liquid the brisket was cooked in. Serve on buns.
Adonna Morgan Meyer (Mrs. Stewart N.)

Bess's Beef Tenderloin with Bordelaise Sauce

Serves 8 to 10

1 large beef tenderloin,
  trimmed
2 tablespoons butter, softened
2 cloves garlic, halved

Lawry's seasoned salt
Onion salt
Seasoned pepper
4 tablespoons butter

Bordelaise Sauce
4 tablespoons butter
2 shallots, chopped
2 cloves garlic, chopped
2 onions, thickly sliced
4 carrots, thinly sliced
2 sprigs parsley
2 cloves
12 black peppercorns

1 bay leaf
4 tablespoons flour
2 10½-ounce cans beef
  bouillon
1 teaspoon salt
¼ teaspoon pepper
½ cup dry red wine
2 tablespoons snipped parsley

Preheat oven to 400 degrees. Rub tenderloin with softened butter and garlic. Heavily shake the seasonings on all sides of the meat until well coated. Heat 4 tablespoons of butter in a large skillet until smoking hot. Brown meat on all sides, rolling over often, until well seared. Bake uncovered in shallow roasting pan at 400 degrees until desired doneness. Bake 20 minutes for rare, 25 to 30 minutes for medium. Do not cook tenderloin well done.

To prepare the Bordelaise sauce melt butter in a large skillet. Saute shallots, garlic, onion slices, carrots, parsley sprigs, cloves, peppercorns and bay leaf until onion is golden and tender. Reduce to low temperature and add flour. Stir constantly until flour is light brown and thickened. Add beef bouillon and simmer until slightly thickened and smooth, stirring often. Pour through a food mill or large strainer. Mash as much through as possible. Add salt, pepper, wine and snipped parsley. Chill until ready to use. Reheat slowly in double boiler.

Marty Clay Conkle (Mrs. Cliff)

Beef Tenderloin and Mushroom Sauce
Yields 1/2 pound beef tenderloin per person

Beef tenderloin

Sauce
6 tablespoons butter
1 clove garlic, minced
1/2 pound mushrooms, sliced
2 medium onions, sliced
2 teaspoons chili sauce
Dried marjoram
Dried thyme
1 teaspoon A-1 sauce

4 drops Tabasco
1/4 teaspoon Worcestershire
  sauce
5 ounces dry red wine
2 beef bouillon cubes
Salt
Pepper
1/2 teaspoon flour

Preheat oven to 450 degrees for at least 15 minutes. Bake tenderloin for 25 minutes. To prepare sauce, melt butter in pan. Saute garlic, mushrooms and onions until tender. Add remaining ingredients and stir until completely blended. Simmer at least 10 minutes. The sauce can be made ahead of time and heated up while cooking the meat. Pour a little sauce over tenderloin the last 10 minutes of cooking. Pass remaining sauce or pour over individual portions.
Linda Meining Zahn (Mrs. Richard L.)

Bistecca Alla Pizzaiola (Italian Roast)
Serves 6 to 8

2 pound sirloin steak, 1 to 1 1/2
  inches thick
1 16-ounce can whole
  tomatoes, undrained
1 teaspoon oregano
1 1/2 teaspoons chopped
  parsley

1/2 teaspoon garlic powder
1 tablespoon minced onion
1/4 teaspoon salt
1/4 teaspoon pepper
2 tablespoons olive oil
1 8-ounce package Mozzarella
  cheese, sliced

Arrange meat in baking dish. Mash tomatoes, including liquid, with fork and spread evenly over meat. Sprinkle with seasonings and oil. Bake tightly covered at 325 degrees for 30 minutes. Remove cover and bake for another 45 minutes. Top meat with cheese slices and bake 20 to 30 minutes more. If you are cooking this on "time bake" and will be gone, it can be cooked uncovered the entire time.
Beth Sherman Wells (Mrs. Edward)

Italian Pot Roast

Serves 4 to 6

¼ cup flour
½ teaspoon salt
¼ teaspoon pepper
1 3- to 4-pound boneless
　chuck or arm roast
2 tablespoons vegetable oil
2 medium onions, sliced
2 4-ounce cans sliced
　mushrooms, drained
½ cup water

¼ cup ketchup
¼ cup dry sherry
¼ teaspoon dry mustard
1 clove garlic, crushed
¼ teaspoon dried rosemary
¼ teaspoon dried thyme
¼ teaspoon dried marjoram
1 bay leaf
1 tablespoon flour
¼ cup cold water

Combine first 3 ingredients. Coat roast with flour mixture. Brown roast on all sides in hot oil in a large Dutch oven. Place onions on top of roast. Combine next 10 ingredients and pour over roast. Cover and bake at 325 degrees for 2½ to 3 hours, or until tender. Remove roast and vegetables to serving platter. Reserve pan drippings. Combine flour and water. Stir until smooth. Pour flour mixture into pan drippings. Cook, stirring constantly, until thickened and bubbly. Serve gravy with roast, pouring some on top of roast.

Debbi Davidson Dale (Mrs. Mark)

Nita's Pot Roast

Serves 6 to 8

1 3- to 5-pound roast, chuck
　or rump
1 envelope Lipton Onion
　Soup Mix
Oregano

Salt
Pepper
1 14½-ounce can stewed
　tomatoes
1 cup red Burgundy wine

Line a 9 x 12-inch ovenproof dish with heavy duty aluminum foil. Put roast in foil. Sprinkle with dry soup mix, pinch of oregano, salt and pepper. Pour tomatoes and wine over roast. Seal with foil and bake at 350 degrees for 4 to 5 hours.

Chris Mills Verity (Mrs. Jidge)

Shawnee Roast
Serves 10 to 12

1 5- to 6-pound boneless
chuck or Pikes Peak roast
1 12-ounce can Coca-Cola
1 5-ounce bottle A-1 sauce
1/2 10-ounce bottle
Worcestershire sauce

2 to 3 cloves
1 18-ounce bottle mild
barbeque sauce
2 teaspoons B-V concentrate
Water
Rye bread

Sauce
11/2 cups mayonnaise
1 tablespoon dry mustard

1 teaspoon horseradish
Half and half

Put all ingredients except bread and sauce ingredients in a large pan and cover. Bake at 300 degrees for 6 to 7 hours. Meat juices can be cooked down, if desired. To prepare sauce, mix well the mayonnaise, mustard and horseradish. Add enough cream to thin sauce to a pouring consistency. To serve, place sliced beef on rye bread. Pour juice over open faced sandwich and put 1 or 2 teaspoons sauce over the sandwich.
Margaret Fisher Eskridge (Mrs. J. B., III)

Pot Roast with Dumplings
Serves 6

1/4 cup butter
1/2 cup chopped onion
1 4-pound chuck roast,
2 inches thick
1 bay leaf, crumbled
1 tablespoon grated orange
peel

1 teaspoon salt
1/8 teaspoon pepper
1/4 teaspoon allspice
1 101/2-ounce can condensed
consomme
2 cups Bisquick
2/3 cup milk

Melt butter over high heat in a 6-quart Dutch oven 4 hours before serving. Lower heat and add onions and brown slightly. Add meat and brown on all sides. Add bay leaf, orange peel, salt, pepper, allspice and consomme. Cover and simmer over low heat 31/2 hours. Add 11/2 cups water to meat and heat to boiling. Meanwhile, stir Bisquick and milk in a medium bowl. Drop by large tablespoons around meat in Dutch oven. Cook over low heat uncovered for 10 minutes. Cover and cook for 10 more minutes. Serve juices from meat as a gravy.
Marjory Pielsticker Feighny (Mrs. James A.)

Roast Beef Au Jus

Yields ½ pound per person

Prime rib roast, well
  marbleized
Salt

Pepper
Parsley

Let prime rib roast stand at room temperature for 1 hour. Preheat oven to 375 degrees. Place roast in a shallow roasting pan. Do not cover or add water. Put roast in oven. Cook for just 1 hour. Turn off heat but do not open oven door at any time until ready to serve. Regardless of length of time roast has been in oven, 30 to 40 minutes before serving, turn oven on at 375 degrees and cook for remaining 30 to 40 minutes. Now open door. Remove roast to warm serving platter and season to taste. Garnish with parsley. The meat will be very brown and crisp on the outside, beautifully pink all the way through, medium rare and very juicy. Use the same procedure for any size roast. It is best to cook the meat in the morning and let it stand in an unopened oven all day. Finish cooking just before serving.

Marty Johnson Margo (Mrs. Robert C.)

Jean Gumerson's Beef and Avocado Blend

Serves 8

2 avocados, peeled and sliced
2 pounds leftover roast beef,
  rare and thinly sliced
1 sweet red onion, thinly
  sliced
½ cup vegetable oil

¼ cup olive oil
½ cup wine vinegar
2 teaspoons Dijon mustard
2 teaspoons salt
Parsley, chopped

Arrange in a glass bowl alternating layers of avocados, beef and red onions. Mix other ingredients and pour over top. Cover and refrigerate several hours.

Susie Ray Graves (Mrs. Jack M.)

Chilled Filet of Beef with Sour Cream Dressing

Serves 6

Salt
Pepper
1 3-pound filet of beef
4 tablespoons butter

1 carrot, finely chopped
1 leek, white part only, finely
    chopped
1 stalk celery, finely chopped

Sour Cream Dressing
1 tablespoon oil
1 clove garlic, crushed
¾ pound bacon, cut in
    1-inch pieces
¼ pound fresh mushrooms,
    sliced
1½ cups sour cream

2 teaspoons horseradish
1 tablespoon grated onion
1 tablespoon finely chopped
    fresh parsley
1 teaspoon dried thyme
1 teaspoon dried chervil

Salt and pepper the beef and dot with 2 tablespoons butter. In a small roasting pan, melt the remaining 2 tablespoons butter. Saute carrot, leek and celery over low heat for 8 minutes. Add the beef and place the pan in the oven at 500 degrees for 25 minutes. Remove the beef from the oven and cool for 1 hour in the pan juices. To prepare dressing, heat the oil and garlic over moderate heat in a heavy medium-sized skillet for 1 minute. Add bacon and saute until barely crisp. Remove the bacon and drain it on paper towels. Pour off all but 3 tablespoons of the fat and saute the mushrooms in the remaining fat over moderate heat for 3 to 5 minutes. Drain mushrooms and set aside. After the meat has cooled, remove it to a cutting board. Pour the pan juices into a medium-sized mixing bowl and add sour cream, horseradish, onion, parsley, thyme and chervil, blending well. Add bacon bits, mushrooms, salt and pepper. To stuff, slice a 1-inch wide, 1-inch deep wedge along the top length of the filet and remove the wedge. Fill the cavity evenly with 3 tablespoons of the dressing. Replace the wedge in the filet. To serve, cut through the filet in complete ¾-inch slices and serve accompanied by the additional dressing.

Carol Craven Wilkinson (Mrs. C. P.)

Beef Boats
Serves 4 to 6

1 pound ground beef
1 large onion, chopped
1 4-ounce can chopped
 green chiles
Seasoned salt

6 French style dinner rolls
3 tablespoons margarine
1/2 pound Cheddar cheese,
 grated

Saute ground beef and onion together. Drain and add green chiles and seasoned salt to taste. Prepare the dinner rolls by removing a lengthwise wedge from top of rolls and scooping out loose filling. Put rolls in 350 degree oven to crisp, then drizzle the cavity with melted margarine. Fill with the meat mixture and top with grated cheese. Bake at 350 degrees for about 40 minutes or until hot. These can be wrapped in aluminum foil before baking and frozen for later use.
Grenda Penhollow Moss (Mrs. Ray)   *Kay Pappan Musser (Mrs. R. Clark)*

Medallions of Beef in White Wine Sauce
Serves 6

18 1/2-inch slices beef
 tenderloin
Salt
Pepper
2 tablespoons butter
1 onion, sliced
2 green peppers, sliced

1/2 pound button mushrooms,
 sliced
2 ounces brandy
1/2 bottle dry white wine
1 pint whipping cream
1 bay leaf

Season medallions of beef on both sides with salt and pepper. Saute beef in butter in a very hot heavy skillet for 1 minute on each side, or longer depending on desired doneness. Transfer to a serving dish and keep warm. Using the skillet, add in onion, peppers and mushrooms and cook until soft. Flame with brandy and add white wine. Cook on high for 5 minutes, uncovered, to reduce liquid by half. Pour in cream, stir and add bay leaf. Bring to a boil and simmer for 10 minutes adjusting the seasoning. Remove bay leaf and pour over the waiting medallions. Serve immediately.
Susan Esco Crain (Mrs. R. Dean)

Daube de Boeuf Provencale

Serves 4 to 6

2 pounds sirloin tips
1 cup dry white vermouth
2 tablespoons olive oil
1 cup sliced onions
1 cup sliced carrots
1 bay leaf
2 cloves garlic, crushed
Freshly ground black pepper
Salt
Flour
1/4 pound bacon, diced

1/2 pound large brown
  mushrooms, sliced
1 1/2 pounds large ripe
  tomatoes
2 cups beef stock
10 anchovies
2 tablespoons capers
2 tablespoons red wine
  vinegar
3 tablespoons olive oil
2 cloves garlic, crushed
1/2 cup chopped parsley

Cut sirloin tips into 2-inch cubes and marinate in dry white vermouth, olive oil, onion, carrots, bay leaf, 2 cloves of garlic, pepper and salt for about 5 hours. Stir occasionally. Remove beef and lightly flour. To prepare daube or stew, simmer bacon in 1 quart of water for 10 minutes. Drain and dry with paper towels. Peel, seed and dice tomatoes. Set aside. Line a 6-quart baking dish with blanched bacon. Arrange part of the marinated vegetables, mushrooms and tomatoes over the bacon. Cover with a layer of floured beef. Repeat layers of bacon, vegetables and beef until all the beef has been used. Pour marinade over layers and add enough beef stock to cover. Bring to a simmer on top of the stove to get stew to cooking temperature. Cover and place in a 325 degree oven for 3 1/2 hours or until meat is tender. Remove from oven and skim fat. To prepare anchovy-caper mixture, mash together anchovies and capers. Add red wine vinegar, olive oil, remaining garlic and parsley. Stir into stew and serve in bowls.

This is a hearty French stew that can be served hot or cold.

Carolyn Clarkson Mee (Mrs. John McHenry)

Sherried Beef
Serves 6 to 8

3 pounds sirloin, cubed and
browned
2 10½-ounce cans golden
mushroom soup
1 package Lipton Onion
Soup mix

1 4-ounce can sliced
mushrooms
1 4-ounce can sliced water
chestnuts
1 cup sherry

Stir all ingredients together. Place in a covered 5-quart Dutch oven and bake for 3 to 5 hours at 325 degrees. Serve over rice.
Cookbook Committee

Hamburger au Poivre
Serves 4

1½ pounds ground chuck
Salt
Crushed peppercorns
3 tablespoons butter
3 tablespoons finely chopped
onions or shallots

¼ cup dry red wine
1 tablespoon brandy
¼ cup beef broth
2 tablespoons minced parsley

Form 4 patties from the chuck. Sprinkle lightly with salt. Press the crushed peppercorns into the meat on both sides, using as much as you like. Heat a heavy skillet to smoking hot and add the patties. Fry 5 minutes on each side for rare, 10 minutes for well done. Remove the patties. Add half the butter and shallots. Cook until shallots wilt. Add wine and boil 1 minute. Add brandy and reduce liquid by half. Add broth and reduce liquid to ¼ cup. Add the remaining butter. Serve over the patties. Sprinkle with the parsley.
Beth Matthews McMullen (Mrs. Harry)

Ratatouille with Sausage
Serves 10 to 12

3 cloves garlic, finely minced
2 onions, thinly sliced
1/3 cup olive oil
1 green pepper, seeded and
   cut into thin rings
2 medium eggplants, diced
   and unpeeled
2 medium zucchini, sliced
   1/4-inch thick
1 20-ounce can whole Italian
   tomatoes, undrained

1 1/2 teaspoons basil
1 1/2 teaspoons parsley
1 1/2 teaspoons salt
Pepper
1 1/2 pounds Italian sausage,
   sliced
1/2 pound whole mushrooms
1 cup grated Swiss cheese

Saute garlic and onions in oil until soft. Add green pepper, eggplant and zucchini and cook five minutes over medium heat, tossing well. Add tomatoes with liquid and seasonings. Simmer 30 minutes, covered for last 15 minutes. Meanwhile cook sausage in frying pan until done and drain well. Add mushrooms to vegetables during last 10 minutes of cooking time. Add sausage to vegetables. Sprinkle with grated cheese. Cover and simmer until cheese melts.

Joy Engle Richardson (Mrs. Jerry)

Ronck's Spaghetti Sauce
Serves 12

2 pounds J.C. Potter mild
   sausage
1 medium onion, chopped
Garlic
1 green pepper, chopped
2 15-ounce cans tomato
   sauce
2 12-ounce cans tomato paste
1 22-ounce can chopped black
   olives

2 1 1/2-ounce envelopes Italian
   style spaghetti mix with
   mushrooms
3 cups water
1 teaspoon oregano leaves
1 bay leaf, crumbled
1 package sliced pepperoni
1 4-ounce can sliced
   mushrooms
1 16-ounce package spaghetti

Brown sausage with onion, green pepper and garlic to taste. Add remaining ingredients. Cook 1 1/2 to 2 hours. Cook spaghetti according to package directions. Serve sauce over spaghetti.

Sandy Simon Childress (Mrs. Bob)

71

Kamp's Ham Loaf with Raisin Sauce
Yields 2 loaves

1½ pounds ground ham
4 ounces ground beef
4 ounces ground pork
2 eggs, beaten
1 cup milk

⅛ teaspoon pepper
½ cup cracker crumbs
1 teaspoon dry mustard
½ cup brown sugar
1 onion, very finely chopped

Sauce
½ cup seedless raisins
1 cup boiling water
¾ cup sugar

1 teaspoon butter
½ teaspoon lemon juice
1 tablespoon cornstarch

Combine all ham loaf ingredients. Shape into at least 2 loaves. Cook with aluminum foil tent at 300 degrees for 4 hours. To prepare sauce, simmer raisins in water with sugar until tender. In separate pan, melt butter. Mix in lemon juice and cornstarch until it becomes a paste. Mix into raisins and stir until thickened. Yields 2½ cups. Serve with ham loaf.
Mary Tolle Walsh (Mrs. Thomas)

Special Ham Loaf
Serves 6 to 8

1½ pounds ground ham
¼ pound ground beef
¼ pound ground pork
½ cup chopped onion
2 eggs
1 cup fine cornflake crumbs

½ cup ketchup
½ cup apple butter
¼ teaspoon ground cloves
⅛ teaspoon pepper
⅓ cup raspberry jelly, melted

Combine all the ingredients except jelly in a bowl. Mix lightly, but well. Pack into a 9 x 5 x 3-inch loaf pan. Bake at 350 degrees for 1 hour. Remove from oven and brush top with melted raspberry jelly. Let stand 15 minutes in pan. Then turn out and brush bottom with jelly. Slice and serve.
Ranell Bules Brown (Mrs. Steve M.)

Hot Ham Sandwich
Serves 2

¼ cup mayonnaise
2 tablespoons horseradish
  mustard
1 tablespoon poppy seeds

2 tablespoons grated onion
Shaved ham
Shaved Swiss cheese
Small hamburger buns

For conventional oven mix first 4 ingredients. On bun, layer the sauce, shaved ham and Swiss cheese. Wrap in aluminum foil and heat at 350 degrees for 15 to 20 minutes. For microwave oven prepare as above except wrap in wax paper and heat on high for 3 to 5 minutes. These freeze beautifully.

Janie Gilbert Axton (Mrs. Jon C.)

Asparagus Rolls
Serves 4

16 stalks asparagus, or more
  if small
2 tablespoons butter
2 tablespoons flour
2 cups milk
8 ounces soft sharp Cheddar
  cheese

2 to 3 drops Tabasco
1 teaspoon Worcestershire
  sauce
8 ⅛-inch slices ham
Cheddar cheese, grated
Parmesan cheese

Cook fresh asparagus and chill. To prepare medium white sauce, melt butter over low heat in skillet. Whisk in flour to prevent lumps, then add milk. Add the soft cheese, Tabasco, Worcestershire and cook for 5 minutes. Roll 2 stalks cool asparagus in each slice of ham. Place in a small ovenproof dish. Pour the cheese sauce over the rolls. Sprinkle a small handful of grated cheese over cheese sauce and top with a small amount of Parmesan. Bake at 375 degrees for 10 minutes.

Tami Aschenbrener Boecking (Mrs. Stephen R.)

Savory Pork Chops
Serves 6

6 pork chops, preferred
   thickness
Salt
Pepper

Brown sugar
Lemon slices
1 cup ketchup
1 cup water

Place pork chops in a flat casserole sprayed with nonstick spray. On each chop place a tablespoon of brown sugar, then top each chop with a lemon slice. Season with salt and pepper. Mix together ketchup and water and pour around chops until they are just covered. Baste occasionally during baking. Bake at 350 degrees for 1 hour or until tender and well done.
   Surprisingly good to be so simple!
Berta Faye Curtis Rex (Mrs. John W.)

Pork Chops and Sauerkraut
Serves 4

4 loin pork chops,
   1/2-inch thick
2 tablespoons unsalted butter
1/2 teaspoon salt
1 teaspoon freshly ground
   pepper
1 tablespoon Dijon mustard

1 tablespoon horseradish
3 1/2 cups sauerkraut, fresh or
   canned, undrained
2 large Red Delicious apples,
   peeled and chopped
1/4 cup finely chopped onion
1 teaspoon caraway seed

Brown pork chops in butter in heavy skillet. Sprinkle with salt and pepper. Stir mustard and horseradish together and spread on browned chops. Combine sauerkraut, apples, onion and caraway seeds. Place in a 2-quart baking dish and lay pork chops on top. Cover and bake at 350 degrees for 30 minutes. Uncover and bake 30 minutes more.
Carol Sue Jennerjahn Taylor (Mrs. Jerry A.)

Marinated Pork Roast
Serves 10 to 12

½ cup soy sauce
½ cup dry sherry
2 cloves garlic, minced
1 tablespoon dry mustard
1 teaspoon ground ginger

1 teaspoon dried thyme,
 crushed
1 4- to 5-pound pork loin roast,
 boned, rolled and tied

Currant Sauce
1 10-ounce jar currant jelly
2 tablespoons sherry

1 tablespoon soy sauce

Blend soy sauce, sherry, garlic, mustard, ginger and thyme. Pour this over roast and let marinate 2 to 3 hours at room temperature or overnight in refrigerator. Turn meat occasionally. Remove from marinade and place on rack in shallow pan. Roast, uncovered at 325 degrees for 2½ to 3 hours or until thermometer reads 170 degrees. Baste with marinade during last hour. To prepare currant sauce, melt currant jelly in a saucepan and add sherry and soy sauce. Stir and simmer 2 minutes. Serve sauce over pork.
Sandy Simon Childress (Mrs. Bob)

Sweet and Sour Pork
Serves 6

1½ pounds lean pork
 shoulder, cut into
 2 x ½-inch strips
¼ cup water
1 20-ounce can pineapple
 chunks
¼ cup brown sugar
2 tablespoons cornstarch

¼ cup vinegar
1 tablespoon soy sauce
½ teaspoon salt
¾ cup green pepper, cut into
 strips
¼ cup thinly sliced onion
2 cans chow mein noodles

Brown pork slowly in hot fat. Add ¼ cup water. Cover and simmer until tender, about 1 hour. Drain pineapple, reserving syrup. Combine brown sugar and cornstarch. Add pineapple syrup, vinegar, soy sauce and salt. Cook and stir over low heat until thick. Pour over hot cooked pork. Let stand 10 minutes. Add pineapple, green pepper and onion. Cook 2 to 3 minutes longer. Serve over chow mein noodles.
Margaret Patzer Holdridge (Mrs. Curtis)

Pork Loin Acapulco
Serves 12 to 16

1 8-pound boneless loin
  of pork
4 slices raw bacon, cut in
  1/4-inch strips
4 garlic cloves, cut in slivers
3 4-ounce cans green chiles,
  cut in 1/2-inch strips
2 tablespoons salt

1/2 teaspoon pepper
1 cup finely minced onion
3 garlic cloves, minced
2 tablespoons chili powder
2 tablespoons paprika
2 tablespoons sugar
Few drops of water

Make 35 1-inch incisions with a sharp knife all over the top of the pork. Place a strip of bacon, sliver of garlic and a strip of green chili into each opening. Rub salt and pepper over pork. In a small bowl combine minced onion, minced garlic, chili powder, paprika and sugar. Stir to make a paste adding drops of water as needed. Spread paste on top of pork. Place pork in an open roasting pan, paste side up. Roast at 325 degrees until meat thermometer reaches 170 degrees, about 1 hour and 45 minutes to 2 hours.

Mary Slattery Price (Mrs. William S.)

Strasburg Pork
Serves 6

2 pounds pork tenderloin
Bacon
1/2 cup soy sauce
1 tablespoon grated onion

1 clove garlic, minced
1 tablespoon vinegar
1/4 teaspoon red pepper
1/2 teaspoon sugar

Wrap tenderloin in bacon. Mix remaining ingredients together and pour over tenderloin. Marinate overnight. Baste with sauce while baking. Bake 2 hours at 325 degrees.

Linda Bloyd Hanna (Mrs. Richard)

Sesame Spareribs
Serves 4

1 package instant meat
  marinade
²/₃ cup pineapple juice
¼ cup soy sauce

1 teaspoon garlic salt
3 pounds pork spareribs
¼ cup toasted sesame seeds

In a shallow pan, thoroughly blend the marinade mixture with the pineapple juice, soy sauce and garlic salt. Place the spareribs in the pan in a single layer and pierce all surfaces thoroughly with a fork. Marinate at least 15 minutes, preferably longer, turning several times. Remove ribs, drain and reserve liquid for basting. Place ribs on a rack in the broiler 4 to 6 inches from the heat and broil 40 to 50 minutes, turning and basting frequently. Do not get too close to broiler as it tends to burn. During the last 10 minutes, brush ribs with marinade and sprinkle generously with sesame seeds. Toast briefly to set seeds. Cut ribs into individual servings with a sharp knife.

Midge Wasson Lindsey (Mrs. Paul B.)

Corn Dogs
Yields 8

½ cup corn meal
½ cup flour
2 teaspoons paprika
1 teaspoon salt
½ teaspoon garlic salt
¼ teaspoon pepper

½ cup milk
1 egg, beaten
2 tablespoons salad oil
8 hot dogs
Flour
Salad oil

Combine corn meal, ½ cup flour, paprika, salt, garlic salt and pepper. Mix lightly. Add milk, egg and 2 tablespoons oil. Beat with a fork until smooth. Roll each hot dog in flour. Coat evenly with batter, allowing excess to drain. Heat 1 inch of salad oil to 375 degrees and fry hot dogs for 2 to 3 minutes or until golden brown. Drain. Insert wooden skewers in the end of each hot dog and serve with mustard or ketchup, if desired.

Margie Pribyl Law (Mrs. Mickey)

Northern Italian Spaghetti
Serves 6

1 12-ounce package spaghetti
1 tablespoon olive oil
6 eggs
¾ cup grated Parmesan
  cheese

¾ pound bacon, cut into
  2-inch pieces
2 tablespoons olive oil

Cook spaghetti in boiling salted water to which 1 tablespoon of olive oil has been added. Beat eggs and Parmesan cheese together. Brown bacon pieces and drain. When spaghetti is cooked, drain and quickly toss spaghetti, egg mixture, 2 tablespoons olive oil and bacon together. Serve immediately.

Jan Rohrer Robinson (Mrs. William J.)

Sausage Rice Casserole
Serves 8 to 10

1 pound hot sausage
1 pound mild sausage
1 cup chopped green pepper
2½ cups sliced celery
¾ cup chopped onion
¼ cup slivered almonds

2 packages Lipton chicken
  noodle soup
4½ cups boiling water
1 cup rice, uncooked
½ teaspoon salt
¼ cup margarine

Crumble sausage and brown. Drain off grease. Add green pepper, celery, and onions to sausage. Continue cooking until vegetables are tender. Add almond slivers, reserving some for garnish. In another pan combine soup, boiling water and rice. Simmer 20 minutes. Add salt and margarine. Stir well. Combine rice and sausage mixture and pour into a greased 3-quart baking dish. Sprinkle reserved almond slivers on top. Bake uncovered at 350 degrees for 1 hour. Freezes well.

Cookbook Committee

Bob Hancock's Country Lamb Pie
Serves 6

1/2 cup chopped onion
1/4 cup butter
1 clove garlic, chopped
1/4 cup flour
2 1/2 cups beef broth
1 tablespoon wine vinegar
3 cups cooked lamb, coarsely
  diced

1/4 teaspoon dill weed
2 tablespoons chopped
  parsley
Salt
Pepper
3/4 pound green beans, cut
  and cooked
1 cup carrots, cooked and
  sliced

Pastry
2 cups flour
1 teaspoon salt
1 teaspoon dill weed

3/4 cup shortening
1/4 cup water
1 egg, slightly beaten

Saute onion in butter until golden. Add garlic and saute 1 minute longer. Stir in 1/4 cup flour. Gradually stir in beef broth. Bring to a boil, stirring constantly. Boil 1 minute. Add vinegar, lamb, 1/4 teaspoon dill weed, parsley, salt and pepper to taste. Cook over low heat for 15 minutes. Add green beans and carrots. Turn into 6 10-ounce baking dishes and set aside. To prepare pastry, combine 2 cups sifted flour, 1 teaspoon salt and 1 teaspoon dill weed in a mixing bowl. Cut in shortening with pastry blender until fairly coarse, but uniform. Sprinkle water over top, toss with a fork and press into a ball. Divide dough in half, then divide each half into thirds. On a lightly floured surface roll each part into a 6-inch circle. Cut air vent in center of each circle. Place one dough circle over each lamb casserole. Trim and press edges under. Flute edges. Slash top and brush with egg. Bake at 425 degrees for 10 to 15 minutes.
Chelin Hancock Satherlie (Mrs. Gregg)

Mint Barbequed Leg of Lamb
Serves 6

1 5¼-pound leg of lamb
1 teaspoon salt

1 or more cloves garlic, cut
   into 8 slivers each

Sauce Number 1
½ cup mint jelly
½ cup cider vinegar
1 tablespoon butter

¼ cup light brown sugar,
   firmly packed
1 teaspoon grated lemon peel
1 tablespoon lemon juice

Sauce Number 2
⅓ to ½ cup butter
⅓ to ½ cup sherry
⅓ to ½ cup mint jelly
1 cup sugar

½ teaspoon salt
1 tablespoon lemon juice
1 teaspoon grated lemon peel
½ teaspoon dry mustard

To prepare either sauce, mix all ingredients together and warm over low heat until jelly is melted. Bring just to boiling, then cool and pour over meat to marinate. Butterfly the leg of lamb and flatten as much as possible to about 2 inch thickness. With sharp knife score the fell or skin side of the lamb in a criss-cross fashion. Wipe with damp cloth and sprinkle with the salt. With the tip of the knife make small gashes in the meat and insert the garlic slivers. Arrange lamb in large baking dish. Cover with either sauce and marinate at least ½ hour, better if 2 or 3. When charcoal is ready, lay lamb flat about 5 inches from the heat, if possible. Cook 1 to 1½ hours to desired doneness. Serve with remaining sauce, heated. Lamb should be tested for doneness after 1 hour and each ½ hour thereafter. Lamb is best when still somewhat pink.
Midge Wasson Lindsey (Mrs. Paul B.)

Butterflied Leg of Lamb
Serves 10 to 12

1 6- to 7-pound leg of lamb,
  boned and butterflied

Marinade

2 tablespoons soy sauce
2 tablespoons Worcestershire
  sauce
1½ teaspoons garlic salt
1 teaspoon Lawry's seasoned
  salt
¾ cup salad oil
¼ cup red wine vinegar

½ cup chopped onion
2 teaspoons Dijon mustard
2 teaspoons salt
½ teaspoon oregano
½ teaspoon basil
1 bay leaf, broken
¼ teaspoon pepper

To butterfly leg of lamb, bone and cut with small incisions to make it lay flat. Place lamb, fat side down in shallow pan. In a small bowl mix marinade ingredients together and pour over lamb. Cover pan tightly and refrigerate overnight. Next day baste several times. Remove lamb from refrigerator at least 1 hour before cooking. The marinade gives the lamb a pungent flavor and tenderizes it. Place meat in broiler pan, fat side up. Broil 4 inches from flame for 5 to 10 minutes. Turn. Baste. Broil 5 to 10 minutes on other side. Lower oven temperature to 425 degrees. Roast meat about 15 minutes. Meat should be pink and juicy. To charcoal grill, cook 20 to 25 minutes on each side, basting at 10-minute intervals. The charcoal grilled leg of lamb is tastier than the oven-cooked lamb.

Mary Davis Nichols (Mrs. John W.)

Lamb Pilaf
Serves 6 to 8

4 tablespoons butter or margarine
1 3-pound boned lamb, cut in 2-inch cubes
1 large onion, thinly sliced and separated into rings
½ teaspoon ground cinnamon
½ teaspoon ground black pepper
2 cups rice, uncooked

1 cup white or golden raisins
2 teaspoons salt
1 10½-ounce can consomme
2 cups water
¼ cup lemon juice
1 3-ounce package sliced almonds, toasted
3 tablespoons chopped parsley

Melt 2 tablespoons butter or margarine in a large skillet. Saute half of the lamb over very high heat until browned. Remove lamb to large bowl lined with paper towels. Drain excess fat from pan. Repeat with remaining 2 tablespoons butter or margarine and remaining lamb. Lower heat to medium. Saute onion, cinnamon and pepper in same skillet until onion is tender. Butter a 2½-quart baking dish lightly. Sprinkle about ½ cup rice over bottom of dish. Layer raisins, meat and onions over rice. Repeat layers. Sprinkle top with salt. Combine consomme and water. Pour over mixture in baking dish. Cover. Bake at 400 degrees for 50 minutes. Remove cover. Sprinkle with lemon juice and almonds. Bake 10 minutes longer. Sprinkle with parsley before serving.
Sally Ames Lenz (Mrs. Bruce)

Fried Shrimp
Serves 4

1 egg
½ cup milk
1 pound large shrimp, uncooked
1 cup flour

1½ teaspoons garlic salt
Salt
Pepper
36 saltines, crushed

Beat egg and milk. Clean shrimp and split to butterfly. Dip in seasoned flour, then egg and milk mixture, then in saltines. Fry in oil until golden brown.
Marty Johnson Margo (Mrs. Robert C.)

Barbequed Shrimp
Serves 12

6 tablespoons Worcestershire
  sauce
6 tablespoons soy sauce
1 clove garlic, pressed, or
  1 teaspoon garlic salt
1 teaspoon salt (omit if
  using garlic salt)
¼ teaspoon pepper

2 tablespoons parsley
1 teaspoon oregano
2 cups Wishbone Italian salad
  dressing
½ pound margarine
1 cup dry white wine
6 pounds shrimp, unpeeled

Mix first 8 ingredients and pour over raw shrimp. Marinate in refrigerator 2 to 3 hours. Add to this melted butter and wine and pour over shrimp in roaster. Bake at 400 degrees for 20 minutes or 15 minutes if shrimp are small. Don't overcook. Serve with French or sourdough bread dipped in sauce.
Karen Cullen Luke (Mrs. Robert)

Shrimp Boiled in Beer
Serves 4

2 pounds shrimp
2 12-ounce cans beer
1 clove garlic, peeled
2 teaspoons salt
½ teaspoon thyme

2 bay leaves
1 teaspoon celery seed
1 tablespoon chopped parsley
⅛ teaspoon cayenne pepper
Juice of ½ lemon

Wash shrimp but do not remove shells. Combine the remaining ingredients and bring to a boil. Add shrimp, return to boil, reduce heat and simmer, uncovered, for 2 to 5 minutes, depending on size of shrimp. Drain and serve hot with plenty of melted butter seasoned with lemon juice and Tabasco sauce, or cold with a mayonnaise and cognac sauce for shrimp. The shrimp may be shelled and deveined before serving.
Marty Rhodes Kavanaugh (Mrs. Daniel P.)

Scampi Spaghetti
Serves 4

4 tablespoons butter
1½ pounds raw shrimp,
  shelled and deveined
Salt
Pepper
2 tablespoons chopped
  shallots
2 tablespoons cognac, warmed
¼ cup tomato puree

¾ cup plus 1 tablespoon
  whipping cream
1 tablespoon chopped fresh
  basil or ½ teaspoon dried
1 tablespoon chopped chives
1 egg yolk
1 pound spaghetti
2 tablespoons chopped
  parsley

Heat half the butter in a skillet and add shrimp, salt and pepper and cook until bright red on both sides, about 3 minutes. Sprinkle with shallots and cook 1 minute, stirring. Add the cognac and flame it. Add the tomato puree and cook 1 minute over high heat. Stir in ¾ cup cream, basil and chives. Beat the egg yolk with the remaining tablespoon of cream and add to shrimp sauce mixture. Stir quickly and do not let boil. Cook spaghetti according to package directions. Drain and return to pan. Toss with remaining butter and turn onto hot platter. Pour shrimp and sauce into center and sprinkle with parsley and serve.
Leslie Meek Wileman

Crab and Spinach Souffle
Serves 10 to 12

1 12-ounce package frozen
  spinach souffle, thawed
1 24-ounce carton small curd
  cottage cheese
6 tablespoons flour
6 eggs, slightly beaten

½ cup butter, diced
½ pound sharp Cheddar
  cheese, grated
2 6½-ounce cans crab meat,
  drained
Seasoned bread crumbs

Mix all ingredients together except bread crumbs. Place in a greased 2½ to 3-quart baking dish. Top with bread crumbs. Bake at 350 degrees for 1 hour, uncovered, or until souffle is set all the way through. Even though the mixture may fit in a smaller dish, it has a tendency to run over. It is best to place it on a cookie sheet with sides.
Janie Gilbert Axton (Mrs. Jon C.)

Eggplant and Crab Casserole
Serves 6 to 8

1 large or 2 medium eggplants	1 pound fresh crab meat

White Sauce

6 tablespoons margarine	1 small onion, grated
3 heaping tablespoons flour	2 tablespoons chopped
1½ cups chicken consomme	parsley
1 13-ounce can evaporated	Salt
milk	Pepper
1 pint half and half	½ cup coarse cracker crumbs
2 egg yolks, slightly beaten	Paprika

Peel and dice eggplant in 1-inch squares. Cover and soak in salted water 30 minutes. Cook until tender, but not mushy, about 20 minutes. Drain in colander. Set aside. To prepare white sauce, melt margarine in a heavy saucepan or skillet and add flour. Brown slightly. Add chicken consomme, evaporated milk and half and half. Bring to a boil and simmer a few minutes. Remove from heat. Gently fold in eggplant and crab meat. Add slightly beaten egg yolks, onion and parsley. Adjust seasonings. Put in buttered baking dish. Sprinkle with cracker crumbs. Dot with butter. Sprinkle with paprika and bake at 400 degrees until brown on top, about 30 minutes.

Virginia Winters Potter (Mrs. A. B., Jr.)

Crab Quiche
Serves 5 to 6

1 9-inch pie shell	3 eggs, beaten
4-ounces Swiss cheese, sliced	1 cup half and half or
or grated	whipping cream, heated
2 green onions with tops,	½ teaspoon grated lemon peel
chopped	½ teaspoon salt
4 thin slices ham, chopped	½ teaspoon dry mustard
or shredded	¼ cup slivered almonds
1 6½-ounce can crab meat	Nutmeg (optional)

Bake pie shell in a 9-inch quiche or pie pan for 10 minutes at 450 degrees. Sprinkle the cheese and onion over bottom of pie shell. Add ham and crab meat. Combine eggs, hot cream, lemon peel, salt and mustard. Beat slightly. Pour over the cheese and meats and let stand for 10 minutes. Top with slivered almonds and bake at 350 degrees for 35 to 45 minutes until custard is set. May sprinkle nutmeg on top before baking, if desired. Let stand 10 minutes after baking before cutting.

Mary Hazel Mitchell Miles (Mrs. W. Howard)

Charcoal Broiled Halibut
Serves 2

1 cup olive oil or salad oil or
  ½ of each
1 cup soy sauce

1 cup dry white wine
2 cloves garlic, minced
2 halibut steaks

Combine oil, soy sauce, wine and garlic. Marinate steaks in mixture for 2 hours. Charcoal broil 10 minutes per side. Albacore fillets may be substituted for halibut steaks.
Carolyn Nichols Bentley (Mrs. Earl W., Jr.)

Liz's Party Salmon Mold
Serves 8

2 7¾-ounce cans salmon
1½ cups finely diced celery
1 cup mayonnaise
¼ cup sweet pickle relish
2 tablespoons chopped onion
2 tablespoons lemon juice

1 teaspoon Worcestershire
  sauce
¾ teaspoon salt
1 envelope unflavored gelatin
¼ cup cold water
½ cup boiling water

Avocado Dressing
1 large or 2 medium ripe
  avocados
1 cup cottage cheese
½ cup mayonnaise
1 tablespoon lemon juice

½ teaspoon horseradish
½ teaspoon salt
¼ teaspoon Worcestershire
  sauce
Dash cayenne

Remove any skin and bones from salmon. Flake finely with a fork. Add celery, mayonnaise, relish, onion, lemon juice, Worcestershire and salt and mix with a fork. In a small bowl, combine cold water and gelatin and let stand 5 minutes or until gelatin softens. Add boiling water and stir until gelatin dissolves. Thoroughly blend dissolved gelatin in salmon mixture. Lightly rub a 4-cup ring mold or 8½ x 4½ x 2½-inch loaf pan with salad oil. Fill with mixture and chill until firm. Unmold on serving platter. To prepare dressing, peel avocado, remove the seed and mash with a fork. Stir in remaining dressing ingredients. Cover bowl and chill to blend flavors. Serve with salmon mold.
Ranell Bules Brown (Mrs. Steve M.)

Salmon Mousse with Dill Sauce
Serves 6 to 8

1 envelope unflavored gelatin
1/4 cup cold water
1/2 cup boiling water
1/2 cup mayonnaise
1 tablespoon fresh lemon
   juice
1/2 teaspoon paprika
1/2 teaspoon Tabasco or hot
   sauce
1 tablespoon plus 1 teaspoon
   grated onion

1 teaspoon salt
2 tablespoons finely chopped
   capers
2 cups fresh or canned
   salmon, well drained
1/2 cup whipping cream,
   whipped stiff but not dry
Lemon wedges
Parsley

Dill Sauce
1 teaspoon salt
1/4 teaspoon white pepper
1/4 cup fresh lemon juice

2 cups sour cream
3 tablespoons finely chopped
   dill

To prepare mousse, sprinkle the gelatin over cold water in a bowl. Let stand to soften, about 5 minutes. Pour boiling water over this and mix well with a wire whisk. Let cool to room temperature. Add mayonnaise, lemon juice, paprika, Tabasco, onion and salt and mix well. Add the capers and salmon. Fold in the whipped cream and pour mixture into a fish mold. With a glass mold, no oiling is necessary. Place mold in refrigerator for several hours until set. To unmold, loosen the edge of the mousse from the mold with the tip of a knife. Place in the freezer section of the refrigerator or in a bowl of ice water for 15 minutes. The additional cold causes the mousse to harden and makes it easier to release. Turn the mold upside down and shake it or tap the edge lightly on a wooden or cushioned surface. When any part of the mousse begins to release, place it over the serving plate, as it is difficult to move once out of the mold. Garnish with lemon wedges and parsley.

To prepare dill sauce combine ingredients, stir well and refrigerate for several hours before using. This lets the flavor develop. If the salmon mousse is to be used as a luncheon entree, this recipe will serve 6 to 8 persons. The dill sauce should be served in a sauce boat or small pitcher to be poured over the mousse after it has been served. As a first course for a more elaborate meal, this mousse will serve from 8 to 12 persons. Serve dill sauce as above. As an hors d'oeuvre, the 1/4 cup lemon juice in sauce should be replaced with grated rind of 1 lemon, about 1 teaspoon and all liquid drained off the sour cream before mixing. This makes a slightly thicker sauce that can be used to outline the fish shape. A bed of lettuce leaves cupped toward the mousse will help to hold the sauce in place. When used in this manner, this recipe will yield 100 to 150 servings.

Carol Craven Wilkinson (Mrs. C. P.)

Baked Salmon Croquettes
Serves 8

1 15½-ounce can pink salmon
Milk
¼ cup butter or margarine
2 tablespoons finely chopped
  onion
⅓ cup flour

½ teaspoon salt
¼ teaspoon pepper
1 tablespoon lemon juice
1 cup crushed corn flakes,
  divided

Drain salmon, reserving liquid. Add enough milk to salmon liquid to measure 1 cup. Set aside. Melt butter in a heavy saucepan over low heat. Add onion and cook until tender. Add flour, stirring until smooth. Cook 1 minute, stirring constantly. Gradually add milk mixture. Cook over medium heat, stirring constantly until thickened and bubbly. Stir in salt and pepper. Set aside. Remove skin and bones from salmon. Flake salmon with a fork. Add lemon juice, ½ cup corn flakes and white sauce, stirring well. Refrigerate mixture until chilled. Shape into croquettes. Roll in remaining corn flakes. Place on a lightly greased baking sheet. Bake at 400 degrees for 30 minutes.

Carole Jo Kerley Evans (Mrs. J. Patrick)

Coquille St. Jacques
Serves 4 to 6

2 pounds fresh scallops
2 cups dry sherry
1 bay leaf
1 pound fresh mushrooms,
  sliced
1 medium onion, chopped
¾ cup butter
3 tablespoons flour

2 tablespoons lemon juice
1 teaspoon salt
½ teaspoon paprika
⅛ teaspoon pepper
Cayenne
Bread crumbs
Grated Parmesan cheese

Simmer scallops in a 12-inch skillet for 10 minutes with sherry and bay leaf. Drain, reserving broth. In the same skillet saute mushrooms and onion in butter. Add flour, stir in reserved wine broth and lemon juice. Cook stirring constantly until thickened. Season with salt, pepper, paprika and cayenne. Add scallops. Place in buttered 2½-quart baking dish. Sprinkle with bread crumbs, Parmesan cheese and paprika. Bake at 325 degrees for 25 minutes.

Marcia Hopping Powell (Mrs. John L.)

Fillet of Sole Stuffed with Scampi
Serves 6

½ cup water
½ cup dry white wine
1 small onion, halved
1 clove
2 bay leaves
Juice of 1 lemon
Rosemary
1 teaspoon salt
6 peppercorns

1 pound scampi
4 tablespoons butter
6 6-ounce fillets of Dover Sole,
 skinned
1 8-ounce can asparagus tips,
 finely chopped
1 pint half and half
3 eggs yolks, beaten

Take a shallow pan and make a court-bouillon by pouring in the water, wine, onion, clove, bay leaves, lemon juice, pinch of rosemary, salt and peppercorns. Bring to a boil. Cover and simmer for 10 minutes. Remove from the heat. In a separate pan saute the scampi in the butter. Remove when lightly golden, reserving the butter. Divide the scampi into 6 equal parts and wrap them in the 6 fillets. Position the stuffed fillets, seam side down, in the hot court-bouillon and cover. Return to a boil and simmer for 5 minutes until the sole is just cooked. Lift the fish out of the juice and place in a shallow ovenproof dish, pouring the reserved hot butter over the top. Keep warm in the oven. To prepare sauce, strain court-bouillon and bring to a boil. Add the chopped asparagus and allow to cool. Stir in the cream followed shortly by the beaten yolks. Return to a low heat stirring constantly. As the sauce begins to thicken, do not allow it to boil. Continue to stir until a coating consistency, a little thicker than whipping cream, has been achieved at which stage the sauce may be poured over the waiting fish. Serve without delay.
Susan Esco Crain (Mrs. R. Dean)

Tuna Almond Casserole
Serves 4 to 6

1/4 cup butter
1/4 cup bread crumbs
2 cups fine noodles
2 61/2-ounce cans tuna
1/2 onion, chopped
1/2 green pepper, chopped
1 2-ounce can sliced
  mushrooms

1 2-ounce jar diced pimentos
1/2 cup sour cream
1 103/4-ounce can cream of
  celery soup
1/4 teaspoon salt
1/2 cup slivered almonds

Saute bread crumbs in butter and reserve. Cook the noodles according to package directions to the al dente stage. Drain the oil from the tuna, or use additional oil if you use water-packed tuna, into a skillet and saute onions and green peppers until tender. Add tuna, breaking up the large chunks. Stir in the mushrooms, pimentos, sour cream, soup and salt. Spread the cooked noodles evenly in a baking dish. Spread the tuna mixture over the noodles and sprinkle the almonds on top. Top with the bread crumbs and bake at 350 degrees for 30 minutes.

Beth Matthews McMullan (Mrs. Harry)

Linguine and Clam Sauce
Serves 4

1/2 pound linguine
1/2 teaspoon salt

1/2 teaspoon olive oil

Clam Sauce
1/4 cup butter
1 clove garlic
1 61/2-ounce can minced clams

11/2 tablespoons chopped
  parsley
1/2 cup evaporated milk
1 tablespoon cornstarch

Cook linguine in 4 quarts boiling, salted water. Add olive oil to water. This prevents it from boiling over. To prepare clam sauce, saute garlic in melted butter in a large skillet. Drain clams and set aside. Reserve clam juice. Soak dry parsley in it. Stir clam juice and parsley into butter and bring to a boil. Reduce heat and simmer uncovered for 10 minutes. Add clams and simmer 5 minutes more. Make cornstarch paste with milk. Add cornstarch paste to clam mixture in skillet. Stir carefully and cook until thickened, about 3 minutes. Butter tends to float, but stir constantly to mix butter into mixture and to avoid sticking. Serve hot clam sauce over cooked linguine.

Carla Chenoweth Splaingard (Mrs. Randy)

Seafood Creole
Serves 8 to 10

1/2 lemon, sliced
Salt
Celery leaves
1/4 onion, sliced
3 or 4 black peppercorns
Garlic salt
3 pounds raw shrimp, shelled
and deveined
4 slices bacon
Flour
2 tablespoons butter
1 clove garlic, finely mashed
1 cup chopped onion
1 1/2 cups chopped green
pepper
1/4 cup finely chopped parsley

1 1/2 cups thinly sliced celery
1 1 3/4-pound can tomatoes
1 6-ounce can tomato paste
1 tablespoon lemon juice
1 tablespoon sugar
1 teaspoon salt
1/4 to 1/2 teaspoon crushed
red pepper
1 bay leaf
1/2 teaspoon dried thyme
leaves
1 10-ounce package frozen
okra
1 or 2 packages frozen crab
meat
1 pint oysters and liquid

In a Dutch oven, boil lemon, salt, celery leaves, onion, peppercorns and a dash of garlic salt with at least 3 quarts of water. Add shrimp. Cover and return to a boil. Simmer 4 to 5 minutes or until firm and opaque. Set shrimp aside. Save 1 cup of the shrimp liquid. Saute bacon and remove from pan, adding enough flour to bacon grease to make a thick, brown roux. To this mixture add butter, garlic, onion, green pepper, parsley and celery. Cook about 5 minutes. Add reserved shrimp liquid, bacon, tomatoes, tomato paste, lemon juice, sugar, salt, pepper, bay leaf, thyme and okra. Bring to boiling. Reduce heat. Cover and simmer 30 minutes. Just before serving add shrimp, crab meat and oysters. Bring to boiling. Reduce heat and simmer until creole is good and hot. Serve over rice.

Carol Rowsey Solomon (Mrs. Stephen G.)

Seafood Casserole
Serves 8

2 cups rice, cooked
½ cup chopped green pepper
½ cup chopped celery
½ cup chopped onion
1 4-ounce can sliced water chestnuts, drained
1 cup mayonnaise
1 cup tomato juice
¼ teaspoon salt
⅛ teaspoon pepper

½ pound shrimp, cooked and shelled
½ pound crab meat, fresh, frozen or canned
½ pound bay scallops, fresh or frozen
¼ cup sliced unblanched almonds
1 cup shredded Cheddar cheese
Paprika

Combine rice, green pepper, celery, onion and water chestnuts. Place in a buttered 2-quart casserole. Combine mayonnaise, tomato juice, salt and pepper. Pour half of this mixture over rice and vegetables in casserole. Arrange shrimp, crab and scallops around edge of casserole, leaving the center free. Pour remainder of tomato juice mixture over seafood. Combine almonds and cheese and put into center of casserole. Sprinkle lightly with paprika. Bake covered at 350 degrees for 30 minutes.
Sally Ames Lenz (Mrs. Bruce)

Stir-Fry Chicken or Shrimp
Serves 4 to 6

1 tablespoon peanut or safflower oil
1 cup chicken or shrimp, cut in chunks
2 cups chopped Chinese cabbage or celery
1 small onion, chopped
1 pimento, chopped

1 medium green pepper, cut in strips
2 ounces water chestnuts, sliced
½ pound raw mushrooms, sliced
2 tablespoons soy sauce
½ teaspoon paprika
1 cup pineapple chunks

Heat oil in wok. Put in chicken or shrimp. Cook 3 to 5 minutes stirring constantly. Add remaining ingredients, stirring constantly. Cook 3 minutes more. Serve immediately.
Mary D. Streich

Chicken Croquettes with Mushroom Sauce
Serves 6 to 8

3 tablespoons butter
3 tablespoons finely
chopped onion
3 tablespoons flour
1½ cups chicken broth
2 chickens, cooked, skinned,
boned and finely chopped
or ground
½ teaspoon salt

½ teaspoon pepper
¼ teaspoon nutmeg
¼ teaspoon red pepper
3 egg yolks
Flour
1 egg, beaten with
3 tablespoons water
2 cups bread crumbs
Oil

Sauce
1 tablespoon butter
2 tablespoons minced onion
¼ pound mushrooms,
chopped
¼ teaspoon salt

¼ teaspoon pepper
2 tablespoons flour
1 cup chicken broth
½ cup half and half

In a large frying pan melt the butter. Saute onion for 2 minutes. Add flour and blend well. Add the chicken broth and stir, making a sauce. Add the chicken and seasonings. Blend well and adjust seasonings to taste. Remove from heat. Add egg yolks carefully, stirring well. Return to heat and cook 2 minutes, stirring constantly. Spread the mixture in an 8 x 8-inch pan, cover and refrigerate 8 to 10 hours. When well chilled, divide into 12 to 14 portions and shape into balls. Coat in flour, smoothing the surfaces. Dip in beaten egg and coat well with the bread crumbs. Chill or freeze until ready to use. If frozen, thaw before frying. Heat 2 or more inches of oil to 375 degrees. Add the croquettes a few at a time and fry until crisp and golden. Serve with mushroom sauce.

To prepare sauce, melt the butter in a skillet and saute onion. Add the mushrooms and saute until liquid has evaporated. Add seasonings and flour and stir briskly. Whisk in the broth and cook 15 minutes, stirring occasionally. Add the cream 5 minutes before serving and simmer.

A great freezer item!
Beth Matthews McMullan (Mrs. Harry)

Aunt Markie's Hawaiian Chicken
Serves 4

Marinade
2/3 cup soy sauce
1/4 cup white wine
1 clove garlic, crushed

2 tablespoons sugar
1/4 teaspoon ginger

1 chicken, cut into pieces

To prepare marinade, combine all ingredients. Cover chicken with marinade and bake at 350 degrees for 1½ hours turning and basting every 20 minutes. This sauce can be used for flank steak or shrimp marinade also.
Sandra Wilkins Lekas (Mrs. Thomas A.)

Patricia Alligood's
Polynesian Chicken and Shrimp
Serves 8

1/2 cup butter or oil
2 chickens, cut into pieces
1/2 cup flour
1/4 cup sesame seeds
1 tablespoon salt
1/2 teaspoon pepper
1 13½-ounce can pineapple rings, packed in heavy syrup
1 green pepper, seeded and sliced into thin rings

1 onion, sliced into thin rings
2/3 cup sliced stuffed green olives
2 cups shrimp, cooked and cleaned
2 10¾-ounce cans tomato soup
1/2 cup chili sauce
1/2 cup pineapple juice reserved from the canned pineapple

Melt the butter or pour oil in 2 9x13-inch pans. Roll the chicken pieces in flour, sesame seeds, salt and pepper. Place in the pans, skin side down and bake uncovered at 375 degrees for 30 minutes. Drain the pineapple rings, reserving the syrup. Turn the chicken skin side up and top with pineapple rings, green pepper rings, onion rings, olives and shrimp. Mix soup, chili sauce and reserved pineapple juice. Pour over chicken, cover the pans and bake until tender, 30 or 45 minutes more.
Beth Matthews McMullan (Mrs. Harry)

Sauteed Chicken Breasts
Serves 6

3 whole chicken breasts,
 halved, boned and skinned
2 eggs, beaten
2 tablespoons water
Flour
Fresh bread crumbs, made
 from French bread or
 English muffins

Butter
Cooking oil
Juice of 1 lemon
¼ cup capers
Parsley
Lemon wedges

Pound chicken breasts between sheets of waxed paper until ¼-inch thick. Combine beaten eggs and water. Dip breasts in flour lightly, then in egg mixture, then in bread crumbs. Cover with waxed paper and refrigerate for 1 hour. Saute chicken breasts over low to medium heat in combined butter and cooking oil. Add a little more butter to pan, then add lemon juice and capers to make sauce. Sprinkle with parsley and serve with lemon wedges for garnish.
Patti Jo Jeter Elder (Mrs. John B.)

Virginia Beach Chicken
Serves 8 to 12

8 whole chicken breasts,
 halved and boned
8 strips raw bacon, halved
1 large jar chipped beef
½ pint sour cream

1 10¾-ounce can golden
 mushroom soup
¼ cup dry sherry
1 2½-ounce can mushrooms,
 drained

Wrap each half of chicken breast in a half piece of raw bacon. Pull apart chipped beef and tear into small pieces. Place pieces in the bottom of a large casserole. Put bacon wrapped chicken on top of beef. Combine sour cream, soup, sherry and mushrooms. Pour over chicken. Bake uncovered at 300 degrees for 2 hours.
Franci King Hart (Mrs. William H.)

Crunchy Chicken Bake
Serves 8

2 10-ounce or 3 8-ounce cans
cut asparagus
1 8-ounce can water chestnuts,
sliced
2 2½-ounce jars sliced
mushrooms or fresh
mushrooms, sauteed
2 cups crushed Triscuits

2 10½-ounce cans cream of
chicken soup
½ cup mayonnaise
2 to 3 cups diced cooked
chicken
3 tablespoons margarine,
melted

Drain asparagus, water chestnuts and mushrooms. Set aside. Spread 1 cup crushed Triscuits in a greased 9 x 13-inch ovenproof dish. Combine soup and mayonnaise and carefully spread half of mixture over Triscuits. Drop by spoonfuls and spread with a knife. Top with layers of chicken, asparagus, water chestnuts and mushrooms. Spread remaining soup mixture over top. Combine remaining Triscuits with melted margarine and sprinkle on top. Cover dish loosely with foil and bake at 350 degrees for 30 minutes. Uncover and bake 15 minutes more or until bubbly.
Linda Polk Klos (Mrs. Tom W.)

Chicken Flambe
Serves 4

½ cup butter
10 pieces chicken, not breasts
2 tablespoons brandy
½ cup Sauterne or other
white wine

2 tablespoons parsley flakes
2 tablespoons chopped chives
1 teaspoon salt
½ teaspoon thyme
½ cup whipping cream

Melt butter in a deep frying pan over high heat. When butter begins to brown, add chicken and brown well. Cover and simmer 15 minutes. Add brandy and flame. Mix together remaining ingredients except cream, and add to pan. Cover and simmer 45 minutes to 1 hour. Remove chicken, keeping warm. Add cream to pan and mix over low heat, but do not boil. Pour mixture over chicken and serve.
Leslie Hood Diggs (Mrs. James Barnes, IV)

Chicken Kiev
Serves 4

½ cup butter, softened
2 tablespoons finely chopped
  fresh parsley
1 clove garlic, mashed
⅛ teaspoon cayenne pepper
2 tablespoons lemon juice
4 whole chicken breasts,
  boned

½ cup flour
2 eggs, slightly beaten
½ cup fine dry bread crumbs
Vegetable oil
Parsley
Lemon wedges

Mix the butter with parsley, garlic and cayenne. Gradually add lemon juice, beating well to blend. Chill until firm enough to shape. Measure out 1 tablespoon of butter mixture and shape into a cube. Divide remainder into quarters and shape each into elongated rolls about 2½ inches long. Refrigerate all shapes overnight or place in freezer for 1 hour. Flatten chicken breasts with meat mallet to ⅛-inch thick. Place a roll of butter on each breast and roll up, tucking in edge to thoroughly seal in butter. Secure loose edges with toothpicks. Roll breasts in flour to coat thoroughly, then coat with beaten eggs. Roll in bread crumbs to cover all sides. Heat 3 to 4 inches vegetable oil in a deep saucepan over moderately high heat or to a temperature of 350 degrees on a frying thermometer. Fry breasts until browned well, about 15 minutes or until juice runs clear when pricked. Remove toothpicks and arrange on a warm platter. Cut the chilled butter into 4 slices and place one on each roll. Garnish with parsley and lemon wedges.
Sandy Simon Childress (Mrs. Bob)

Honeyed Chicken Breasts
Serves 4

2 whole chicken breasts,
  halved
2 tablespoons butter
¼ cup lemon juice

1 teaspoon soy sauce
¼ cup honey
1 egg yolk

Brown chicken breasts in butter. Pour off excess butter. Mix together lemon juice, soy sauce, honey and egg yolk. Place chicken in baking dish, pour honey mixture over chicken. Bake covered at 350 degrees for 1½ hours.
Lisa Davis Pierce (Mrs. Mark H.)

Aloha Broiled Chicken
Serves 4

2 2-pound broiler chickens,
  split in half
Melted butter
Salt

Pepper
1 20-ounce can pineapple
  rings, packed in syrup
1 16-ounce can peach halves

Pineapple Sauce
½ cup butter
1 teaspoon cornstarch
1 teaspoon grated lemon peel
¼ cup lemon juice
⅓ cup pineapple syrup

2 tablespoons finely chopped
  onion
1 teaspoon soy sauce
¼ teaspoon thyme

Brush chicken with melted butter. Season with salt and pepper. Place skin side down on broiler pan, using no rack. Broil 5 to 7 inches from heat for 25 minutes, or until lightly browned. Brush occasionally with melted butter. Turn. Broil 15 to 20 minutes longer. While chicken is broiling, prepare pineapple sauce.

To prepare pineapple sauce, melt butter and blend in cornstarch. Add remaining ingredients. Cook 5 minutes over low heat, stirring constantly. About 5 minutes before end of cooking time for chicken, place canned pineapple rings and peach halves beside chicken. Brush chicken and fruits with pineapple sauce. Broil 5 minutes longer. Pass with the sauce.
Sally Morrison Stringer (Mrs. Edward H., Jr.)

Fancy Chicken Breasts
Serves 4

2 whole chicken breasts
  halved, skinned and boned
4 slices Swiss cheese
1 10¾-ounce can chicken
  mushroom soup or cream
  of mushroom soup

¼ cup cooking sherry
2 cups Pepperidge Farm
  croutons
½ cup butter, melted

Place chicken breasts in ovenproof pan and top with cheese. Mix soup and sherry together and pour over top. Put croutons on top and drizzle with melted butter. Bake at 350 degrees for 1 to 1¼ hours.
Linda Meining Zahn (Mrs. Richard L.)

Chicken Breasts with Rice and Almonds
Serves 8

6 whole chicken breasts, halved
1/4 cup butter
1 1/4 cups Uncle Ben's converted rice, uncooked
1 10 3/4-ounce can cream of chicken soup

1 10 3/4-ounce can cream of celery soup
1 10 3/4-ounce can cream of mushroom soup
1/4 cup sherry
1/4 cup slivered almonds
1/2 cup grated Parmesan cheese

In a 3-quart baking dish, melt the butter and sprinkle the uncooked rice over it. In a separate pan, mix the soups and sherry and heat, but do not boil. Spread 1/2 of the soup mixture over the rice and butter and mix thoroughly. Place the chicken breasts on this and cover with the remaining soup mixture. Sprinkle almonds, then cheese on top. Cover with heavy duty foil and bake at 275 degrees for 2 1/2 hours. Remove foil for the last 15 minutes of cooking to brown.

Patsy Eskridge King (Mrs. Arthur E., Jr.)

Chicken a la Swiss
Serves 6

6 whole chicken breasts, halved and boned
1 10 3/4-ounce can cream of celery soup

1 10 3/4-ounce can cream of chicken soup
1/3 cup sherry
Swiss cheese

Place chicken breasts in a 3-quart baking dish that has been sprayed with Pam. Mix the soups and sherry together. Pour over chicken. Grate enough cheese to amply cover the entire top of the dish. Bake uncovered at 275 degrees for 2 1/2 to 3 hours. This recipe may be made the night before, refrigerated, then cooked the next day after coming to room temperature. (Flavor is stronger then.)

Great company dish! There's nothing last minute to do.

Nita Forrest Folger (Mrs. Doug)

Chicken and Grapes
Serves 4

4 whole chicken breasts,
  halved and boned
2 tablespoons butter
1½ tablespoons orange
  marmalade
½ tablespoon tarragon

½ cup dry white wine or
  champagne
½ pint whipping cream
2 teaspoons cornstarch
1½ cups seedless green
  grapes

Skin chicken breasts. Brown lightly on both sides in 2 tablespoons of butter. Add marmalade, tarragon and wine to chicken. Cover and simmer 20 minutes or until tender. Remove chicken and keep warm. Add whipping cream to pan. Bring to rolling boil. Add cornstarch, dissolved in a little water. Return to boil. Simmer until thickened. Add grapes and chicken. Heat thoroughly. Serve with rice.
Libby Berry Payne (Mrs. Morton, III)

Medallions of Chicken Breasts Piquant
Serves 12

6 whole chicken breasts,
  halved and skinned
Seasoned flour
½ pound butter
1 pound fresh mushrooms,
  sliced
1 bottle capers

1 cup dry white wine
1 bay leaf
Salt
Pepper
1 cup chicken stock
Parsley, chopped

Bone chicken breasts separating the tenderloin. Cut each piece into small round pieces. Dry. Dust lightly with seasoned flour. Melt ¼ cup butter in a skillet and saute mushrooms with half of the capers. Remove with slotted spoon and set aside. Add remaining butter to skillet and brown chicken breast pieces until golden brown. Remove chicken to a shallow casserole and set aside. Deglaze pan with the white wine, remaining capers and bay leaf, bringing to a rapid boil and scraping pan. Return mushroom mixture to pan and boil to reduce liquid by half. Pour half of this sauce over chicken. Stir chicken stock into remaining sauce mixture. Boil to reduce some more. Check for seasonings and season more if needed. Pour over chicken. Let stand 30 or more minutes. Reheat to serve with chopped parsley on top.
Aileen Westbrook Malloy (Mrs. John Francis)

Favorite Chicken Spaghetti
Serves 10

1 3- or 4-pound hen or fryer
½ pound spaghetti
1 large onion, diced
1 cup celery, chopped
6 tablespoons butter or
chicken fat
1 4-ounce can mushrooms, or
¼ pound fresh mushrooms,
sliced

6 tablespoons flour
1 quart chicken broth
1 tablespoon Lawry's
seasoned salt
½ pound sharp Cheddar
cheese, grated

Stew chicken until tender. Remove meat from bones. Cook spaghetti according to package directions. Do not overcook. Brown onion and celery in butter or chicken fat. Add mushrooms. Add flour and mix. Add chicken broth to make thin gravy. Add Lawry's salt, cheese, chicken and cooked spaghetti. Bake at 350 degrees for 45 minutes to 1 hour in a 3-quart casserole.

Nancy Frantz Davies (Mrs. Frank L., Jr.)

Chicken Mozzarella
Serves 2

2 whole chicken breasts,
halved
¼ cup seasoned flour
¼ cup butter
4 slices Mozzarella cheese,
¼-inch thick

Salt
Pepper
½ teaspoon paprika
Parsley

Bone and skin the chicken breasts. Roll in seasoned flour. Melt ¼ cup butter in skillet. Place a slice of cheese in each breast and bring the ends together and secure with toothpicks. Brown breasts in the butter. Transfer to an ovenproof dish or small casserole. Sprinkle with paprika, salt and pepper to taste. Cook at 350 degrees for 30 minutes. Garnish with parsley.

Pat Gallagher

Chicken Tetrazzini
Serves 8

1 3½-pound stewing hen
2 teaspoons salt
⅛ teaspoon pepper
½ pound fine egg noodles
7 tablespoons butter
½ pound mushrooms, sliced
¼ cup flour

½ teaspoon salt
1 cup half and half
¼ cup sherry
1½ cups grated Longhorn
  cheese
Paprika

In a large covered kettle simmer hen in 2 quarts water, salt and pepper for 3 to 4 hours. Remove chicken, reserving broth, and let cool. Break into pieces after removing from bones. Bring broth to a boil, add noodles and cook according to package directions. Drain, reserving broth. Boil broth down to 2 cups and strain. Saute mushrooms in 3 tablespoons butter. Into 4 tablespoons melted butter, stir flour, salt, 2 cups strained broth and half and half. Stir sauce and cook until thickened. Add chicken, mushrooms and sherry. Heat. Place noodles in shallow 3-quart baking dish. Pour on sauce. Top with cheese and paprika. Bake at 450 degrees for 10 minutes. If dish is made ahead, refrigerated or frozen, thaw, then bake at 350 degrees for 30 minutes.
Barbara Pannage Stanfield (Mrs. Neil)

Chicken Supreme
Serves 4 to 6

1 cup sour cream
2 teaspoons celery salt
2 tablespoons lemon juice
1 teaspoon paprika
1 clove garlic, crushed

2 teaspoons salt
¼ teaspoon pepper
6 chicken breast halves, boned
1 cup bread crumbs
½ cup butter, melted

Combine sour cream, celery salt, lemon juice, paprika, garlic, salt and pepper. Coat chicken well with mixture and refrigerate overnight, uncovered. Next day, roll chicken in bread crumbs and arrange in a shallow baking dish. Spoon half of the butter over chicken. Bake uncovered at 350 degrees for 40 minutes. Spoon remaining butter over chicken and bake 15 minutes longer. Serve hot.
Debbi Davidson Dale (Mrs. Mark)   *Ann Connolly Henry (Mrs. John A., III)*

Sour Cream Chicken Divine
Serves 2

2 whole chicken breasts,
   halved and boned
4 tablespoons butter
1/2 cup white wine
1/4 teaspoon tarragon
1/4 teaspoon thyme
1/2 bay leaf

Salt
Pepper
1/2 cup sour cream
1 egg yolk
1/4 teaspoon Dijon mustard
1 4-ounce can mushroom
   pieces, or 1/4 pound fresh
   mushrooms, sliced

Saute chicken breasts in butter. Add white wine, tarragon, thyme, bay leaf, salt and pepper. Simmer 45 minutes. Remove breasts from pan and set aside. Mix remaining ingredients and add to sauce in pan. Reheat. Pour over chicken and serve with wild rice.

Jane Covington White (Mrs. James U., Jr.)

Sour Cream Enchiladas
Serves 6 to 8

4 to 5 whole chicken breasts
Celery salt
Onion flakes
1 10³/4-ounce can cream of
   mushroom soup
1 10³/4-ounce can cream of
   chicken soup
1/2 cup sour cream

1/2 cup chopped onion
1 to 2 jalapeno peppers,
   seeded and chopped
1 package corn tortillas
4 ounces Cheddar cheese,
   grated
4 ounces Swiss cheese, grated

Season chicken breasts with celery salt and onion flakes to taste. Place in a casserole. Cover with foil and bake at 325 degrees for 1 hour. Bone chicken and cut into bite size pieces. Add soups, sour cream, onion and jalapeno peppers. Mix together. Tear tortillas into quarters. Layer tortillas, chicken mixture and cheeses. Layer twice, ending with cheeses. Bake at 350 degrees for 30 to 45 minutes.

Linda Huper Reece (Mrs. Robert A.)

Swiss Enchiladas
Serves 6

1 pound green tomatillos
3 green Serrano chiles, or
  2 jalapenos
1 clove garlic
1 tablespoon chopped onion
1 tablespoon chopped
  coriander
2 tablespoons oil
Baking soda
Sugar

2 cups white sauce
1 cup half and half
1 cup shredded Cheddar
  cheese
Salt
Pepper
2 whole chicken breasts,
  cooked and shredded
Corn tortillas

Peel tomatillos and chiles. Boil with enough water to cover. When tender, drain and mix in blender with garlic, onion and coriander. Pour mixture into medium saucepan and saute with 2 tablespoons cooking oil, adding a pinch of baking soda and sugar. Add prepared white sauce, half and half and half of cheese. Season with salt and pepper to taste. Roll corn tortillas with chicken and place in casserole. Pour sauce over and top with remaining cheese. Bake at 350 degrees for 30 minutes or until bubbly.

Green tomatillos are found in the fresh produce section. They are slightly greener and larger than cherry tomatoes.
Stephanie Irwin Neville (Mrs. Drew)

Easy Chicken Curry
Serves 6

2 tablespoons butter
3 teaspoons curry powder
1 red apple, finely chopped
½ onion, finely chopped
1 10¾-ounce can cream of
  mushroom soup

1 cup milk
Salt
3 whole chicken breasts,
  halved and boned

Melt butter in a saucepan. Add curry powder, apple and onion. Saute until the onion is transparent. Add soup, milk and salt. Place the 6 chicken breasts in 1 layer in a shallow baking dish and pour sauce over them. Bake uncovered at 350 to 375 degrees for 1 hour.
Gayle Semtner (Mrs. B. L., III)

Chicken Ole Casserole
Serves 4

3 chicken breasts, boned and
  cut into 1-inch squares
Poultry seasoning
Olive oil
Garlic powder
1/2 cup white rice, uncooked
1 10-ounce package frozen
  chopped broccoli

1 small jar Jalapeno Cheese
  Whiz
1 10³/4-ounce can cream of
  mushroom soup
Salt
Pepper
3/4 cup bread crumbs
2 tablespoons butter, melted

Season chicken with poultry seasoning and saute in olive oil and garlic powder until lightly browned. Drain and set aside. Cook rice and broccoli according to package directions. Mix rice, broccoli, cheese, soup and chicken. Add salt and pepper to taste. Put in casserole dish and top with bread crumbs and melted butter. Bake at 350 degrees for 1 hour.
Lisa King Brashear (Mrs. Herb)

Hattie's Never Fail Southern Fried Chicken
Yields 2 pieces of chicken per adult

Chicken pieces
Bacon grease or bottled oil
  or combination
Flour

Salt
Pepper
Lawry's seasoned salt

The key to this recipe is an electric skillet. Rinse and pat dry chicken. Pour bacon grease or combination to 1/2-inch depth. Turn temperature to 325 degrees and heat oil. Shake chicken pieces in flour only and place in electric skillet skin side or most fleshy part up. Sprinkle with salt and pepper then liberally with Lawry's seasoned salt. Cover skillet leaving air vents open. Cook without opening for 25 minutes. Remove cover, turn chicken over to brown for 10 minutes or less. Drain on brown paper bags. If using only oil you must watch the temperature as it will cook hotter and faster. Bacon grease is recommended.
Ginger Parker Johnson (Mrs. William J.)

Baked Cornish Hen
Serves 2

2 thawed Cornish hens,
giblets removed
Celery salt
Lemon pepper
Bouquet Garni seasoning

2 slices bread (English muffins
are best)
1/4 cup butter
1/4 yellow onion, cut in chunks

Clean Cornish hens inside and out and pat dry. Sprinkle cavity with celery salt, lemon pepper and Bouquet Garni. Tear bread into pieces. In back of cavity place in layers small amount of bread, pat of butter, a few onion chunks, a dash of lemon pepper and Bouquet Garni. Repeat layers ending with the bread. Place in a roasting pan with dash of Bouquet Garni and cook at 350 degrees for 45 minutes to 1 hour, basting with butter after the first 10 minutes and then twice more.
Sharon Fitkin Boecking (Mrs. H. E., III)

Roast Pheasant with Apples and Calvados
Serves 4

2 pheasants
2 bay leaves
1/2 cup butter
Salt
Pepper
6 Delicious apples
1/4 pound mushrooms

6 shallots
Sprig of thyme or 1 teaspoon
dried thyme
1 cup Calvados cognac
3/4 cup dry white wine
12 ounces whipping cream

Place a bay leaf and 1/4 cup butter inside each pheasant. Season with salt and pepper. Peel, core and slice the apples. Chop mushrooms and shallots. Set aside. Roast the pheasants side by side, but not touching, at 350 degrees for 1 1/4 hours or until tender. Remove from roasting pan and keep warm. Retain the juices and place the roasting pan over moderate heat. Add the shallots, mushrooms, apples and thyme. Cook until soft. Flame with the Calvados. Add wine and bring to a boil. Continue to boil until liquid is reduced by half. Stir in cream and serve.
Susan Esco Crain (Mrs. R. Dean)

Riverview Plantation Quail
Serves 2 to 4

4 quail
Salt
Pepper
Flour
Butter

1 teaspoon Worcestershire
    sauce
Garlic salt
2 slices lemon
1 cup water
1 to 2 tablespoons flour

Salt and pepper birds and flour lightly. Brown in butter. Add a small amount of water, Worcestershire sauce, dash of garlic salt and 2 slices of lemon. Place in a roaster, cover and cook at 350 degrees for 1 to 1¼ hours. Baste birds often. Water may be added if necessary while cooking in order to have enough juices to make gravy.

To prepare gravy, mix water and flour together well. Add to juices in roasting pan. Stir until thickened. Serve over birds.
Barbara Workman Vose (Mrs. Charles A., Jr.)

Steamed Quail
Serves 4

12 quail
Salt
Pepper
Flour
Margarine
Oil

1 small white onion, thinly
    sliced
White wine
1 tablespoon instant chicken
    broth, dissolved in ½ cup
    hot water

Salt, pepper and flour the quail. In a large cast iron skillet, saute quail in a small amount of margarine and oil. When browned, cover with thin slices of onion rings. Add chicken bouillon and ½ cup or more white wine. Quail should be covered in liquid. Place cover on skillet and steam about 45 minutes to 1 hour.
Judy Monroe Pitts (Mrs. H. Craig)

Quail in Wine
Serves 4 to 6

½ pound butter
4 green onions, chopped
2 cloves garlic
4 bay leaves
12 whole cloves

8 quail
1 pint white Port wine
1 tablespoon flour
1 pint whipping cream

Melt butter and add onions, garlic and seasonings. Let simmer 10 minutes. Salt birds lightly and brown in butter. Pour wine over birds. Cover and let simmer for 30 minutes or until tender. Remove birds and strain sauce. Make gravy by thickening sauce with flour and adding cream. Return birds to gravy and heat through.
Sandy Simon Childress (Mrs. Bob)

Wild Duck
Yields 1 duck per person

Duck
Salt
Pepper
1 onion, quartered
2 tart apples, quartered

3 tablespoons raisins
  (optional)
1 strip bacon or salt pork
½ cup red wine
Parsley

Wash and dry duck. Rub duck thoroughly with salt and pepper. Let stand in refrigerator several hours or overnight. Stuff with onion, apples and raisins, if desired. Use 2 parts apple to 1 part onion. Place in casserole or electric cooker with slice of bacon or salt pork over each duck. Cover tightly and bake at 500 degrees until the duck is hot through, then turn down to 300 degrees, pour wine over each duck after it starts to cook and cook 2 to 4 hours for well done duck. Stuffing may be removed before serving. Garnish with parsley.
Virginia Winters Potter (Mrs. A. B., Jr.)

Barbequed Dove

Dove
Salt
Pepper
Cayenne

Woody's concentrated
  cooking sauce
Bacon
Toothpicks

Season dove to taste and marinate in Woody's cooking sauce several hours. Wrap in bacon, securing with toothpicks, and charcoal about 10 to 15 minutes to preferred doneness.
Sandy Simon Childress (Mrs. Bob)

Quiche Lorraine
Serves 8

1 9-inch pie crust
1/2 pound Swiss cheese, grated
1 onion, sliced
2 tablespoons flour
4 eggs
1 teaspoon salt
Ground pepper

1 1/2 cups milk
1/2 teaspoon curry powder
1/4 teaspoon ground nutmeg
2 drops Tabasco
Slivered ham, crisp bacon
    or chicken

Make pie crust or use prepared 9-inch crust. Mix grated cheese with flour and spread in bottom of pie shell. Arrange onion rings on top. Beat eggs lightly. Beat in remaining ingredients. Pour egg mixture over cheese and onion rings. Add slivered ham, bacon or chicken. Bake at 350 degrees for 45 minutes.
Patsy King Hosman (Mrs. Thomas D.)

Country Swiss Fondue
Serves 4

1 large clove garlic
8 ounces Emmental (Swiss)
    cheese, grated
8 ounces Gruyere cheese,
    grated
8 ounces dry white wine
    (Chablis is good)

1 to 2 tablespoons cornstarch
1 to 2 tablespoons Kirsch
    liqueur
Fresh baked French bread,
    cut into bite-sized pieces

Rub a pottery fondue pot thoroughly with garlic. Discard the garlic. Put the grated cheese and all but 2 tablespoons wine into the pot. Melt slowly on the range over medium heat, stirring occasionally. Make a mixture of the cornstarch and 2 tablespoons of white wine. After the cheese has melted, about 15 minutes, add cornstarch mixture and stir until the cheese and wine have bonded. Stir in Kirsch and remove from the stove. Put the pot over the fondue fire and serve immediately with crusty French bread.
Suzie Chandler Sargent (Mrs. John, Jr.)

Picture Perfect Pasta Primavera
Serves 6 to 8

1/2 cup unsalted butter
1 medium onion, minced
1 large clove garlic, minced
1 pound thin asparagus, ends trimmed and cut diagonally into 1/4-inch slices. Leave tips intact.
1/2 pound mushrooms, thinly sliced
1 small cauliflower or 1/2 larger head broken into small flowerets
3 small zucchini, cut diagonally into 1/4-inch slices
3 thin carrots, cut diagonally into 1/8-inch slices

1 cup whipping cream
1/2 cup chicken stock
2 tablespoons chopped fresh basil, or 2 teaspoons dried basil
1 cup tiny frozen peas, thawed
4 to 6 ounces Prosciutto or cooked ham, chopped
5 green onion tops, sliced
Salt
Pepper
1 pound fettuccine or linguini, cooked al dente and drained
1 1/4 cups freshly grated Parmesan cheese

Melt butter in a large, deep skillet over medium-high heat. Add onions and garlic and saute until onion is softened, about 3 minutes. Mix in asparagus, mushrooms, cauliflower, zucchini and carrots. Stir fry 3 to 5 minutes. Remove several asparagus tips for garnish. Increase heat to high. Add cream, chicken stock and basil and allow mixture to boil until liquid is slightly reduced, about 3 minutes. Stir in peas, ham and green onion and cook 1 more minute. Season to taste with salt and pepper. Add cooked pasta and Parmesan cheese, tossing until thoroughly combined and pasta is heated. Add more chicken stock if necessary. Turn onto large serving platter, garnish with reserved vegetables and serve immediately.

Polly Puckett Nichols (Mrs. Larry)

Pasta Primavera
Serves 6 to 8

1 bunch broccoli, flowerets
  only
1 bunch asparagus, tips only
1 small zucchini, sliced
1 summer squash, cubed
1 cup cut fresh green beans
1/2 cup peas, fresh or frozen
1 pound vermicelli, cooked
  al dente
1 cup thinly sliced
  mushrooms
1 bunch scallions, chopped
2 cloves garlic, minced
2 tablespoons butter

2 cups cherry tomatoes,
  cut in half
1/4 cup chopped parsley
2 tablespoons fresh chopped
  basil or 1 teaspoon dried
  basil
1/2 teaspoon dried red pepper
  flakes
1/4 cup butter
2 tablespoons chicken broth
3/4 cup whipping cream
2/3 cup freshly grated
  Parmesan cheese
Salt
Pepper

Cook each of the first 6 vegetables separately in boiling, salted water until tender, but still crisp. Rinse in cold water until chilled. Drain well. This may be done in advance and each vegetable wrapped separately and refrigerated. Place cooked vegetables in bowl. In a medium sized skillet saute mushrooms, scallions and garlic in 2 tablespoons butter for 2 to 3 minutes. Add tomatoes and cook 1 more minute, stirring gently. Add to the bowl of vegetables along with parsley, basil and red pepper flakes. In a large Dutch oven melt 1/4 cup butter. Add chicken broth, cream, cheese, salt and pepper to taste. Stir with a whisk until smooth, but do not boil. Add vegetables only to heat through, then add the cooked pasta. Adjust seasonings. Serve immediately dividing among heated plates. Pass extra cheese.

Lisa Davis Pierce (Mrs. Mark H.)

Reniers' Enchiladas
Serves 6

1½ pounds ground beef
Oil
Salt
2 medium yellow onions,
  diced

Sauce
4 tablespoons Mazola oil
½ cup flour
1 pint water
1 10-ounce can enchilada
  sauce

Garnish
Sour cream
Chopped green chiles
Salsa

1 4-ounce can sliced black
  olives
1 pound sharp Cheddar
  cheese, grated
12 corn tortillas
4 green onions, chopped

1 8-ounce can tomato sauce
2 tablespoons chili powder
1 tablespoon cumin powder
Salt

Guacamole
Sliced black olives

Cook beef in oil, salt to taste. Set aside in a large bowl and let cool. Add onions, olives and half of the cheese. To prepare sauce, combine ingredients. Cook until thick. Cool. Heat tortillas in oven for 1 minute then run through sauce. Put ½ cup meat mixture in the middle of each tortilla. Roll and place seam side down in a 9 x 13-inch ovenproof dish. Spread remaining sauce on top, then sprinkle with remaining cheese and chopped green onions. Bake at 350 degrees for 45 minutes. Top with any or all of the garnishes, if desired.
Anne Reniers Lee (Mrs. Robert E., Jr.)

Enchilada Casserole
Serves 6

Cheese Sauce
1 1/2 cans Cheddar cheese soup
1/4 teaspoon paprika

3/4 15-ounce can enchilada
  sauce

Meat Mixture
1 pound ground beef
1 small onion, chopped
1 15 1/2-ounce can refried
  beans
1/2 teaspoon salt

1/4 teaspoon pepper
1 cup salad oil
12 flour tortillas
1 medium tomato, chopped

Garnish
3/4 cup sliced black olives

Green pepper rings

To prepare cheese sauce, combine ingredients and cook until smooth and bubbly. Cook ground beef and onion in skillet until meat is brown and onion is tender. Stir in beans, salt and pepper. In another skillet heat oil until it sizzles. Quickly dip each tortilla in hot oil just until it is softened. Then remove to paper towel. Place about 1/3 cup meat mixture on each tortilla. Top meat with chopped tomato. Then roll tortilla tightly and place seam side down in a 9 x 13-inch baking dish. Pour cheese sauce over tortillas. Casserole may be refrigerated at this time. Bake uncovered for 20 to 25 minutes at 350 degrees, or until cheese is bubbly in middle. May be garnished with ripe olives and green pepper rings.
Genie McBee Stone (Mrs. Frank P.)

Easy Enchiladas
Serves 6

1 pound hamburger meat
1 large onion, chopped
1 10-ounce can mild enchilada
  sauce
1 16-ounce can chili con carne
10 to 12 tortillas, thawed

8 ounces Cheddar cheese,
  grated
Optional: top each enchilada
  with 1 tablespoon sour
  cream before serving

Brown hamburger meat and ½ of the onion. Add the enchilada sauce and chili and let simmer, stirring occasionally, for 15 minutes. Lightly grease a 9 x 13-inch baking dish. Fill tortillas with meat mixture, sprinkling each with onion and ½ of the cheese. When filled, lightly roll them and place seam side down side by side in the baking dish. Pour remaining sauce over all and sprinkle with the rest of the cheese. Bake at 350 degrees for 20 to 25 minutes.
Sally Frye Bentley (Mrs. Steven J.)

Diana's Mexican Casserole
Serves 12

12 corn tortillas
1½ pounds ground beef
1 onion, chopped
1 tablespoon chili powder
Salt
Pepper

1 10-ounce can Ranch Style
  beans
1 pound Velveeta cheese,
  sliced
1 10¾-ounce can cream of
  chicken soup
1 10-ounce can Rotel tomatoes

Line the bottom of a greased 9 x 13-inch baking dish with 6 tortillas. Brown ground beef with onion, chili powder, salt and pepper to taste. Drain and spread meat mixture over tortillas. Layer beans, undrained. Layer sliced cheese over beans. Cover with remaining tortillas. Combine soup and Rotel tomatoes and pour over casserole. Cover with foil and bake at 350 degrees for 1 hour.
Debbi Davidson Dale (Mrs. Mark)

Taco Casserole
Serves 6 to 8

2 pounds ground chuck
1 onion, chopped
1 teaspoon salt
1/2 teaspoon garlic powder
2 8-ounce cans tomato sauce
1 tablespoon wine vinegar
2 tablespoons chili powder

1 1/2 cups Mexican kidney
  beans
1 4-ounce can chopped green
  chiles
1 11-ounce package corn chips
1/2 pound Cheddar cheese,
  grated

Garnish
2 cups shredded lettuce
Black olives
Green onions

Sour cream
Guacamole

Saute ground chuck and chopped onion until brown. Drain the grease and add the next 5 ingredients. Cover and simmer 15 minutes. Mix in the beans and chiles. Grease an 8 1/2 x 11-inch baking dish. Cover the bottom with corn chips and sprinkle with cheese. Spoon over half the meat sauce. Add more chips, then meat sauce and top with remaining grated cheese. Bake uncovered at 375 degrees for 20 minutes. Top with any or all of the garnishes.
Kristen Van der Hoof Freeland (Mrs. Royden R.)

Favorite Company Casserole
Serves 6

1 1/4 pounds ground beef
1 clove garlic
2 8-ounce cans tomato sauce
1 tablespoon sugar
1 teaspoon salt
1 teaspoon pepper

6 ounces egg noodles,
  medium or wide
6 to 8 green onions
1 cup small curd cottage
  cheese
1 cup sour cream
3/4 cup grated Cheddar cheese

Brown ground beef. Add garlic, tomato sauce, sugar, salt and pepper. Simmer about 10 minutes and remove garlic. Cook noodles according to package directions. Chop onions, including tops and mix with cottage cheese and sour cream. Grease a 9 x 12-inch baking dish. Layer noodles, sour cream mixture and beef sauce. Repeat layers and top with Cheddar cheese. Bake at 350 degrees for 30 minutes.
Ruth McKissick Commander (Mrs. A. C.)

Zucchini and Green Chile Quiche
Serves 6 to 8

Pastry for 9-inch pie, baked
for 6 minutes
3 cups coarsely grated,
unpeeled zucchini
(3/4 pound)
Salt
1 4-ounce can chopped
green chiles
3/4 cup sliced green onions,
tops and bottoms

1 1/2 tablespoons butter
1 tablespoon flour
1 cup grated Cheddar cheese
1/2 cup grated Monterey Jack
cheese
3 eggs
1 1/2 cups whipping cream
Black pepper, freshly ground
Salt

Grate zucchini and sprinkle with salt. Let stand 30 minutes. Squeeze out moisture and pat dry. Blot dry green chiles. Cook green onions slowly in butter, about 2 minutes. Stir in zucchini and heat a few minutes, only until zucchini is glazed with butter. Blend in flour and spread mixture into pastry shell. Sprinkle with green chiles and half of the cheeses. Beat eggs with cream and season very lightly with salt and pepper. Pour into pastry shell and sprinkle with remaining cheeses. Bake at 400 degrees for 15 minutes. Reduce heat to 350 degrees and bake about 20 to 25 minutes longer, until custard is set and slightly puffed. Cool at least 15 minutes before cutting.
Polly Puckett Nichols (Mrs. Larry)

Microwave Mexican Eggs
Serves 4

4 tablespoons butter
1 4-ounce can chopped green
chiles
2 tomatoes, diced
8 eggs, beaten
1 tablespoon onion flakes

1/2 cup milk
Garlic salt
Salt
Pepper
Cheddar cheese, grated

Microwave butter on high in a round dish. Cook chiles and tomatoes in melted butter on high for 1 minute and 30 seconds. Add eggs, onion, milk and seasonings to taste. Cook on high for 1 minute. Stir outside of eggs to the center. Cook on high for 2 minutes or until done. Eggs need to be moist. Sprinkle with grated cheese. Serve at once.
Kay Davies Oliver (Mrs. Gates E.)

Italian Zucchini Pie
Serves 6

4 cups thinly sliced, unpeeled
zucchini
1 cup coarsely chopped onion
½ cup butter
½ cup fresh chopped parsley
or 2 tablespoons parsley
flakes
½ teaspoon salt
½ teaspoon black pepper

¼ teaspoon garlic powder
¼ teaspoon sweet basil
¼ teaspoon oregano
2 eggs, well beaten
2 cups shredded Muenster or
Mozzarella cheese
1 8-ounce can refrigerated
crescent dinner rolls
2 teaspoons Dijon or prepared
mustard

In a 10-inch skillet, cook zucchini and onion in butter until tender, about 10 minutes. Stir in parsley and seasonings. In large bowl, blend eggs and cheese. Stir in vegetable mixture. Separate crescent dough into 8 triangles. Place in ungreased 11-inch quiche pan, 10-inch pie pan or 8 x 12-inch baking dish. Press over bottom and up sides to form crust. Spread crust with mustard. Pour vegetable mixture evenly into crust. Bake at 375 degrees for 18 to 25 minutes, or until knife inserted near center comes out clean.

Peggy Richardson

South of the Border Eggs
Serves 2

3 patties hot sausage, cut
½-inch thick
¼ green pepper, seeded and
chopped
1 small onion, chopped

1 teaspoon chili powder
1 teaspoon flour
1 cup tomato juice
Salt
Eggs

Crumble sausage into skillet over low heat. Add green pepper and onion and saute slowly until onion is clear. Add chili powder mixed with flour, stirring. Pour in tomato juice. Salt to taste. Cover and simmer over very low heat while you prepare eggs, either scrambled, fried or poached. Serve sauce over eggs.

Carol Rowsey Solomon (Mrs. Stephen G.)

Scrambled Egg Casserole
Serves 10 to 12

Cheese Sauce
2 tablespoons butter
2½ tablespoons flour
½ teaspoon salt
⅛ teaspoon pepper

2 cups milk
1 cup shredded American cheese

1 cup crisp bacon or chopped ham
¼ cup chopped green onion
3 tablespoons butter, melted
12 eggs, beaten

1 4-ounce can mushrooms, drained
2¼ cups lightly buttered bread crumbs
Paprika

To prepare cheese sauce, melt butter. Blend in flour and add salt and pepper to taste. Gradually stir in milk. Cook until bubbly and sauce starts to thicken. Stir in American cheese.

Saute bacon or ham and onion in butter. Add eggs and lightly scramble. Fold in cheese sauce and mushrooms. Turn into a 9 x 13-inch glass casserole. Top with bread crumbs and paprika. Cover and chill until ready to bake. Bake uncovered at 350 degrees for 30 minutes.
Cookbook Committee

Eggs Au Gratin
Serves 8

White Sauce
2 tablespoons butter
3 tablespoons flour
1½ cups milk

¾ teaspoon salt
⅛ teaspoon paprika

8 eggs, hard-boiled
½ cup grated Cheddar cheese

Paprika

To prepare white sauce, melt butter and add flour, stirring constantly. Add milk a little at a time, stirring until sauce is smooth. Add salt and paprika. Slice hard-boiled eggs. Arrange layers of sliced eggs in a greased 3-quart baking dish. Pour white sauce over them and sprinkle with cheese and paprika. Bake at 350 degrees for 20 minutes.
Diane Blinn Kenney (Mrs. Hebert K.)

Charlotte's Egg Casserole
Serves 10

1 pound hot Jimmy Dean
  sausage
1 pound regular Jimmy Dean
  sausage
2½ cups Brownberry onion
  and garlic croutons
4 eggs
2½ cups milk

¾ teaspoon dry mustard
2 cups grated sharp Old
  English cheese
2 cups grated Velveeta cheese
1 10¾-ounce can cream of
  mushroom soup
½ cup milk

Brown and drain sausage. Place sausage in a 9 x 13-inch ovenproof casserole. Pour croutons over sausage. Beat eggs, milk and mustard. Pour over croutons and sausage. Sprinkle grated cheese over casserole. Cover with foil and refrigerate overnight. Before baking, combine soup and milk and pour over casserole. Bake uncovered at 350 degrees for 45 minutes.

Nancy Key deCordova (Mrs. Edwin W.)

Jim's Breakfast
Serves 4

1 tablespoon butter
4 large mushrooms, chopped
¼ green pepper, seeded and
  chopped
2 green onions, chopped,
  including tops
½ tablespoon chopped
  pimentos or ¼ red bell
  pepper, chopped

6 eggs, beaten
Salt
Pepper
Seasoned salt
Flour tortillas, warmed
8 strips bacon, cooked
Picante sauce, or other
  Mexican sauce

Melt butter in frying pan. Saute mushrooms. Add green pepper, onion and pimentos. Stir in eggs. Salt and pepper to taste. Continue to cook until eggs are done, stirring occasionally. Serve immediately with warmed tortillas, bacon and picante sauce.

To assemble, put eggs in middle of tortilla, crumble bacon, add sauce and roll up.

Leslie Hood Diggs (Mrs. James Barnes, IV)

Foolproof Cheese Souffle
Serves 6

2 cups grated Cheddar cheese
1 10¾-ounce can cream of
mushroom soup

5 eggs, separated
Red pepper
Salt

Melt cheese and soup in double boiler and let cool thoroughly. Beat egg yolks until fluffy. Beat egg whites until stiff. Pour cheese mixture into yolks. Fold egg whites into yolk and cheese mixture, add a dash of red pepper and a pinch of salt. Bake in buttered souffle dish at 300 degrees for 30 minutes. If not browned enough in 30 minutes, increase oven temperature to 350 degrees.

Ginger Smith Shaw (Mrs. James Crawford)

Chile Egg Puff
Serves 8 to 10

10 eggs, beaten
1 tablespoon butter
½ cup flour
1 teaspoon baking powder
½ teaspoon salt
16 ounces small curd cottage
cheese
½ cup butter, melted

½ pound Monterey Jack
cheese, grated
½ pound Monterey Jack
jalapeno cheese, grated
1 pound sausage, ham or
bacon, cooked
4 jalapeno peppers, chopped

Butter a 9 x 13 x 2-inch glass baking dish with 1 tablespoon butter. Mix remaining ingredients together in large mixing bowl. Pour in baking dish, then bake at 350 degrees for 35 to 40 minutes, until slightly browned. Cut into squares.

*Carla Chenoweth Splaingard
(Mrs. Randy)*

*Marian Whitten Cathcart
(Mrs. William R.)*

Compatibles

Salads
Vegetables
Sauces
Breads

Caesar Salad
Serves 6 to 8

Dressing

1 clove garlic
1/2 cup salad oil
1 egg
2 tablespoons lemon juice
1/2 cup grated Parmesan
cheese

1 teaspoon Worcestershire
sauce
1/2 teaspoon salt
1/2 teaspoon pepper

1 head romaine lettuce

1 cup croutons

To prepare dressing blend ingredients in order given in food processor or blender. Chill well. Toss with lettuce and add croutons. Dressing may also be served on hamburgers.
Nancy Key deCordova (Mrs. Edwin W.)

Italian Salad
Serves 6

Dressing

4 ounces crumbled bleu
cheese
1/2 cup salad oil
2 tablespoons lemon juice

1/2 teaspoon sugar
1/2 teaspoon salt
Dash of pepper
Dash of paprika

2 medium onions, thinly
sliced and separated
into rings
1/2 cup sliced fresh
mushrooms

1 head romaine, torn into
pieces
2 cups sliced raw zucchini
1/2 cup sliced radishes

To prepare dressing, combine bleu cheese, salad oil, lemon juice, sugar, salt, pepper and paprika.

In bowl combine onion and mushrooms. Pour dressing on top and marinate overnight. Before serving, combine romaine, zucchini and radishes in salad bowl. Pour dressing and marinated vegetable mixture over and toss.
Judy Weilert Savage (Mrs. Robert L.)

Spinach and Cottage Cheese Supreme
Serves 6 to 8

Dressing
1/4 cup sugar
1/3 cup vinegar
1/2 to 3/4 cup oil

1 package fresh spinach
1 head iceberg lettuce, or less
   to equal amount of spinach

1 teaspoon salt
1 teaspoon dry mustard
2 to 3 green onions, chopped

1/4 pound bacon, cooked crisp
   and crumbled
1/2 cup cottage cheese

To prepare dressing, mix ingredients at least 6 hours ahead so that flavors will blend. At serving time, toss salad ingredients together and add dressing. Toss again and serve.
Elizabeth Lane Hoover   *Jane Covington White (Mrs. James U., Jr.)*

Fresh Spinach Salad
Serves 6 to 8

2 pounds fresh spinach
2 hard-boiled eggs, finely
   chopped
1/3 cup finely chopped celery

Dressing
1/4 teaspoon salt
1/4 teaspoon Tabasco
1 teaspoon vinegar

1/3 cup finely chopped onion
1/2 cup finely cubed Cheddar
   cheese
Crisp leaves of romaine lettuce

1/3 cup mayonnaise
1 tablespoon prepared
   horseradish

Thoroughly wash spinach leaves in warm water, discarding any bruised leaves. Using only the fresh inner leaves, trim the roots and coarse stems. Dry spinach leaves and chop fairly fine to make 3 cups. Combine spinach with hard-boiled eggs, celery, onion and cheese.

To prepare dressing, blend the salt, Tabasco and vinegar into the mayonnaise with the prepared horseradish. Fold into the chopped vegetables, mixing well. Chill. Serve on crisp leaves of romaine.
Linda Huper Reece (Mrs. Robert A.)

Savory Red Onion Salad
Serves 6

1/2 pound bacon
1 head lettuce

1 large red onion, sliced
2 hard-boiled eggs, chopped

Dressing
1 egg
1/4 cup sugar

3 tablespoons vinegar
4 tablespoons bacon
   drippings, cooled

Dice and fry bacon until crisp. Drain and cool. Reserve drippings. Add onion to lettuce which has been torn into pieces in salad bowl.

To prepare dressing, beat egg. Add sugar and vinegar. Cook in saucepan over low heat until thickened, stirring constantly. Cool. Add cooked dressing mixture to cooled bacon drippings. Mix thoroughly. Set aside. Do not refrigerate. Add bacon and chopped eggs to lettuce and onions. Pour dressing over mixture. Toss well.

Leslie Hood Diggs (Mrs. James Barnes, IV)

Harriet Abrahms' Salad
Serves 6 to 8

Dressing
1 large avocado, mashed
1/2 cup sour cream
3 tablespoons Italian dressing

1 tablespoon chopped onion
3/4 teaspoon chili powder
1/4 teaspoon salt

1 head lettuce, torn
2 tomatoes, chopped
1 tablespoon chopped green
   chiles
1/2 cup sliced black olives
1 1-pound can kidney beans,
   drained

Salt
Pepper
1 cup grated Cheddar cheese
1 to 2 cups regular size
   corn chips

To prepare dressing, mix ingredients and refrigerate overnight for flavors to blend. At serving time toss remaining salad ingredients with dressing and top with grated cheese and corn chips.

Barbara Pannage Stanfield (Mrs. Neil)

Canlis' Special Salad
Serves 4 to 6

2 tablespoons olive oil
Salt
1 clove garlic
2 tomatoes, peeled

2 heads romaine lettuce
1/2 cup croutons, homemade
    if possible

Condiments
1/4 cup chopped green onion
1/2 cup Romano cheese,
    freshly grated

1/2 cup crisp bacon, finely
    chopped

Dressing
3/4 cup olive oil
Juice of 2 1/2 lemons
1/2 teaspoon freshly ground
    pepper

1/4 teaspoon chopped fresh
    mint
1/4 teaspoon oregano
1 coddled egg

Into a large wooden bowl, pour approximately 2 tablespoons of good imported olive oil, sprinkle with salt and rub sides of bowl firmly with a large clove of garlic. The oil will act as a lubricant and the salt as an abrasive. Discard garlic and in the bottom of the bowl first place the tomatoes cut in eighths. Add romaine, slice in 1-inch strips. Add condiments.

To prepare dressing, pour olive oil, lemon juice and seasonings into a bowl. Add coddled egg and whip vigorously. When ready to serve, pour dressing over salad. Add croutons and toss.

This is a variation of Caesar Salad from Canlis' Charcoal Broiler Restaurant, Honolulu, Hawaii.

Barbara Butcher Beeler (Mrs. Claude E., Jr.)

Monterey Sweet and Sour Salad
Serves 6 to 8

4 tablespoons sugar
3½ teaspoons garlic salt
⅔ cup vegetable oil
1 cup apple cider vinegar
¼ cup water

3 tablespoons sesame seeds
1 head iceberg lettuce, torn
  into pieces
2 cups shredded Monterey
  Jack cheese

Mix first 5 ingredients in a pint jar. Shake well and refrigerate at least 2 hours. Toast sesame seeds. At serving time, place lettuce in bowl. Shake dressing and pour half over lettuce. Top with cheese and sesame seeds. Toss. Refrigerate remaining dressing for later use.
Sally Rapp Story (Mrs. Scott)

Mandarin Orange Salad
Serves 10 to 12

1 20-ounce can crushed
  pineapple (in its own juice)
2 11-ounce cans mandarin
  oranges
3 egg yolks
⅓ cup sugar
1 tablespoon flour

1 cup boiling water, or less, if
  using pineapple juice
1 3-ounce package orange
  Jell-o
1 cup whipping cream
1½ cups miniature
  marshmallows

Drain pineapple, reserving liquid. Drain mandarin oranges. Place pineapple and oranges in a saucepan and add egg yolks, sugar and flour. Cook until thickened. Add enough water to reserved pineapple juice to make one cup. Bring to a boil and pour over orange Jell-o, stirring until dissolved. Add gelatin mixture to fruits and refrigerate until almost set. Whip cream and add marshmallows. Fold into Jell-o mixture and pour into oiled mold. Refrigerate again until firm.
Debbi Wehba Reed (Mrs. Edward A.)

Christmas Pretzel Salad
Serves 20

2 cups crushed pretzels
¾ cup melted butter
3 tablespoons sugar
1 3-ounce package strawberry Jell-o
2 cups very hot water

1 16-ounce package frozen strawberries, partially thawed
1 8-ounce package cream cheese, softened
½ cup sugar
1 8-ounce container Cool Whip

Mix pretzel crumbs, butter and sugar and pat into bottom of a 9 x 13-inch pan. Bake for 10 minutes at 400 degrees. Cool and set aside. Dissolve Jell-o in hot water and add partially thawed strawberries. Refrigerate mixture for 20 minutes. Combine cream cheese, sugar and Cool Whip. Mix until well blended and smooth. Spread cream cheese layer over cooled crust, sealing edges. Pour and spread strawberry mixture over the top. Refrigerate until set.
Ginger Parker Johnson (Mrs. William J.)

Anita's Raspberry Salad
Serves 12 to 16

2 6-ounce boxes raspberry Jell-o
2 cups boiling water
2 10-ounce packages frozen raspberries

1 20-ounce can crushed pineapple
2 medium bananas
1 pint sour cream
½ 6¼-ounce package miniature marshmallows

Combine Jell-o and boiling water. Dissolve completely. Add frozen raspberries and stir until Jell-o begins to thicken. Add crushed pineapple, including juice. Mash bananas and stir into sour cream. Add marshmallows to sour cream mixture. Using 9 x 13-inch pan or 12-cup mold, place half of Jell-o mixture in container, then spread with sour cream mixture. Top with remaining Jell-o and refrigerate until firm.
Anita Dow Johnson (Mrs. Milo Mike)

Delectable Frozen Fruit Salad
Yields 9 quarts

4 20-ounce cans crushed
  pineapple
2 16-ounce cans sliced peaches
2 cups halved fresh white
  seedless grapes
1½ cups maraschino cherries,
  cut into eighths
½ pound marshmallows,
  quartered, or equal
  amount of miniature
  marshmallows
2 teaspoons finely chopped
  crystallized ginger

1 envelope unflavored gelatin
¼ cup cold water
1 cup orange juice
¼ cup lemon juice
2½ cups sugar
½ teaspoon salt
2 cups coarsely chopped
  pecans
2 quarts heavy cream,
  whipped
3 cups mayonnaise

Drain all fruit, reserving 1½ cups pineapple juice. Cube peach slices. Combine fruit with marshmallows and ginger. Soften gelatin in cold water. Heat pineapple juice to boiling, add gelatin and stir to dissolve. Add orange and lemon juice, sugar and salt and stir to dissolve. Chill. When mixture starts to thicken, add the fruit mixture and nuts. Fold in whipped cream and mayonnaise. Spoon into 9 1-quart cylindrical cartons (paper, plastic or metal). Cover and freeze. To serve, thaw sufficiently to allow salad to slip out of carton. Cut in 1-inch slices and serve on lettuce.

Midge Wasson Lindsey (Mrs. Paul B.)

Fruit Salad Dressing
Serves 6 to 8

1 cup sugar
1 tablespoon dry mustard
1 tablespoon celery seed
1 tablespoon paprika
1 scant tablespoon salt

1 tablespoon tarragon
3 tablespoons white vinegar
1 tablespoon grated onion
2 cups Wesson oil

Mix dry ingredients. Add vinegar and onion and mix thoroughly with a fork. Gradually add Wesson oil, stirring until thickened.

Sherri Fain Norville (Mrs. Richard S.)

Apple Nutty Spinach Salad
Serves 8

Dressing
3 tablespoons lemon juice
1/2 cup safflower oil
2 tablespoons sugar

1 clove garlic, pressed
1/2 teaspoon salt

1 16-ounce package fresh
spinach, washed and stems
trimmed
1 medium red onion, sliced
very thin

1 cup walnuts, halved
1 large red apple, cored
and sliced thin

Combine dressing ingredients and pour over salad mixture. Toss well.
Karel Frank Love (Mrs. Joe R.)

Berke's Cranberry Salad
Yields 2 to 3 quarts

1 pound fresh cranberries
2 cups sugar
1 quart whipping cream

3 cups miniature
marshmallows, cut in half
1 cup chopped pecans

Chop cranberries in food processor or blender. Mix in sugar and let stand in refrigerator at least 2 hours or overnight. Whip cream and combine with cranberries and sugar. Add marshmallows and pecans. Store in refrigerator 2 to 3 hours before serving.
Debby Downing Goodman (Mrs. Jim K.)

Kansas City Apricot Salad
Serves 12 to 15

1 20-ounce can crushed
   pineapple
1 6-ounce package apricot
   gelatin
1 8-ounce package cream
   cheese

1 cup diced celery
1 cup chopped pecans
½ pint whipping cream,
   whipped

Heat pineapple and gelatin to boiling. (No extra water is needed.) Cool in refrigerator until slightly congealed. Add crumbled cream cheese and beat with electric mixer. Add celery and pecans. Fold in whipping cream. Pour into mold or 9 x 13-inch pan. Refrigerate until firm. Cut in squares and serve on a lettuce leaf.
Darlene Trammell Parman (Mrs. Larry V.)

Florida Frozen Fruit Salad
Serves 40

1 12-ounce can frozen orange
   juice concentrate, thawed
1 can water
1 cup sugar
2 tablespoons lemon juice
6 bananas, cut up

1 20-ounce can crushed
   pineapple, do not drain
2 16-ounce cans apricot halves,
   drained and quartered
Mayonnaise (optional)
Paprika (optional)

Mix all ingredients except mayonnaise and paprika together and pour into muffin tins lined with paper cups. Freeze. After frozen, remove from muffin pans and return to freezer in plastic bags. When ready to serve, place upside down on lettuce leaf, remove paper and top with mayonnaise and a dash of paprika, if desired.
Mary Margaret Smith Ledbetter (Mrs. Eugene P., Jr.)

Salads/Vegetables/Sauces/Breads **Compatibles**

Candied Apple Salad
Serves 12

½ cup red hots
2 cups water
1 6-ounce package cherry
  Jell-o
1 cup cold water

3 apples, chopped (may or
  may not be peeled)
½ cup chopped nuts (pecans
  or walnuts)
1 cup chopped celery

Add red hots to 2 cups water and bring to a boil. Keep at a low boil, stirring frequently until all red hots are melted. Pour mixture over cherry Jell-o which is in a large mixing bowl. Stir until Jell-o is completely dissolved. Add cold water and then chill until slightly thickened. Mix in apples, nuts and celery. Pour mixture into a 5-cup mold, 12 individual molds or a 9 x 13-inch glass pan. Chill until firm.
Beccy Ricks Brown (Mrs. Dale)

Mandarin Salad
Serves 6 to 8

1 cup mandarin oranges,
  drained
½ head lettuce, may use
  several types
1 cup chopped celery

1 tablespoon parsley flakes
2 green onions, tops only,
  chopped
¼ cup toasted almonds

Dressing
¼ cup salad oil
¼ teaspoon Tabasco
½ teaspoon salt

2 tablespoons sugar
2 tablespoons tarragon
  vinegar

Combine all salad ingredients in bowl. Mix dressing ingredients together and pour over salad just before serving.
Marty Sanger McCharen (Mrs. John, III)

131

Betty Townsend's Winter Fruit Bowl
Serves 12 to 16

4 medium grapefruit,
  sectioned and cut in half
1 cup grapefruit juice and water
1 cup sugar

½ cup orange marmalade
2 cups fresh cranberries
3 medium bananas, sliced

Prepare grapefruit, reserving juice, and set aside. Add water to juice to make 1 cup. Combine with sugar and marmalade. Heat to boiling. Add cranberries and cook 5 minutes or until skins burst. Cool completely. Add grapefruit. Chill. Add bananas when ready to serve.
Ranell Bules Brown (Mrs. Steve M.)

Poached Pears
Serves 6

1 6-ounce or 2 3-ounce
  packages strawberry gelatin
1½ cups boiling water
1 cup cranberry juice cocktail

3 pieces cinnamon stick
6 whole cloves
6 fresh pears, pared and cored

In deep 2-quart casserole combine gelatin and boiling water, stirring until gelatin is dissolved. Stir in cranberry juice, cinnamon stick and cloves. Add pears. Bake at 350 degrees for 45 to 50 minutes, basting pears often with syrup. Cool pears in syrup, turning frequently. Serve warm or cool.
Debbi Davidson Dale (Mrs. Mark)

Purple Lady Salad
Serves 8 to 10

2 3-ounce packages raspberry
  Jell-o
1 cup hot water
1 1-pound can blueberries

1 8-ounce can crushed
  pineapple
1 cup finely chopped nuts
½ pint whipping cream

Dissolve Jell-o in one cup hot water. Add the can of blueberries with syrup and can of crushed pineapple. Refrigerate until almost set. Whip the cream and fold it and the nuts into the Jell-o. Refrigerate in individual molds or a 9 x 13-inch glass dish until firm.
Olive Kees Austin (Mrs. Gerald G.)

Bacon/Green Pea Chiller
Serves 6

1 cup sour cream
1 teaspoon seasoned salt
1/4 teaspoon lemon pepper
1/4 teaspoon garlic powder
1 20-ounce package frozen
  peas, thawed

1/2 pound bacon, cooked
  and crumbled
1 small tomato, diced
1/4 cup minced red onion

Mix all ingredients. Chill overnight and serve cold.
Chelin Hancock Satherlie (Mrs. Gregg)

Sally's Tomato Mousse
Serves 8

1 package unflavored gelatin
1/2 cup warm water
1 10 3/4-ounce can tomato soup
1/2 cup mayonnaise
1/2 green pepper, finely
  chopped

2 stalks celery, finely chopped
1 onion, finely chopped
1 tablespoon lemon juice
1 cup sour cream
Parsley
Dill

Soften gelatin in warm water. Heat soup and pour gelatin into it. Whisk in mayonnaise, then fold in vegetables, lemon juice, sour cream and spices. Place in a well-greased mold or greased 9 x 11-inch casserole. Chill and serve. Can be used as an appetizer spread on crackers.
Franci King Hart (Mrs. William H.)

Marinated Mushrooms and Artichoke Hearts
Serves 16 to 20

3 14-ounce cans artichoke
  hearts, drained and halved
2 pounds fresh mushrooms,
  halved
1½ cups water
1 cup cider vinegar
½ cup salad oil

1 clove garlic, halved
1½ tablespoons salt
½ teaspoon peppercorns
½ teaspoon dried thyme
½ teaspoon oregano
2 tablespoons chopped fresh
  parsley

Combine all ingredients. Refrigerate overnight, stirring occasionally. Drain and serve.

Linda Lee Rooker (Mrs. Barry)   *Barbara Pannage Stanfield (Mrs. Neil)*

Marinated Mushroom Salad
Serves 8

¼ to ⅓ cup salad oil
1 teaspoon salt
1¼ teaspoons dried basil
1¼ teaspoons Dijon mustard
¼ teaspoon pepper
¼ teaspoon paprika
3 tablespoons white wine
  vinegar

2 teaspoons lemon juice
1 pound fresh mushrooms,
  sliced
¾ cup thinly sliced green
  onions, including tops
½ basket cherry tomatoes

To prepare marinade, combine first 8 ingredients. Mix mushrooms and onions. Add to marinade. Marinate at room temperature for 1 hour. Refrigerate until serving time. When ready to serve, add halved cherry tomatoes. Stir enough to cover tomatoes with marinade and drain. If you wish, leave marinade in vegetables and serve with slotted spoon.

Mary D. Streich

Cauliflower Combo
Serves 6 to 8

Dressing

½ cup oil
3 tablespoons lemon juice
3 tablespoons wine vinegar

2 teaspoons salt
½ teaspoon sugar
¼ teaspoon pepper

4 cups cauliflower, chopped
    fine
1 cup sliced black olives

½ cup diced pimentos
⅔ cup chopped green pepper
½ cup chopped green onions

Mix dressing. Pour over salad ingredients. Stir well.
Carla Smith Pickrell (Mrs. Nelson)

Oriental Vegetable Salad
Serves 12

1 16-ounce can sliced carrots
1 15-ounce can red kidney
    beans
1 17-ounce can tiny green peas
1 16-ounce can Blue Lake
    green beans
1 16-ounce can seasoned
    French style green beans
1 12-ounce can white shoepeg
    corn

1 14-ounce can bean sprouts
1 8-ounce can sliced water
    chestnuts
1 2-ounce jar chopped red
    pimentos
1 cup finely chopped bell
    pepper
1 cup finely chopped onion
1 cup finely chopped celery

Marinade

½ cup water
1 cup sugar
1 cup vegetable oil
1 cup wine vinegar

2 teaspoons salt
1 teaspoon Tabasco
1 teaspoon pepper

Open the canned vegetables. Drain and toss in a large container. Add bell pepper, onion and celery. To prepare marinade, mix ingredients in a saucepan. Bring to a boil. Cool and pour over vegetables. Refrigerate 24 hours before serving. This will keep for several weeks in refrigerator.
Gail Price Fine (Mrs. Douglas P.)

Shoepeg Corn Salad
Serves 10

2 12-ounce cans white
shoepeg corn
1 16-ounce can French style
green beans
1 16-ounce can small green
peas

1 2-ounce jar diced pimentos
1 medium size onion,
chopped
1 green pepper, chopped

Dressing
¾ cup sugar
¾ cup salad vinegar
½ cup vegetable oil

1 teaspoon salt
1 teaspoon pepper
1 tablespoon celery seed

Drain all cans of vegetables and set aside.

To prepare dressing blend ingredients together and bring to a boil. Allow to cool. Pour over vegetables and chill overnight.

Linda Polk Klos (Mrs. Tom W.)

Copper Carrot Coins
Serves 20

2 pounds carrots
Salt

1 green pepper
1 medium onion

Dressing
1 10¾-ounce can tomato soup
½ cup salad oil
1 cup sugar
¾ cup vinegar
1 teaspoon prepared mustard

1 teaspoon Worcestershire
sauce
½ teaspoon salt
Pepper

Peel and slice carrots into rounds. Cook in lightly salted water until barely tender and still crisp. Rinse with cold water and drain. Slice green pepper and onion very thinly.

To prepare dressing combine tomato soup, salad oil, sugar, vinegar, mustard, Worcestershire, salt and pepper in bowl. Add vegetables and mix well. Refrigerate overnight.

Mary Elizabeth Miller Brown (Mrs. Wilbur P.)   *Barbara Louise Ketchum*

Mother's Potato Salad
Serves 8 to 10

6 potatoes, boiled, skinned
and cubed
6 hard-boiled eggs, sliced
14 sweet pickles, sliced
2 bunches green onions,
chopped

2 2-ounce jars chopped
pimentos
½ tablespoon salt, per layer
½ tablespoon pepper,
per layer
½ tablespoon celery seed,
per layer

Dressing
1 pint jar Miracle Whip
2 tablespoons mustard

4 tablespoons sweet pickle
juice
4 tablespoons sugar

This is made in 3 layers. Start with ⅓ of the potatoes and follow with
⅓ of each of the vegetable ingredients and eggs. Cover with ⅓ of
the dressing mixture. Repeat 2 more times, making sure you sprinkle
each layer with salt, pepper and celery seed. Refrigerate. Just before serving, mix layers together. Preparing the salad in layers is the secret to the
success of this recipe.
Michele Moore Hughes (Mrs. Jack)

Beer Potato Salad
Serves 8

3 pounds potatoes
2 cups diced celery
1 small onion, chopped
2 teaspoons salt
1 cup mayonnaise

2 tablespoons mustard
¼ teaspoon Tabasco
½ cup beer
2 tablespoons chopped
parsley

Boil potatoes in skins until tender. Peel and dice. Add celery, onion
and salt. Set aside. Blend together mayonnaise, mustard and Tabasco.
Gradually stir in beer. Add parsley. Pour sauce over potato mixture and
mix lightly until blended. Refrigerate.
Susan Barnhart Wade

Meg's Egg Salad
Serves 8 to 12

12 eggs
1 cup mayonnaise
1 tablespoon Durkee's Famous
  Sauce
2 teaspoons Dijon mustard
2 tablespoons sweet pickle
  relish
1/3 cup crumbled bacon

Cavender's All-Purpose Greek
  Seasoning
Coarsely ground black pepper
Salt
Freeze-dried chives
Garlic powder
Accent
Onion powder

Hard boil eggs, allow to cool and remove shells. Put eggs through food processor, remove to separate bowl and add remaining ingredients. All seasonings are added to taste. Chill at least 1 hour before serving to blend flavors. You may substitute sweet pickles for pickle relish. Add one pickle for every 3 to 4 eggs as you put them through the food processor. You may want to add some pickle juice when combining eggs with spices. Makes attractive luncheon fare served on top of individual tomato aspic.

Mary Tolle Walsh (Mrs. Thomas)

Bombay Chicken Salad
Serves 6

1 cup brown rice
1 8-ounce can sliced
  pineapple, cut in
  1/2-inch strips
2 cups cooked chicken, cut in
  1/4 to 1/2-inch strips
1 cup sliced celery
1/3 cup sliced green onions

1/3 cup toasted slivered
  almonds
1/4 cup pineapple juice, saved
  from can
1/3 cup mayonnaise
1/4 cup chopped chutney
1 teaspoon curry powder

Cook the brown rice according to package but without using any butter. Add pineapple pieces, chicken, celery, green onions and toasted almonds to cooked rice. Mix and stir pineapple juice, mayonnaise, chopped chutney and curry powder into rice mixture. Chill at least 4 hours before serving.

Carolyn Nichols Bentley (Mrs. Earl W., Jr.)

Chicken Pasta Charmer
Serves 10 to 12

6 chicken breast halves, about
 1½ pounds
1 onion, quartered
1 carrot, halved
1 celery stalk, halved
⅓ cup pine nuts
1 teaspoon butter
⅓ pound snow peas
1 pound linguine
1 15-ounce can garbanzo
 beans, drained

½ pound fresh mushrooms,
 sliced
1 2-ounce jar stuffed green
 olives, drained and sliced
1 2-ounce can pitted black
 olives, drained and sliced
1 red or green bell pepper, cut
 into thin strips
1 jar marinated artichoke
 hearts, drained

Dressing
1 cup olive oil
5 tablespoons red wine
 vinegar
½ cup minced fresh parsley
4 teaspoons Dijon mustard

½ teaspoon curry powder
1½ teaspoons salt
1 teaspoon pepper
½ teaspoon garlic powder

Boil chicken in water with onion, carrot and celery until done. Cool. Skin and bone chicken and cut into bite-size pieces. Saute pine nuts in butter until nuts begin to brown. Cool. Cook snow peas in boiling water for 1 minute. Cool in ice water and drain. Cook linguine until al dente. Drain and rinse in cold water. Mix chicken, pine nuts, peas, linguine, beans, mushrooms, olives, bell pepper and artichoke hearts in large bowl and toss to blend thoroughly.

To prepare dressing, mix all ingredients in a small bowl. Pour dressing over salad and toss well. Refrigerate. Can be prepared one day ahead and refrigerated.

Gennie LeForce Johnson (Mrs. Robert M.)

Seaside Salad
Serves 6 to 8

1 7¼-ounce package Kraft macaroni and cheese dinner
¼ cup margarine
¼ cup milk
1 10-ounce package frozen peas, uncooked, thawed
1 7-ounce can tuna, drained
1 cup chopped celery

1 cup Miracle Whip salad dressing
2 tablespoons finely chopped onion
Dash salt
¼ cup pickle relish, drained (optional)
2 tablespoons chopped pimentos (optional)

Prepare macaroni and cheese dinner according to package directions, using margarine and milk. Add all other ingredients, mix lightly and chill.
Margo Maidt Winfrey (Mrs. Ron)

Chinese Chicken Salad
Serves 4 to 6

2 tablespoons soy sauce
1 tablespoon oil
1 tablespoon sherry
1 clove garlic, minced
¼ teaspoon ginger
¼ teaspoon Chinese 5-spice powder

4 to 6 boneless chicken breasts
¼ cup sesame seeds
6 cups shredded lettuce
3 green onions, sliced
1 bunch fresh parsley chopped
1 cup cashews, toasted, unsalted if possible

Lemon Dressing
½ teaspoon dry mustard
1 teaspoon sugar
1 teaspoon grated lemon peel
2 teaspoons soy sauce

1 tablespoon lemon juice
4 tablespoons oil
Salt
Pepper

Mix first 6 ingredients and rub mixture over chicken breasts. Place chicken skin side up in baking pan. Pour remaining soy sauce mixture on top of chicken. Bake at 400 degrees for 20 minutes. Cool. Skin chicken and cut into thin strips. Spread sesame seeds in frying pan and toast. Mix chicken in bowl with lettuce, onion and parsley. Add sesame seeds and ¾ cup of the cashews. Prepare lemon dressing. Pour over chicken mixture and toss lightly, adding salt and pepper to taste. Top with remaining ¼ cup cashews.
Elizabeth White Hoffman (Mrs. Kent)

Bengal Salad
Serves 6

1 cup crab meat
1 cup sliced celery
1 cup shrimp
1/2 cup sliced water chestnuts
4 tablespoons chutney
1 can pineapple tidbits

Juice of 1 lemon
2 tablespoons Bar-Le-Duc
   currants
1/2 cup almonds, sauteed in
   2 teaspoons butter
Salt

Dressing
1 cup mayonnaise
1/4 cup sour cream

1 teaspoon curry powder

Combine all ingredients with dressing mixture. Chill and serve on lettuce cups.
Florence Potter Sutton (Mrs. William J.)

Cold Shrimp (or Chicken) and Pasta Medley
Serves 10 to 12

2 cups fresh tomatoes, peeled
   and cut up (may use cherry
   tomatoes)
1 can artichoke hearts,
   drained and quartered
3/4 pound fresh mushrooms,
   sliced
1 1/2 cups snow peas
1 1/2 cups bottled Italian
   dressing

3/4 pound vermicelli, broken
   in half
3 cups shrimp, cooked, peeled
   and deveined or 4 whole
   chicken breasts, boiled,
   skinned and boned
3/4 cup pine nuts (also called
   Pignolia nuts)
1/3 cup fresh basil or
   3 teaspoons dried basil
1/4 cup minced fresh parsley

Toss cut up tomatoes, artichoke hearts, mushrooms and snow peas (thawed, if frozen, or blanched if using fresh) with 1 cup of Italian dressing. Refrigerate. Cook vermicelli according to package directions. Drain. Toss with remaining 1/2 cup Italian dressing while still warm. Refrigerate separately. Before serving toss all ingredients together.
Marty Johnson Margo (Mrs. Robert C.)

Crab Louis
Serves 4

Dressing
1/4 cup whipping cream
1 cup mayonnaise
1/4 cup chili sauce

1/4 cup chopped green onions
1/4 cup chopped green pepper
1 teaspoon lemon juice

1 large head lettuce, shredded
4 Bibb or romaine lettuce cups
2 to 3 cups fresh, shelled crab
　legs or frozen king crab
2 large tomatoes, cut in
　wedges

2 hard-boiled eggs, quartered
1 15-ounce can hearts of palm
　or white asparagus spears
Salt
Paprika
4 to 8 stuffed olives

To prepare dressing, mix whipping cream, mayonnaise, chili sauce, green onions, green pepper and lemon juice. Set aside. Arrange shredded lettuce on Bibb or romaine lettuce cups. Arrange chunks of crab on lettuce. Circle with tomatoes, eggs and hearts of palm. Sprinkle tomatoes and eggs with salt. Pour Louis dressing on top and sprinkle with paprika and garnish with stuffed olives.
Ruth McKissick Commander (Mrs. A. C.)

Hearty Tuna Salad
Serves 4

1 6½-ounce can tuna
1 10-ounce package frozen
　peas
1 cup thinly sliced celery
1/2 cup chopped green onion
3/4 cup mayonnaise
2 tablespoons lemon juice

1 teaspoon curry powder
1/8 teaspoon garlic salt
1 teaspoon soy sauce
1/4 cup toasted slivered
　almonds
1 cup chow mein noodles

Drain tuna, break into large pieces. Cook peas according to package directions, cool. Add peas, celery and onions to tuna. Combine mayonnaise, lemon juice, curry powder, garlic salt and soy sauce. Add to tuna mixture. Refrigerate at least 2 hours. At serving time, add noodles and almonds. Toss lightly and serve.
Becky Jenkins Stith (Mrs. David)

Rice and Artichoke Salad Royale
Serves 8

1 package chicken-flavored
 rice or 1½ cups long grain
 rice cooked in chicken
 broth
4 green onions, sliced
½ green pepper, seeded and
 finely chopped

12 stuffed green olives, sliced
2 6-ounce jars marinated
 artichoke hearts, drained,
 reserving liquid
¾ teaspoon curry powder
⅓ cup mayonnaise

Prepare rice and let cool. In large bowl mix rice with onions, green pepper and olives. Cut artichokes in half. Combine reserved liquid with curry powder and mayonnaise. Add artichoke hearts to rice and vegetable mixture and toss with dressing. Chill until ready to serve.

Sally Morrison Stringer *Pam Stone Weatherholt*
(Mrs. Edward H., Jr.) *(Mrs. William)*

Premiere Pasta Salad
Serves 12

1 pound medium bow tie or
 shell macaroni
1 small jar diced pimentos,
 drained

1 bunch fresh broccoli, cut
 into flowerets
½ cup toasted pine nuts or
 toasted slivered blanched
 almonds

Dressing
½ cup olive oil
½ cup salad oil
½ cup white wine vinegar
2½ teaspoons salt

1 teaspoon Dijon mustard
½ teaspoon ground white
 pepper
1 cup Parmesan cheese

Cook macaroni according to package directions. Drain and rinse with cold water. Drain again and set aside.

To prepare dressing, combine ingredients in a food processor. Cover and blend for 30 seconds. In a large bowl combine macaroni and pimentos. Pour on dressing and toss gently. Cover and let stand at least 4 hours. Can be made ahead to this point and refrigerated for up to 24 hours. Blanch broccoli in a large saucepan of boiling salted water for 1 minute. Drain and cool. Add broccoli and ¼ cup of nuts to salad 30 minutes before serving. Toss. Sprinkle remaining nuts over top of salad. Let stand at room temperature until ready to serve.

Debby Gambulos Dudman (Mrs. Paul)

Artichokes Langford
Serves 6 to 8

2 10-ounce packages frozen
  chopped spinach
1 bunch green onions, white
  part only
1/4 cup butter
1 cup whipping cream
Salt

Pepper
1/8 teaspoon horseradish
4 dashes Tabasco
2 14-ounce cans artichoke
  bottoms
Parmesan cheese

Cook spinach according to directions. Drain well. Chop green onions. Puree onions and cooked spinach in food processor or blender. Lightly brown butter in heavy skillet, then add puree. Stir in whipping cream and season to taste with Tabasco, salt, pepper and horseradish. Stuff artichoke bottoms with spinach mixture and top with generous amount of Parmesan cheese. Toast on a buttered cookie sheet at 350 degrees for approximately 20 minutes.

Catherine Coburn Langford (Mrs. Dennis)

Artichoke Hearts Florentine
Serves 6 to 8

2 10 1/2-ounce packages
  frozen chopped spinach
1 onion, chopped
Butter

1 8-ounce package cream
  cheese, cut in small pieces
1 14-ounce can artichoke
  hearts, cut up
Parmesan cheese or croutons

Cook chopped spinach according to package directions. Drain. Saute onion in butter. Add onion and cream cheese pieces to spinach. Add artichoke hearts. Pour into a greased 2-quart casserole and top with Parmesan cheese or crushed croutons. Bake at 350 degrees for 20 to 30 minutes or until hot.

Marty Johnson Margo (Mrs. Robert C.)

Cheddar Asparagus Casserole
Serves 8

3 16-ounce cans cut asparagus
1 10½-ounce can cream of
  mushroom soup
⅓ cup milk

3 hard-boiled eggs, sliced
1 cup grated Cheddar cheese
1 ⅝-ounce package potato
  chips

Layer half of asparagus in a 9 x 13-inch buttered casserole. Combine soup and milk. Layer half of eggs, half of soup and milk mixture, and half of cheese. Repeat and end with cheese and potato chips on top. Bake at 350 degrees for 20 to 30 minutes, or until bubbly and brown.
Lee Ann Naifeh Kuhlman (Mrs. James E.)

Asparagus Mushroom Casserole
Serves 8 to 10

4 cups fresh mushrooms,
  cleaned and sliced thickly
1 cup finely chopped onion
4 tablespoons unsalted butter
2 tablespoons flour
1 teaspoon chicken bouillon
  granules
½ teaspoon salt
Dash pepper

½ teaspoon nutmeg
1 cup milk
2 8-ounce packages frozen
  asparagus, cooked and
  drained, cut in 3-inch pieces
¼ cup chopped pimentos
2 teaspoons fresh lemon juice
¾ cup fresh soft bread crumbs
2 tablespoons butter, melted

Cook mushrooms and onions in 4 tablespoons butter about 10 minutes. Remove mushrooms and onions from pan, leaving butter and liquid. Using whisk mix in flour, bouillon, salt, pepper and nutmeg. Slowly add milk. Cook and stir over medium heat until bubbly. Add mushrooms, onions, cooked asparagus, pimentos and lemon juice. Stir until well mixed. Place mixture in buttered 2-quart glass dish. Combine bread crumbs and 2 tablespoons melted butter. Sprinkle bread crumb mixture on top of casserole. Bake at 350 degrees for 35 to 40 minutes.
Carol Sue Jennerjahn Taylor (Mrs. Jerry A.)

Asparagus with Pine Nuts
in Lemon Vinaigrette
Serves 4

1 pound fresh asparagus

Lemon Vinaigrette
¼ cup olive oil
1 tablespoon fresh lemon
  juice
1 clove garlic, mashed to
  a paste

3 tablespoons pine nuts

½ teaspoon dried oregano,
  crumbled
½ teaspoon dried basil,
  crumbled
½ teaspoon salt
Freshly ground pepper

Steam asparagus 7 minutes. Toast pine nuts in a dry heavy skillet over medium heat. Toss frequently until golden brown, about 3 minutes. Set aside.

To prepare lemon vinaigrette whisk all ingredients together in a bowl or shake in a tightly closed jar until blended. Heat the vinaigrette in a non-corrosive medium saucepan over medium heat until hot, about 3 minutes. Toss asparagus with dressing. Place asparagus on serving dish. Sprinkle with pine nuts. Let stand at room temperature until serving time.
Margie Pribyl Law (Mrs. Mickey)

Beets in Mustard Cream
Serves 8 to 10

1 pound fresh beets, about
  4 medium
Salt
2 tablespoons Dijon mustard
1 tablespoon tarragon vinegar

½ teaspoon salt
½ teaspoon black pepper
¼ cup olive oil
1 cup plain yogurt

Cut off tops and roots of beets and scrub them under cold water with a vegetable brush. Boil them in a saucepan filled with cold water and a good pinch of salt for about ½ hour or until beets are just tender. Put them in a colander and rinse with cold water. Slice them thinly, leaving skins on, into a medium-sized bowl. In a smaller bowl thoroughly combine mustard, vinegar, salt and pepper. Add the olive oil slowly, beating with a whisk, as in making mayonnaise. Stir in yogurt to finish the sauce. Pour the mustard cream sauce over the beets, toss, cover and refrigerate.
Susan Esco Crain (Mrs. R. Dean)

Broccoli and Onion Casserole
Serves 6

2 10-ounce packages frozen
    cut broccoli
2 cups frozen small whole
    onions
1/4 cup butter, divided
2 tablespoons flour
1/3 teaspoon salt

Pepper (optional)
1 cup milk
1 3-ounce package cream
    cheese
3/4 cup shredded sharp
    American cheese
1 cup bread crumbs

Cook frozen broccoli according to package directions. Drain. Cook onions according to directions. Drain. Melt half the butter. Stir in the flour, salt and pepper, if desired. Add milk and stir constantly until thick and bubbly. Reduce heat and stir in cream cheese. Stir until mixture is smooth. Put vegetables in a 2-quart casserole. Pour sauce over all and mix. Sprinkle with American cheese. Top with bread crumbs. Bake at 350 degrees for approximately 40 minutes.
Mary Slattery Price (Mrs. William S.)

Souffled Broccoli Ring
Serves 12

2 1/2 pounds broccoli
1/2 cup sour cream
Onion salt
Seasoned salt

Ground pepper
4 eggs, beaten
Creamed onions (optional)

Cook broccoli in boiling salted water about 14 minutes, or cook in microwave until tender. Drain and cool. Puree broccoli and add sour cream and seasonings to taste. Mix in beaten eggs. Pour into a 4-cup buttered ring mold. Cook in hot water bath at 350 degrees for 30 minutes. Cover mold with aluminum foil while cooking. Mold should set like custard. Unmold and fill center with creamed onions.
Peg Malloy

Easy Broccoli Casserole
Serves 8

2 10-ounce packages frozen
chopped broccoli
1 cup cream of mushroom
soup

½ cup mayonnaise
1 tablespoon lemon juice
½ cup grated Cheddar cheese
1 cup Cheez-it cracker crumbs

Cook broccoli, drain, and place in buttered casserole. Mix soup, mayonnaise, lemon juice and cheese. Spoon over the broccoli. Top with cracker crumbs. Bake at 350 degrees for 20 minutes.
Betty Lou Morgan Stewart (Mrs. Michael M.)

Mother's Carrots
Serves 6

1 pound carrots, peeled
½ cup butter
2 tablespoons brown sugar
1 tablespoon chopped chives
1 teaspoon dry mustard

¾ teaspoon salt
⅛ teaspoon cayenne pepper
1 8-ounce can water chestnuts,
slivered or halved

Diagonally slice peeled carrots. Saute in butter at least 10 minutes. Add brown sugar, chives, mustard, salt and cayenne pepper. Cook until tender. Toss gently with water chestnuts before serving.
Stacey Shannon Blake (Mrs. Joe)

Sweet and Sour Celery and Onions
Serves 4 to 6

1 bunch fresh celery
6 strips bacon
1 cup onions, sliced into rings
3 tablespoons cider vinegar

1 tablespoon sugar
¼ teaspoon salt
¼ teaspoon pepper

Trim leaves off celery. Cut stalks into 1-inch pieces and set aside. Fry bacon until crisp and drain on paper towels. Reserve 3 tablespoons bacon fat. Saute celery and onion rings in bacon fat over moderate heat for 5 minutes. Reduce heat. Cover and cool 12 to 15 minutes or until vegetables are crisp and tender. Stir in vinegar, sugar, salt and pepper. Heat until hot. Crumble bacon over top and serve.
Kay Pappan Musser (Mrs. R. Clark)

Mexican Corn Casserole
Serves 6

2 10-ounce boxes frozen corn,
   white or yellow, thawed
1/2 cup butter, melted
2 large eggs
1/2 pound Monterey Jack
   cheese, cubed
1/2 cup cornmeal
1 cup sour cream

1 4-ounce can chopped green
   chiles for mildly hot flavor,
   2 cans for more intense
   flavor
1 1/2 teaspoons salt
Black pepper
Paprika

Grease a 2-quart casserole or loaf pan. Puree half the corn with butter
and eggs. Combine remaining ingredients including corn, except paprika,
and blend with the puree. Pour into the prepared pan and sprinkle with
paprika. Bake uncovered for 50 to 60 minutes at 350 degrees or until
firm. Can be cooked in microwave on high for 20 minutes or until firm.
Be sure to use microwave-proof dish.
Beth Matthews McMullan (Mrs. Harry)

Patrick's Cauliflower Souffle
Serves 8

3 tablespoons butter
3 tablespoons flour
1/2 cup milk
1/2 cup grated Cheddar cheese
1/2 cup mayonnaise
2 cups cauliflower, cooked
   and mashed
1/4 cup chopped parsley
1 tablespoon finely chopped
   onion

3 eggs, slightly beaten
1 tablespoon lemon juice
1 teaspoon Worcestershire
   sauce
Salt
Pepper
1 10-ounce can Rotel tomatoes
   and green chiles (optional)

Heat butter, flour and milk to make a thick white sauce. Combine
remaining ingredients and add to white sauce. Pour in a greased ring
mold or ovenproof dish and set in a hot water bath. Bake at 375 degrees
for 45 minutes or until top is firm and set when shaken. This can be
made the day before and then baked.
Mary Tolle Walsh (Mrs. Thomas)

Creamed New Cabbage
Serves 6

1 small, firm white head of
cabbage
2 tablespoons butter
Salt
Aromatic pepper

Sugar
1/2 cup whipping cream
Toasted sesame seeds
Paprika

Remove core of cabbage. Slice in a food processor using the thick slicing blade. Melt butter in a large skillet. Add cabbage, pinch of salt aromatic pepper to taste and a good pinch of sugar. Cover and cook over moderately high heat until cabbage is well-coated with butter and begins to cook down. Add 1/2 cup whipping cream and simmer until cream is reduced and cabbage is cooked but still crisp. Sprinkle with toasted sesame seeds and garnish with paprika. Serve hot.
Anne Wileman Schafer

Cabbage Casserole
Serves 8

1 large head cabbage, cored,
cooked in salted water
and drained
1 10½-ounce can cream of
mushroom soup
2 to 4 tablespoons milk

1 2-ounce jar pimentos
1½ cups grated Velveeta
cheese
4 to 6 crackers, crushed
2 to 4 tablespoons butter

Mix mushroom soup with milk and pimentos until consistency of gravy or until mixture pours easily. Place half of cabbage on bottom of a 2-quart casserole. Pour half of soup mixture over this. Sprinkle half of grated cheese on top. Top with half of cracker crumbs. Repeat. Dot with butter. Bake at 350 degrees for 1 hour.
Stacey Shannon Blake (Mrs. Joe)

Low Calorie Baked Okra
Serves 6

3 cups okra, cut in 1-inch
  pieces
1 medium green pepper, diced
1 medium onion, diced

3 medium tomatoes, diced
Salt
Pepper
1 tomato, sliced

Layer okra, green pepper, onion and diced tomatoes in a 2-quart baking dish. Season with salt and pepper. Top with slices of tomato. Cover with aluminum foil or casserole lid. Bake at 325 degrees for 45 minutes.
Patsy Eskridge King (Mrs. Arthur E., Jr.)

Lemon Green Beans
Serves 4

2 to 3 pounds fresh green
  beans
1/2 cup butter
1/2 cup bread crumbs

2 lemon rinds, grated
Salt (optional)
Pepper (optional)

Steam and drain green beans. Arrange on platter. Brown bread crumbs in melted butter. Add the grated rinds of lemon. Add salt and pepper. Pour or sprinkle this mixture over hot beans.
Tami Aschenbrener Boecking (Mrs. Stephen R.)

Pepper Corn
Serves 4

2 12-ounce cans white
  shoepeg corn
2 3-ounce packages cream
  cheese
1/4 cup milk

2 tablespoons butter or
  margarine
1 4-ounce can chopped
  green chiles
Buttered bread crumbs
Paprika

Mix corn, cream cheese, milk, butter and chopped chiles in the top of a double boiler. Stir until cream cheese melts. Pour into a 1-quart baking dish. Top with buttered bread crumbs and paprika. Bake at 325 degrees for 15 to 20 minutes until bubbling.
Karen Keitz Lawler (Mrs. Wayne D.)

Eggplant Parmigiana
Serves 8

2 tablespoons Bertolli virgin olive oil
½ cup finely chopped onion
1 clove garlic, minced
½ pound extra lean ground beef
1 1-pound 12-ounce can Progresso Italian tomatoes, undrained
1 6-ounce can tomato paste
2 teaspoons oregano leaves
1 teaspoon dried basil
1 teaspoon salt
¼ teaspoon freshly ground pepper
1 tablespoon brown sugar
1 large fresh eggplant
2 eggs, slightly beaten
1 tablespoon water
½ cup seasoned dry bread crumbs
1½ cups grated fresh Parmesan cheese, divided
⅓ cup olive oil
8 ounces Mozzarella cheese, grated and divided

Saute onion and garlic in 2 tablespoons olive oil. Add ground beef, stirring until browned, about 5 minutes. Add tomatoes, tomato paste, oregano, basil, salt, pepper and brown sugar. Bring to a boil, stirring occasionally. Reduce heat and simmer covered 35 minutes. Grease a 9 x 13-inch baking dish. Slice unpeeled eggplant into ¼-inch slices. Combine eggs with 1 tablespoon water. Combine bread crumbs and ½ cup of the Parmesan cheese. Mix well. Dip eggplant into egg and then crumb mixture. Saute in olive oil until crisp. Drain. Arrange half of cooked eggplant onto bottom of baking dish. Pour half of tomato sauce over eggplant, sprinkle with half of remaining Parmesan cheese and top with half of Mozzarella cheese. Repeat process ending with Mozzarella on top. Bake uncovered at 350 degrees for 30 minutes. If cooked frozen, bake at 350 degrees for 45 minutes covered, 15 minutes uncovered.
Carol Sue Jennerjahn Taylor (Mrs. Jerry A.)

Oklahoma Baked Beans
Serves 10 to 15

1 53-ounce can pork and beans
1 12-ounce bottle of chili sauce
1 large onion, chopped
⅔ cup brown sugar
1 tablespoon dry mustard
Chopped bacon (optional)

Mix together the ingredients and pour into an ovenproof casserole. Bake at 300 degrees for 1 to 2 hours.
Linda Lee Rooker (Mrs. Barry)

Parmesan Spinach Souffle
Serves 8 to 10

2 10-ounce packages frozen
  spinach
2 tablespoons grated onion
4 eggs
4 tablespoons butter

2 tablespoons flour
1 cup sour cream
1¾ cups grated Parmesan
  cheese

Cook spinach and grated onion together in boiling water until thawed. Drain thoroughly. Beat eggs. Melt butter and mix with flour. Fold butter and flour mixture, sour cream and Parmesan cheese into eggs. Gently mix in drained spinach. Pour into greased 1½ quart souffle dish. Bake at 350 degrees for 30 minutes or until center is set.
Mary Hart Reeves (Mrs. William George)

Riverview Plantation's English Pea Casserole
Serves 4 to 6

½ cup margarine
2 15-ounce cans baby English
  peas, drained but reserving
  liquid
Salt
Pepper

1 10½-ounce can cream of
  mushroom soup, heated
1½ cups grated Cheddar
  cheese
Saltines, crumbled

Melt margarine and pour over drained peas that have been put in a 2-quart baking dish. Add a dash of salt and pepper. Pour mushroom soup, slightly thinned with liquid from the peas, over peas. Sprinkle grated cheese and cracker crumbs on top. Bake at 350 degrees for 30 minutes.
Marion Joullian

Microwave Zucchini
Serves 6

3 medium zucchini, grated
3 tablespoons butter or
  margarine
½ teaspoon salt

¼ teaspoon pepper
1½ tablespoons Parmesan
  cheese

Grate zucchini by hand or in food processor. Spoon grated zucchini into greased rectangular baking dish. Dot with butter. Sprinkle with salt, pepper and cheese. Cover with plastic wrap. Microwave on high for 4 to 5 minutes. Serve immediately while hot.
Gail Price Fine (Mrs. Douglas P.)

Zucchini Au Gratin
Serves 6 to 8

2 tablespoons olive oil
4 medium zucchini, sliced
1 large onion, sliced
12 ounces Mozzarella or
  Monterey Jack cheese,
  cubed

½ cup grated Parmesan
  cheese
½ cup fresh minced parsley
Salt
Pepper
½ cup fresh bread crumbs
Butter

Pour oil into a 9 x 13-inch baking dish. Layer half of the zucchini, onion, Mozzarella cheese, Parmesan cheese and parsley. Lightly season with salt and pepper. Repeat layer. Cover with bread crumbs. Dot with butter. Bake uncovered at 350 degrees for 40 minutes.
Gennie LeForce Johnson (Mrs. Robert M.)

Squash and Green Chile Casserole
Serves 4 to 6

8 to 10 summer squash
1 pound Cheddar cheese,
  grated
2 4-ounce cans chopped
  green chiles

Salt
Pepper
2 tablespoons butter

Clean and slice squash. Boil until soft. Drain and mash. Put in small deep baking dish. Mix with cheese and chiles. Season to taste. Dot with butter and bake at 350 degrees until cheese melts.
Elizabeth White Hoffman (Mrs. Kent)

Squash Casserole Supreme
Serves 6

2 pounds yellow squash, steamed, drained and mashed
1 10½-ounce can cream of chicken soup
1 cup sour cream
2 tablespoons brown sugar
Salt
¼ cup butter or margarine, softened
2 carrots, peeled and grated
1 medium onion, grated
Pepperidge Farm Herb Stuffing

Add other ingredients to squash, reserving some of the stuffing. Mix well and put in a shallow 8 x 12-inch baking dish and top with reserved stuffing mix. Bake at 350 degrees for 30 to 45 minutes, or until top is brown.

Linda Tresenwriter Cheatham (Mrs. James E., Jr.)

Herbed Cucumbers with Crookneck Squash
Serves 6

1 hothouse or English cucumber
1 pound yellow squash
¼ cup butter
1 clove garlic, minced
1 tablespoon chopped parsley
1 tablespoon chopped chives
Freshly squeezed lemon juice
Salt
Pepper

Take cucumber and squash and slice on the bias into ½-inch thick pieces. Melt ¼ cup butter and add garlic. Add vegetables. Turn them over once or twice and shake the pan so they do not stick. When they are tender, stir in parsley and chives and a good squeeze of lemon juice. Season with salt and pepper.

Katherine Walbert Walker (Mrs. Russell)

Aunt Fanny's Cabin Baked Squash
Serves 6 to 8

3 pounds yellow squash,
  cooked until tender
1/2 cup chopped onion
1 cup cracker crumbs
1/2 teaspoon black pepper

2 eggs, beaten
1/2 cup butter, divided
1 tablespoon sugar
1 teaspoon salt

Mash squash. Add onion, 1/2 cup cracker crumbs, pepper, eggs, 1/4 cup butter, sugar and salt. Combine well. Pour in buttered 2-quart baking dish. Melt remaining butter and spread on top. Sprinkle with additional cracker crumbs to suit taste. Bake at 375 degrees for 1 hour.
Patricia Hadlock Ramsey (Mrs. Christian, Jr.)

Stuffed Tomatoes
Serves 4

4 tomatoes
5 strips bacon, cooked crisp
1/2 pound mushrooms, minced
3 tablespoons butter
3 to 4 tablespoons Italian
  bread crumbs
3 green onions, chopped

Pinch fresh parsley, minced
Salt
Pepper
1/4 cup freshly grated
  Parmesan cheese
Dill weed

Slice off top of tomatoes and scoop out all of the pulp. Turn over to drain tomatoes. Cook bacon and drain. Saute mushrooms in butter in small frying pan for 2 to 3 minutes. Add bread crumbs, green onions and pinch of fresh parsley. Season with salt and pepper, if desired. Crumble bacon and add to mixture. Stuff tomatoes with cooked bacon and mushroom mixture. Top with freshly grated Parmesan cheese and sprinkle with dill weed. Dot with butter. Place stuffed tomatoes in a muffin tin to hold tomatoes' shape and prevent spilling. Bake at 350 degrees for about 20 minutes.
Sharon Fitkin Boecking (Mrs. H. E., III)

Tomatoes Florentine
Serves 12

12 small tomatoes
¼ cup prepared mustard
12 strips bacon, diced and
  sauteed
2 12-ounce packages frozen
  spinach souffle, thawed
  1 hour

¼ cup grated Parmesan
  cheese
Parsley sprigs

Cut a thin slice from the top of each tomato. Carefully scoop out pulp to make a shell. Drain shells upside down 15 minutes. Spread inside of each with 1 teaspoon mustard. Divide bacon evenly into tomatoes. Spoon spinach souffle into tomatoes. Sprinkle teaspoon of cheese over each top. Arrange tomatoes in 2 8-inch round baking dishes or any ovenproof dish. Bake uncovered at 375 degrees for 20 to 30 minutes or until golden brown on top. Garnish with parsley sprigs.

Sally Morrison Stringer (Mrs. Edward H., Jr.)

Ratatouille
Serves 8 to 10

Olive oil
2 onions, thinly sliced
2 green peppers, thinly sliced
2 eggplants, peeled and cubed
3 large zucchini, cut into strips
½ pound fresh mushrooms,
  sliced
4 cloves garlic, minced

½ teaspoon salt
¼ teaspoon pepper
2 tablespoons minced parsley
½ teaspoon basil
1 teaspoon garlic salt
4 10-ounce cans Italian
  tomatoes, undrained

In a heavy skillet saute onion and green pepper in olive oil. Remove to a separate pot. Stir-fry each vegetable quickly in the olive oil and remove to the same pot. When all vegetables are stir-fried, add garlic, salt, pepper, parsley, basil and garlic salt. Add tomatoes. Cook on low heat 20 to 30 minutes. Be careful not to overcook or make mushy. The squash and eggplant should have a little bit of al dente left to them. Serve hot or cold. It freezes nicely.

Lee Ann Naifeh Kuhlman (Mrs. James E.)

Christmas Eve Vegetable Pie
Serves 6 to 8

Pate Brisee
3³/₄ cups flour
1¹/₂ cups plus 2 tablespoons
  unsalted butter

1 tablespoon salt
3 whole eggs

Vegetable Filling
Cooking oil
2 large yellow onions, sliced
  thin, separated into rings
1 eggplant, peeled and sliced
  in ¹/₄-inch rounds
3 fresh tomatoes, peeled and
  sliced thick
¹/₄ cup freshly grated
  Parmesan cheese, divided

1 package Birds Eye whole
  kernel frozen corn
2 green peppers, seeded and
  sliced into rings
2 cloves garlic, minced
Salt
Pepper
2 tablespoons butter, divided

To prepare Pate Brisee place flour, cold butter and salt in food processor. Process with on and off motions until dough looks like meal. Add eggs and process until dough forms a ball. Do not over process. Wrap in plastic wrap and let rest in refrigerator for 1¹/₂ hours. Roll out dough and place in 2 deep-dish fluted quiche or pie pans. Cover with buttered weighted foil and blind bake for 6 minutes at 400 degrees. Remove foil, prick with fork and bake 3 to 4 minutes longer. Cool. This will make 2 crusts. Freeze one empty crust for later use.

To prepare vegetable filling, saute onions in oil until lightly browned. Add eggplant and tomatoes and saute until slightly soft. Sprinkle 1 tablespoon of Parmesan into empty crust. Then layer eggplant, tomatoes, half box of frozen corn, onions and green pepper. Mix remaining Parmesan with garlic and sprinkle 1 tablespoon over vegetables and dot with 1 tablespoon butter. Add another layer of vegetables in same order. Sprinkle with rest of cheese, salt and pepper and dot with last tablespoon of butter. Bake for 40 to 45 minutes at 350 degrees or until done.
Carol Sue Jennerjahn Taylor (Mrs. Jerry A.)

Emergency Vegetables
Serves 4 to 6

Stokely's Vegetables Del Sol,
  carrots, broccoli,
  cauliflower

1 1-ounce package Hidden
  Valley Original Dressing Mix
1 cup mayonnaise
1 cup milk

Cook vegetables one half the time indicated on package or until just under crunchy. Drain vegetables and spread on paper towels. Blot with towels until they are very dry. Chill. Prepare Hidden Valley dressing according to package directions and chill for 20 to 30 minutes. Stir in enough dressing to coat vegetables – probably about half of the dressing for each package of vegetables. For microwave, cook vegetables one half the time indicated on package or until just under crunchy. Then proceed as above. Serve chilled.

Mary Tolle Walsh (Mrs. Thomas)

Green Cheese Enchiladas
Serves 6 to 12

1 dozen corn tortillas
1/2 cup oil
3/4 cup chopped onion
12 ounces Monterey Jack
  cheese, grated
1/4 cup flour

1/4 cup butter or margarine,
  melted
2 cups chicken broth
1 cup sour cream
1 4-ounce can chopped
  green chiles

Soften tortillas by heating 15 seconds on each side in hot oil. When done drain on paper towels. Put 2 tablespoons grated cheese and small amount of onion on each tortilla. Roll, placing seam side down in greased baking dish. Melt margarine in saucepan. Stir in flour and add chicken broth. Cook, stirring constantly, until thickened and bubbly. Add sour cream and chiles. Heat thoroughly but do not boil. Pour sauce over enchiladas. Bake at 425 degrees for 20 minutes. Remove, sprinkle with remaining cheese and return to oven until melted.

Ann Savage Holbrook (Mrs. Lester Win)

Chiles Rellenos
Serves 8

1-pound 10-ounce can whole
  green chiles
1 pound Monterey Jack
  cheese, cut in 1/2-inch
  thick strips
5 eggs
1 1/4 cups milk

1/4 cup flour
1/2 teaspoon salt
1/8 teaspoon pepper
1/2 pound Cheddar cheese,
  grated
Paprika

Rinse seeds from chiles and dry. Stuff each chile with Jack cheese. Beat eggs and gradually add milk, flour, salt and pepper. Beat thoroughly. Arrange 1/2 of the stuffed chiles in a 2-quart casserole. Sprinkle with half of Cheddar cheese. Sprinkle with paprika. Repeat layers ending with cheese and paprika. Pour egg mixture over all. Bake uncovered at 350 degrees for 45 minutes or until knife inserted between chiles in custard comes out clean.

Karen Keitz Lawler (Mrs. Wayne D.)

Green Chile Rice
Serves 6

2 cups long grain instant rice
2 cups water
1/2 teaspoon salt
1 tablespoon butter
8 ounces Monterey Jack
  cheese, cubed

1 cup sour cream
1 4-ounce can chopped green
  chiles
Paprika

Cook rice with water, salt and butter according to package directions. Let stand 5 minutes. Mix cheese, sour cream and chiles with rice. Pour into a buttered 2-quart casserole and top with paprika. Bake at 350 degrees for 30 minutes.

Linda Gist Kerran (Mrs. Michael L.)

Really Wild Rice
Serves 8

¾ cup butter
1 10½-ounce can beef
  consomme
1 10½-ounce can onion soup
1 8-ounce can water chestnuts,
  drained and sliced

1 8-ounce can sliced
  mushrooms, drained
1 6-ounce box Uncle Ben's
  long grain wild rice

Melt butter. Mix all ingredients in a 1½-quart baking dish. Stir to mix well. Bake at 350 degrees for 1 hour.
Mary Hart Reeves (Mrs. William George)

Brown Rice and Mushroom Medley
Serves 6

1 onion, chopped
1 cup Uncle Ben's converted
  rice, uncooked
1 cup soy sauce

1 2.5-ounce jar sliced
  mushrooms
1 10½-ounce can beef
  consomme
⅔ can water

Chop onion and saute in small amount of oil. Add uncooked rice, soy sauce and mushrooms. Heat consomme and water to boiling and add to rice mixture. Pour into a 1½-quart baking dish and bake at 400 degrees for 30 minutes.
Michele Moore Hughes (Mrs. Jack)

Mushroom and Onion Rice Bake
Serves 6

½ cup margarine or butter
1 10½-ounce can onion soup
1 10½-ounce can beef broth

1 4-ounce can sliced
  mushrooms
1¼ cups Uncle Ben's
  converted rice

Melt butter. Add onion soup, beef broth, mushrooms and rice. Mix together in a 2-quart casserole. Cover and bake at 350 degrees for 1 hour.
Lee Ann Naifeh Kuhlman (Mrs. James E.)

Nancy Breen's Onion Pie
Serves 8

1/2 cup butter or margarine
1 1/4 cups saltine cracker
   crumbs
2 1/2 cups sliced onions
3 eggs, beaten

1 1/4 cups milk
1/2 pound sharp Cheddar
   cheese, grated
1 teaspoon salt
1/4 teaspoon pepper

Melt butter in skillet. Reserve 2 tablespoons and pour remaining butter into a bowl with cracker crumbs. Mix well. Put into a 9 or 10-inch pie pan. Press on bottom and sides. Cook onions in 2 tablespoons butter until transparent. Place onions evenly on pie crust. Combine eggs, milk, cheese, salt and pepper. Pour over onions. Bake at 325 degrees for 45 minutes.

Leslie Hood Diggs (Mrs. James Barnes, IV)

The Best Friend A Steak Ever Had
Serves 2

1 4-ounce can button
   mushrooms
1 4-ounce can sliced
   mushrooms
3 1/2 tablespoons butter
1 tablespoon soy sauce

1 tablespoon Worcestershire
   sauce
2 to 3 tablespoons sherry
Onion powder
Accent
Coarse ground black pepper
Garlic powder

Drain all mushrooms well. Slice buttons in half if large. Melt butter in a 7-inch skillet. Saute buttons 2 to 3 minutes, add slices and continue to saute until all are browned. Reduce heat, add dry seasonings to taste, stir and simmer 2 to 3 minutes. Add soy and Worcestershire sauces and, increasing heat slightly, simmer another 2 to 3 minutes. Add sherry, stir well, reduce heat to simmer and cover. Cook covered 3 to 5 minutes until sherry cooks down. May be kept on range until steak is done. By reducing heat to warm and adding small amounts of sherry, mushrooms can be kept on range for extended period. May be increased in quantity 50% in the 7-inch pan, or 2 to 3 times in a 9-inch pan while maintaining approximately the same cooking times.

Mary Tolle Walsh (Mrs. Thomas)

Fettucini Alfredo
Serves 4 to 6

6 tablespoons butter or
margarine
1½ cups whipping cream,
divided
3 to 4 cups hot, cooked egg
noodles, drained

1 cup shredded Parmesan
cheese
Salt
Pepper
Freshly grated nutmeg or
ground nutmeg

In a wide frying pan or chafing dish over high heat, melt butter until it is lightly browned. Add ½ cup of the cream and boil rapidly until large shiny bubbles form; stir occasionally. (You can make this part of the sauce earlier in the day and then reheat.) Reduce heat to medium or place chafing dish over direct flame. Add noodles to the sauce. Toss vigorously with 2 forks. Pour in the cheese and the remaining cream, a little at a time, about 3 additions. The noodles should be kept moist but without too much liquid. Season with salt and pepper and grate nutmeg generously over the noodles or use about ⅛ teaspoon ground nutmeg. Serve immediately.
Sally Morrison Stringer (Mrs. Edward H., Jr.)

Bill's Fettucini Surprise
Serves 4 to 6

¼ cup butter or margarine
1 cup sliced ham
1 6½-ounce jar chopped
pimentos
1 10-ounce package frozen
peas
1 cup heavy whipping cream

½ teaspoon salt
¼ teaspoon pepper
1 pound fettucini noodles or
½ regular and ½ spinach
noodles
1 cup grated Parmesan cheese

Melt butter in skillet and stir fry ham about 1 minute. Add pimentos and peas and cook another minute. Stir in cream, salt and pepper and bring to a boil. Lower heat and simmer, stirring occasionally until sauce thickens slightly, about 3 minutes. Remove sauce from heat while cooking pasta. Cook pasta according to package directions and drain. Return pasta to pot and add sauce and cheese. Toss until well blended over low heat.
Marilyn Novak Sullivan (Mrs. William H.)

Cheddar Potatoes
Serves 10 to 12

1 32-ounce package frozen
hash brown potatoes,
shredded or chopped
1/2 cup margarine, melted
1 10¾-ounce can cream of
chicken soup

10 ounces Cheddar cheese,
grated
8 ounces sour cream
1 teaspoon salt
1 small onion, grated

Topping
2 cups cornflakes, crushed

1/4 cup margarine, melted

Mix all the ingredients together, except topping, and pour into a 9 x 12-inch ungreased baking dish. Mix crushed cornflakes and melted margarine and sprinkle on top. Bake at 350 degrees for 45 minutes.
Joann Davies Graham (Mrs. Greg)

Gourmet Cheese Potatoes
Serves 10 to 12

6 large white potatoes
2/3 cup chopped green onion
1/2 cup margarine or butter
2 cups grated sharp Cheddar
cheese

2 cups sour cream
1½ teaspoons salt
1/2 teaspoon pepper

Boil potatoes in their skins. Cool, peel, shred potatoes and set aside. Saute onion in butter. Add cheese, stirring until cheese has melted. Add sour cream and mix well. Fold in shredded cooked potatoes. Add salt and pepper. Bake in a 3-quart oblong baking dish at 350 degrees for 30 minutes or until heated through.
Gretchen Bennett

Marty Johnson Margo (Mrs. Robert C.)

Lemon Sweet Potatoes
Serves 8

4 pounds sweet potatoes,
  cooked, peeled and mashed
3 tablespoons lemon juice
1 teaspoon salt

¼ cup butter, softened
2 egg yolks
Lemon slices
Butter, melted

In a bowl combine sweet potatoes, lemon juice and salt. Beat in butter and egg yolks. Taste for seasoning. Transfer mixture to buttered 1½-quart casserole. Top with lemon slices and brush the top with melted butter. Bake at 325 degrees for 45 minutes, or until heated through.
Debbi Davidson Dale (Mrs. Mark)

Patrician Potatoes
Serves 6 to 8

8 to 10 potatoes
1 8-ounce package cream
  cheese
1 cup sour cream
Salt

Pepper
Garlic salt
Chives
Butter
Paprika

Peel potatoes, cook and drain. While potatoes are boiling, beat sour cream and cream cheese until fluffy. Add hot potatoes gradually and beat constantly until light and fluffy. Season to taste with salt, pepper and garlic salt. Add chives and spoon into a 2-quart casserole. Brush top with melted butter and sprinkle with paprika. Bake at 350 degrees for 30 minutes.
Linda Huper Reece (Mrs. Robert A.)

Thyme Potatoes
Serves 4

2 potatoes
2 tablespoons and 2 teaspoons
  butter, melted

Garlic salt
Thyme
2 bay leaves

Slice unpeeled potatoes like fries. Place potatoes in butter sprinkled with garlic salt. Brown lightly under broiler. Add thyme and bay leaves. Bake at 300 degrees for 1 hour.
Betty Lou Lee Upsher (Mrs. Sidney)

Potatoes Romanoff
Serves 10 to 12

5 cups potatoes, cooked and
diced
2 teaspoons salt, divided
2 cups small curd cottage
cheese
1 cup sour cream

¼ cup finely chopped green
onion
1 small clove garlic, minced
½ cup grated mild cheese
Paprika

Cook unpeeled potatoes only until tender. Cool, peel and cut into small cubes. Sprinkle with 1 teaspoon salt. Combine cottage cheese, sour cream, onion and garlic with the remaining 1 teaspoon salt. Fold in potato cubes and pour into buttered 2½-quart or 9 x 13-inch baking dish. Top with cheese and sprinkle lightly with paprika. Bake at 350 degrees for 40 to 45 minutes or until thoroughly heated and lightly browned on top.

Carole Jo Kerley Evans (Mrs. J. Patrick)

Potato Spinach Casserole
Serves 8

6 large potatoes
1 10-ounce package frozen
chopped spinach, thawed
and drained
½ cup butter
2 tablespoons dill weed
1 tablespoon salt

1 teaspoon pepper
8 ounces sour cream
1 cup shredded Cheddar
cheese
1 teaspoon paprika
1 teaspoon cayenne pepper

Cook potatoes and mash. Add thawed spinach, butter, dill weed, salt and pepper. When blended, fold in sour cream. Pour into a 2 to 3-quart baking dish. Top with cheese and sprinkle on paprika and cayenne mixed together. Cook covered at 375 degrees for 20 minutes. Uncover and cook 10 more minutes.

Mary Montgomery Rockett (Mrs. D. Joe)

Best Beef Marinade
Yields ½ cup

4 tablespoons soy sauce
2 tablespoons salad oil
1 tablespoon wine vinegar
2 tablespoons chopped
    parsley
2 large garlic cloves, minced

½ teaspoon Lawry's seasoned
    salt
½ teaspoon Lawry's seasoned
    pepper
¼ teaspoon ginger

Mix together all ingredients and pour over meat of your choice. Meat needs to marinate at least 30 minutes, preferably all day or overnight. If marinade is made ahead of time, store in a jar in the refrigerator.
Susan Rosman Edwards (Mrs. Carl)

Sprehe's Meat Sauce
Yields 7 pints

24 tomatoes
4 green peppers
4 large onions
1 red pepper
2 cups sugar
1 tablespoon salt

1½ cups vinegar
2 teaspoons cinnamon
2 teaspoons ground cloves
2 teaspoons allspice
2 teaspoons nutmeg

Drop tomatoes individually into boiling water for 1 minute. Remove and drop into cold water. When tomatoes are cool, remove skins and cores. Chop tomatoes and place in a 2½-gallon pot. Chop green peppers, onions and red pepper and add to tomatoes. Add all other ingredients and bring to a boil. Reduce heat to simmer and cook for 2½ to 3 hours. Sterilize 7 pint jars and lids while the sauce is cooking. Put sauce into jars, filling within ½ inch from the top. Place canning lids on top and close tightly when sauce is warm, not hot. Sauce can be kept in pantry or refrigerator for 1 year.
Montine Price Sprehe (Mrs. Paul F.)

Pulliam's Barbeque Sauce
Yields 1 gallon

2 14-ounce bottles ketchup
1 12-ounce bottle chili sauce
1/3 cup prepared mustard
2 tablespoons dry mustard
2 tablespoons coarse ground
   pepper
1 tablespoon soy sauce
1/2 cup vinegar
1/2 cup brown sugar

1/2 cup lemon juice
1/2 cup bottled steak sauce
1 tablespoon red pepper
2 tablespoons salad oil
4 whole cloves
1 medium onion, chopped
1 12-ounce can beer
1/4 cup Worcestershire sauce
1 clove garlic, minced

Combine all ingredients in a large kettle and cook over medium heat for 10 minutes. Lower heat to simmer for 15 more minutes. Sauce keeps well in the refrigerator for 2 to 3 weeks.
Janyce Shorbe Coffeen (Mrs. Henry, Jr.)

Old Smokey Barbeque Sauce
Yields 1 cup

1 clove garlic, minced
2 teaspoons mustard
1 teaspoon sugar
1 teaspoon salt
1 teaspoon red pepper

1 teaspoon black pepper
2 teaspoons flour
Juice of 1 lemon
Vinegar
1 cup margarine

Mix first 8 ingredients together in a 1 cup measure. Add enough vinegar to make 1 cup. In a saucepan, melt 1 cup margarine and add the vinegar mixture. Boil for 3 minutes. This is excellent on charcoaled meats, chicken or fish.
Nancy Frantz Davies (Mrs. Frank L.)

Barbeque Sauce
Yields 1 quart

1 32-ounce bottle ketchup
1 ketchup bottle of water
3 tablespoons A-1 steak sauce
3 tablespoons vinegar
Juice of 1 lemon
1 tablespoon butter

1 tablespoon sugar
1 tablespoon Liquid Smoke
2 tablespoons mustard
3 bay leaves
1 teaspoon cumin powder

Mix all ingredients together in a saucepan and heat. Sauce is excellent on brisket.
Sue Coury Homsey (Mrs. Gary Ben)

Apple Syrup
Yields 1 cup

1 cup apple juice
2 sticks cinnamon, broken
12 whole cloves

½ cup sugar
2 tablespoons light Karo

Mix apple juice, cinnamon sticks and cloves in a saucepan. Cover and simmer for 10 minutes. Cool and strain. Add sugar and Karo to juice and boil briskly for 4 to 6 minutes, uncovered. For a thicker syrup cook a little longer.
Carolyn Nichols Bentley (Mrs. Earl W., Jr.)

Nectarine Magic
Yields 3 cups

8 fresh nectarines
¼ cup sugar
¼ cup light corn syrup
¼ cup ketchup
2 tablespoons vinegar

1 tablespoon grated onion
1 teaspoon salt
¼ teaspoon allspice
2 tablespoons butter

Peel and slice nectarines. Mash in food processor or blender to make 2 cups puree. In a large saucepan, blend puree and remaining ingredients, except butter. Simmer 8 to 10 minutes. Use as a glaze for chicken or ham, basting meat as it cooks. Add butter to remainder and serve hot as sauce.
Polly Puckett Nichols (Mrs. Larry)

Steve's Monkey Bread
Serves 8 to 10

1 cup milk
1/2 cup butter
1 package yeast
1/4 cup warm water
2 eggs, beaten

1/2 cup sugar
1/2 teaspoon salt
3 cups flour
1/2 cup butter

Scald milk and 1/2 cup butter. Dissolve yeast in warm water. Beat together eggs, sugar and salt. Add milk and butter to egg mixture. Add 1 1/2 cups flour to mixture. Add yeast. Let rise uncovered 1 hour. Add 1 1/2 cups more flour. Cover with damp cloth and store in refrigerator overnight. Remove from refrigerator 3 hours before cooking. Let stand. After 2 hours, melt 1/2 cup butter in bundt pan. Place batter in the pan and let rise for 1 hour. Bake at 350 degrees for 30 to 35 minutes.
Ranell Bules Brown (Mrs. Steve M.)

Poppy Seed Dinner Rolls
Yields 18 large rolls

1 package yeast
1/4 cup warm water
1 teaspoon sugar
1 cup milk, scalded
1/2 cup Crisco

1/4 cup sugar
1 3/4 teaspoons salt
1 egg, beaten
3 1/4 cups flour
Poppy seeds

Sprinkle yeast over water in a small bowl. Add 1 teaspoon sugar and stir well. Set aside to dissolve for 5 to 10 minutes. Combine milk, Crisco, 1/4 cup sugar and salt in large bowl. Stir well until shortening is melted and lukewarm. Stir in egg and yeast mixture. Gradually add flour, beating well after each addition. Continue to beat until batter is smooth. Cover and let rise 1 1/2 hours in a warm place. Stir down with a spoon and let rise another 30 minutes. Spoon into lightly greased muffin tins, half full. Let rise 20 minutes. Brush with butter and poppy seeds. Bake at 425 degrees for 12 to 15 minutes.
Laurel Johnson Kallenberger (Mrs. David)

Mary Ann's Magic Rolls
Yields 3 dozen

1 package dry yeast
1 cup cool tap water
1 cup potato water
2/3 cup Crisco, melted
1 cup mashed potatoes

2/3 cup sugar
2 eggs, well beaten
1 teaspoon salt
4 to 5 cups sifted flour

Orange Cream Icing
3 cups powdered sugar
1/3 cup butter or margarine
1 1/2 teaspoons vanilla

2 to 3 tablespoons fresh
   orange juice
Grated orange peel

Dissolve yeast in the tap water. Let potato water and melted Crisco cool and add mashed potatoes, yeast mixture and sugar. Let stand for 2 hours. Then add the eggs and salt and mix well. Add sifted flour, one cup at a time, and knead until dough is stiff. Put in greased mixing bowl and let stand 2 hours. Place in refrigerator until 2 hours before serving. Pinch out in cloverleaf rolls and put in greased muffin tins. Let rise 1 to 1 1/2 hours; then bake at 400 degrees for 10 to 12 minutes. This dough will keep for 5 days in the refrigerator. To prepare Orange Cream Icing, combine the icing ingredients to a spreadable consistency. About 1 minute before the rolls are done, put a dollop of icing on the top of each roll and return them to the oven until the icing has melted. Serve warm. You may also serve the Orange Cream Icing on the side with the butter.
Helen Ford Sanger (Mrs. Fenton)

Pauline McLean's Sally Lunn Muffins
Yields 70

3/4 cup margarine or
   Wesson oil
2/3 cup sugar

3 eggs
3 cups self-rising flour
1 cup milk

Cream margarine or oil and sugar. Add remaining ingredients. Spoon into 1 1/2-inch greased muffin tins or into paper-lined tins. Bake at 400 degrees for 10 minutes.
Beth Matthews McMullan (Mrs. Harry)

No Need to Knead Rolls
Yields 30 rolls

1 package yeast
1/4 cup warm water
2 eggs
1/2 cup sugar

1 teaspoon salt
1/2 cup vegetable oil
1 cup warm water
4 cups sifted flour

Dissolve yeast in 1/4 cup warm water. Beat eggs slightly and add to the dissolved yeast. Add sugar, salt, oil and 1 cup warm water. Mix ingredients, add flour and mix well. Let stand at room temperature 8 hours or overnight. Divide dough into 4 parts and roll as if making pie crust into 8-inch circles. Cut each circle into 8 pie-shaped wedges. Start with wide edge and roll to the point like crescent rolls. Place on greased cookie sheet and let rise about 4 to 6 hours. Bake at 350 degrees for 10 to 15 minutes.

Mary Hazel Mitchell Miles (Mrs. W. Howard)

Ice Box Rolls
Yields 24

2 packages yeast
1 cup warm water
1 tablespoon sugar
2 cups milk, scalded
1/2 cup melted shortening

1/2 cup sugar
1 tablespoon salt
1 egg, well beaten
7 cups flour
Butter

Mix yeast, warm water and 1 tablespoon sugar. Let stand 20 minutes to dissolve. While cooling scalded milk, add shortening, 1/2 cup sugar and salt. When cool, add egg and yeast mixture. Add flour and mix well. It will be sticky. Cover and refrigerate in large bowl overnight. Two hours before serving, knead on floured board and roll out. Spread with soft butter and roll up jelly roll fashion. Cut into 1-inch slices and place in well-greased muffin tins. Allow to rise 2 hours. Bake at 425 degrees for 10 to 12 minutes.

Suzanne Lucas Nelson (Mrs. Jay)

Basic Dinner or Sweet Rolls
Yields 4 to 5 dozen

1/2 cup warm water
1 package yeast
1/2 teaspoon sugar
1/2 cup Crisco
1/2 cup sugar

1 egg, beaten
2 cups warm milk
1 1/2 teaspoons salt
6 cups flour

Frosting
2 to 4 tablespoons butter
4 cups powdered sugar

1/2 teaspoon vanilla
Drops of milk

Mix water, yeast and 1/2 teaspoon sugar. Let stand for 45 minutes. Cream Crisco and 1/2 cup sugar. Add egg and yeast mixture. Mix well. Add remaining ingredients. Place in a greased bowl in the refrigerator for at least 4 to 6 hours. It will rise in the refrigerator. To prepare dinner rolls, take a portion of the dough, knead and roll out on a floured board until desired thickness. Cut with cutter. Spread with melted butter, fold over and place in a greased pan. Let rise until double in size. Bake at 400 degrees for 15 to 20 minutes. To prepare sweet rolls, take a portion of the dough, knead, roll out and brush with melted butter. Sprinkle sugar and cinnamon across the dough. Roll the dough jelly roll fashion and cut into 1/2-inch slices. Place in a greased pan. Let rise until double in size. Bake at 400 degrees for 15 to 20 minutes. While cooling, frost with mixture of sifted powdered sugar, butter, vanilla and drops of milk.
Gayle Lucas Semtner (Mrs. B. L., III)

Gracie's Brown Bread
Yields 8 small loaves

1 cup All Bran
1 cup buttermilk
1 tablespoon dark molasses
1/2 cup sugar

1 cup flour
1 teaspoon baking soda
1/4 teaspoon salt

Combine all ingredients and pour into small round cans about the size of empty baking powder cans. Set cans on rack in large pan containing water just below the rack level. Place lid on pan and steam on top of stove 3 to 4 hours.
Grace Thatcher Hoffman (Mrs. Roy, Jr.)

Easy No-Knead French Bread
Yields 1 loaf

1 tablespoon honey or sugar
1 teaspoon salt
1 1/2 tablespoons margarine
1 cup boiling water
1/4 cup lukewarm water

1 package yeast
Sugar
3 cups plus 2 tablespoons flour
Cornmeal

In a bowl mix honey or sugar, salt and margarine. Pour 1 cup boiling water over this mixture. Let mixture cool to lukewarm. Meanwhile dissolve yeast and pinch of sugar in the 1/4 cup of lukewarm water. When the first mixture is lukewarm, mix the two together. Gradually add the flour and beat well. Cover with plastic wrap. Stir with a spoon every 10 minutes for an hour. Place dough on a floured board and pat or roll into a rectangular shape about 12 x 8 inches and about 1/2-inch thick. Roll into a roll, jelly roll style, pressing out the air as you go. Place on a cookie sheet sprinkled with cornmeal and let rise until double in size. Make 4 diagonal slashes with a very sharp knife just before putting in oven. Bake at 400 degrees for 20 minutes or until bread sounds hollow.
Linda Wright Elliot (Mrs. Earl)

Buttermilk Bread
Yields 2 loaves

1 package yeast
1/2 cup warm water
2 tablespoons sugar

1 tablespoon salt
1 1/2 cups buttermilk
5 cups flour, white or whole wheat

In a large bowl pour yeast into 1/2 cup warm water. Stir until dissolved. Add sugar, salt and buttermilk and stir. Add flour, 1 cup at a time, stirring until well mixed. Cover and let rise 2 to 3 hours. Knead down 2 or 3 times. Let rise again for 2 to 3 more hours. Knead down again 2 or 3 times. Divide dough and shape into 2 loaves. Place in bread pans and let rise 2 or 3 hours. Bake at 375 degrees for 10 minutes. Lower heat to 350 degrees and bake 35 to 50 more minutes.
Eve Edwards Patterson (Mrs. William)

Mother's Biscuits
Serves 4

2 cups flour
4 teaspoons baking powder
1 teaspoon salt
2 teaspoons sugar

1/8 teaspoon baking soda
6 tablespoons Crisco
1 cup buttermilk

Mix dry ingredients and Crisco with a fork. Cut together until mixture resembles coarse crumbs. Add buttermilk all at once. Beat with a fork. Turn out on a floured surface. Roll out 1/2 inch thick. Cut with a floured biscuit cutter. Bake on a greased cookie sheet at 450 degrees for 10 minutes.

Patsy King Hosman
(Mrs. Thomas D.)

Patsy Eskridge King
(Mrs. Arthur E., Jr.)

Bread Sticks
Yields 32 sticks

1 5/8 cups unsifted white flour
1 5/8 cups unsifted whole wheat
  flour
1 tablespoon sugar
1 tablespoon salt
2 packages yeast

1/4 cup margarine
1 1/4 cups hot water
1 egg white, beaten with
  1 tablespoon cold water
Sesame seeds or poppy seeds
Kosher coarse salt

Mix white and whole wheat flours together. Combine 1 cup flour, sugar, salt and yeast in bowl. Add margarine and hot water. Beat with mixer 2 minutes at medium speed. Add 1/2 cup flour and beat on high another 2 minutes. Add remaining flour until dough is soft. Turn out onto floured board. Knead it for 5 minutes. Shape into long fat log. Cut into 32 pieces. Pour a little oil on cookie sheet. Roll dough pieces into sticks. Roll in oil on sheet and let rise 20 minutes. Brush with egg whites, seeds and salt. Bake at 350 degrees for 20 minutes or until golden brown.

Toni Mack Wizenberg (Mrs. Morris J.)

Miniature Dill Loaves
Yields 10

4 tablespoons butter
½ teaspoon dill weed

1 package refrigerator flaky
biscuits

Melt butter. Add dill. Dip each biscuit into butter and stand 3 each in ungreased miniture loaf pans. Put pans on cookie sheet for easy handling. Bake at 375 degrees for 15 minutes until golden brown. Break loaves back into biscuits before serving.
Mary Davis Nichols (Mrs. John W.)

Parmesan Toast
Serves 12

Pepperidge Farm hard rolls,
  6 to a package
½ cup butter, softened

Parmesan cheese
Sesame seeds (optional)

Slice each uncooked or leftover cooked roll into 4 lengthwise pieces. Spread with softened butter and sprinkle generously with Parmesan cheese. Top with sesame seeds, if desired. Bake at 350 degrees for 15 to 20 minutes or until nicely browned.
Sandra Wilkins Lekas (Mrs. Thomas A.)

Parmesan Toast Strips
Serves 10 to 15

1 8-ounce package cream
  cheese
½ cup butter

1 package Hidden Valley
  Ranch dressing mix
1 loaf bread
Parmesan cheese

Blend cream cheese, butter and dressing mix together. Trim crusts off bread slices. Toast one side of bread, which has been cut into 4 strips. Spread untoasted side with cream cheese mixture and dip in Parmesan cheese. Freeze on cookie sheets. When ready to serve, bake at 350 to 400 degrees for 10 to 15 minutes, or until golden.
Sandy Simon Childress (Mrs. Bob)

Onion Bread
Yields 2 loaves

¾ cup milk
1 1⅜-ounce envelope onion
    soup mix
½ cup sugar
½ cup soft butter or margarine

2 packages yeast
½ cup warm water
1 egg, beaten
4 cups unsifted flour

Scald milk. Stir in onion soup mix and blend well. Stir in sugar and butter, mixing until butter melts. Cool to lukewarm. Sprinkle yeast over warm water and stir to dissolve. Add lukewarm milk mixture, egg and half the flour. Beat until smooth. Add remaining flour to make a stiff batter. Cover tightly and chill at least 2 hours. Cut dough in half. Flatten and press each half evenly into well-greased 1½-quart casseroles or 2 loaf pans. Brush with melted butter. Cover with a clean towel. Let rise in a warm place until double in size. Bake at 375 degrees for about 35 minutes. Remove from casserole to rack. Brush with butter again. Cool completely before cutting or serving.
Sue Ann White Hyde (Mrs. James Dudley)

Ann's Zucchini Bread
Yields 2 loaves

3 eggs, beaten
1 cup oil
1¼ cups brown sugar
1¼ cups sugar
3 cups flour
1 teaspoon salt

1 tablespoon cinnamon
1 teaspoon baking powder
1 teaspoon baking soda
1 tablespoon vanilla
2 cups grated zucchini
1 cup chopped nuts (optional)

Combine eggs, oil and sugars. Sift together dry ingredients and add to first mixture. Add remaining ingredients. Bake in 2 greased bread pans at 350 degrees for 60 to 70 minutes.
Sally Gilbert Flynn (Mrs. Edmund W.)

Danish Puff

½ cup butter or margarine,
  softened
1 cup flour
2 tablespoons water
½ cup butter

1 cup water
1 teaspoon almond extract
1 cup flour
3 eggs
Chopped nuts

Glaze
1½ cups powdered sugar
2 tablespoons butter, softened

1½ teaspoons vanilla
1 to 2 tablespoons warm water

Cut ½ cup butter into 1 cup flour. Sprinkle 2 tablespoons water over this mixture. Mix. Shape into round ball and divide in half. On an ungreased baking sheet, pat each half into a 12 x 3-inch strip. Place 3 inches apart. Heat ½ cup butter and 1 cup water to rolling boil in a medium saucepan. Remove from heat and quickly stir in almond extract and 1 cup flour. Stir vigorously over low heat until mixture forms a ball, about 1 minute. Remove from heat. Beat in eggs all at once until smooth and glossy. Divide in half. Spread each half evenly over other strips. Bake at 350 degrees for 60 minutes or until top is crisp and brown. Cool. Top will shrink and fall, forming custardy top of puff. Prepare glaze and frost. Sprinkle generously with nuts. This will freeze.
Marty Johnson Margo (Mrs. Robert C.)

Cinnamon Sticks
Yields 28 pieces

7 to 8 bread slices
½ cup butter

¾ cup sugar
1½ teaspoons cinnamon

Remove the crusts and cut each slice into 1-inch sticks. Melt butter in skillet. Remove from heat. Dip each breadstick in the butter on all sides very quickly. Then roll the buttered sticks in the mixture of sugar and cinnamon. Place on ungreased cookie sheet and bake at 350 degrees for 15 minutes. Store in an airtight container.
Stacey Shannon Blake (Mrs. Joe)

Applesauce Muffins
Yields 4 dozen

1 cup shortening
2½ cups sugar
4 eggs, beaten
2 cups thick applesauce
4 cups flour
½ teaspoon salt

2 teaspoons baking powder
1 teaspoon baking soda
2 teaspoons cinnamon
1 teaspoon cloves
2 cups raisins or Royal Ann
  cherries

Cream together shortening and sugar. Add beaten eggs and applesauce. Sift and add next 6 ingredients. Beat until smooth. Then add raisins or cherries that have been drained and dusted with flour. Pour into greased and floured muffin tins. Bake at 350 degrees for 20 to 25 minutes.
Patsy King Hosman (Mrs. Thomas D.)

Luscious Lemon Muffins
Yields 2 dozen

1 cup unsalted butter
1 cup sugar
4 large eggs, separated
½ cup fresh squeezed lemon
  juice (about 6 lemons)

2 cups flour
2 teaspoons baking powder
1 teaspoon salt
2½ teaspoons grated lemon
  rind

Cream butter and sugar. Add egg yolks which have been well-beaten. Add lemon juice alternately with flour, baking powder and salt mixture. Be careful not to overmix. In a separate bowl, beat egg whites until stiff but not dry. Fold egg whites and lemon peel into batter by hand using a wooden spoon or paddle. Fill buttered or paper-lined muffin tins ¾ full. Bake at 375 degrees about 20 minutes.
Carol Sue Jennerjahn Taylor (Mrs. Jerry A.)

Banana Rolls
Yields 12

6 tablespoons butter, melted
8 tablespoons brown sugar
36 pecan halves
2 cups Bisquick

2 bananas, mashed
½ cup brown sugar
Chopped pecans

Put 1½ teaspoons melted butter, 2 teaspoons brown sugar and 3 pecan halves in the bottom of each muffin tin. Mix 2 cups Bisquick with mashed bananas, using your hands if necessary. Knead and roll into a large rectangle. Sprinkle with ½ cup brown sugar and chopped pecans. Roll up jelly roll style and cut into 12 slices. Place in muffin tins. Bake at 450 degrees for 10 minutes. Turn upside down for a few seconds on a cookie sheet before taking out of pan to let the sugar run down over rolls.

Ranell Bules Brown (Mrs. Steve M.)   *Ann Whiting Hargis (Mrs. V. Burns)*

Apple Coffee Cake
Serves 12

2 cups sugar
1 cup butter
2 eggs
2 cups flour
1 teaspoon baking soda

1 teaspoon cinnamon
1 teaspoon nutmeg
4 to 6 medium apples
1 cup coarsely chopped
   walnuts or pecans

Cream sugar and butter together. Add eggs and mix well. Sift dry ingredients together and fold into first mixture. Core and dice the apples. Stir in the apple pieces and nuts. Pour into a 9 x 13-inch baking dish that is lightly greased and floured. Bake at 375 degrees for 45 to 60 minutes. Test but leave moist.

Beth Sherman Wells (Mrs. Edward)

Banana Bread
Serves 12

1/2 cup shortening	1/2 teaspoon baking powder
3/4 cup sugar	1/2 teaspoon salt
2 eggs	1/2 cup buttermilk
2 cups flour	1 cup mashed bananas
3/4 teaspoon baking soda	1 teaspoon vanilla

Cream shortening and sugar. Add eggs. Sift together flour, baking soda, baking powder and salt. Add to sugar mixture. Add buttermilk, bananas and vanilla. Pour into greased bundt pan, angel food cake pan, loaf pan or small loaf pans. Bake at 350 degrees for approximately 50 minutes.
Linda Gist Kerran (Mrs. Michael)

Strawberry Nut Bread with Strawberry Cream
Yields 6 small loaves or 2 large loaves

3 cups flour, sifted	1 1/4 cups oil
1 teaspoon baking soda	2 16-ounce packages frozen
1 teaspoon salt	strawberries, thawed and
1 teaspoon cinnamon	mashed
2 cups sugar	1 1/4 cups pecans, chopped
4 eggs, beaten	

Strawberry Cream

1/2 cup or more strawberry juice	1 8-ounce package cream cheese, softened
	1/4 cup sugar

Sift flour, baking soda, salt, cinnamon and sugar into a large bowl. In a separate bowl, combine eggs, oil, strawberries and pecans. Make a well in the center of the dry ingredients. Add liquids, stirring just enough to moisten. Pour into 2 greased 9 x 5 x 3-inch pans and bake at 350 degrees for 1 hour. If using smaller pans, bake for 40 minutes. Remove from oven and let stand 5 minutes before removing from pans. To prepare strawberry cream, combine the juice, cream cheese and sugar in a blender or food processor. Serve as a side dish with the bread.
Ranell Bules Brown (Mrs. Steve M.)   *Berta Faye Curtis Rex (Mrs. John W.)*

Orange Banana Bread
Yields 1 loaf

3 cups Bisquick
½ cup sugar
3 eggs

½ cup fresh orange juice
2 large, very ripe bananas
¾ cup chopped pecans

Combine Bisquick and sugar in a large mixing bowl. Add remaining ingredients and beat for 2 minutes, scraping bowl often. Pour batter into a greased and floured loaf pan. Bake at 350 degrees for 60 to 70 minutes. Cool 10 minutes before removing from pan. Remove and cool completely on wire rack.

Carol Sue Jennerjahn Taylor (Mrs. Jerry A.)

Orange Coffee Cake
Serves 12 to 18

½ cup shortening or butter
1 cup sugar
2 eggs
½ cup buttermilk
1 cup sour cream
1 6-ounce can frozen orange juice concentrate, thawed

½ teaspoon grated orange peel
2 cups flour
1 teaspoon baking soda
1 teaspoon salt
1 cup raisins
½ cup chopped nuts (optional)

Topping
⅓ cup sugar
1 teaspoon cinnamon

½ cup chopped nuts

Cream shortening and sugar. Add eggs and beat. Stir in buttermilk, sour cream, ½ cup of orange juice concentrate and orange peel. Mix flour, baking soda, salt and raisins together. Fold into mixture. Pour into a 9 x 13-inch greased and floured pan. Bake at 350 degrees for 30 to 40 minutes. To prepare topping combine ingredients. While still hot pour rest of orange juice concentrate over cake and sprinkle with topping.

Beth Sherman Wells (Mrs. Edward)

Gammy's Orange Cranberry Bread
Yields 1 loaf

2 cups flour, sifted
1 cup sugar
1/2 teaspoon salt
1 1/2 teaspoons baking powder
1/2 teaspoon baking soda
1 cup coarsely chopped
  pecans or walnuts

1 cup whole fresh cranberries
2 tablespoons oil
Hot water
2 tablespoons grated orange
  peel
1/2 cup orange juice
1 egg, slightly beaten

Sift first 5 ingredients into large bowl. Combine nuts and cranberries in small bowl and toss 1/2 cup of flour mixture with nuts and berries. Put 2 tablespoons oil in a 3/4 cup measuring cup and fill with hot water. Mix oil and water with orange peel and juice. Stir egg into flour mixture, just enough to moisten. Gently stir in orange mixture, cranberries and nuts. Pour into large greased loaf pan. Bake at 325 degrees for 1 hour. Cool completely before removing from pan. Wrap in foil and store in refrigerator or freeze.

Beth Sherman Wells (Mrs. Edward)

Raspberry Cream Cheese Coffee Cake
Serves 8

1 3-ounce package cream
  cheese
4 tablespoons butter, softened

Glaze
1 cup powdered sugar
1 1/2 tablespoons milk

2 cups Bisquick
1/3 cup milk
1/2 cup raspberry preserves

1/2 teaspoon vanilla

Cut cream cheese and butter into Bisquick until crumbly. Blend in milk. Turn onto floured surface and knead 8 to 10 times. Place on wax paper and roll to a 12 x 8-inch rectangle. Turn onto greased jelly roll pan and remove paper. Spread preserves down center of the dough. Make 2 1/2-inch cuts at 1-inch intervals along each side. Fold sides over filling, closing sides tightly with fingers. Bake at 425 degrees for 12 to 15 minutes. To prepare glaze, combine remaining ingredients and drizzle over cake.

Marjory Pielsticker Feighny (Mrs. James A.)

Poppy Seed Cake
Serves 16

¼ cup poppy seeds
1¼ cup cold water
1 package yellow cake mix

¼ cup Mazola oil
3 eggs

Glaze
1 cup powdered sugar
1 tablespoon freshly squeezed
   lemon juice

1 teaspoon freshly grated
   lemon peel
1 to 2 teaspoons water

Soak poppy seeds in the cold water for 3 minutes. Preheat oven to 350 degrees. Blend cake mix, oil, eggs and poppy seed liquid in large mixer bowl and beat 4 minutes. Pour into a greased and floured bundt pan or angel food cake pan. Bake 40 to 45 minutes on center oven rack. Cool 10 minutes. Remove from pan and cool completely on wire rack. To prepare the glaze, mix the powdered sugar, lemon juice and lemon peel. Stir in just enough water to make a smooth consistency to drizzle over the cake.

Carol Sue Jennerjahn Taylor (Mrs. Jerry A.)

Sweet Poppy Seed Bread
Yields 2 loaves

3 cups flour
1½ teaspoons salt
1½ teaspoons baking powder
2½ cups sugar
1½ teaspoons vanilla

1½ cups milk
1⅓ cups salad oil
1½ tablespoons poppy seed
3 eggs
1½ teaspoons almond extract

Glaze
½ cup sugar
¼ cup orange juice
½ teaspoon vanilla

½ teaspoon almond extract
½ teaspoon butter extract

Combine all bread ingredients in electric mixing bowl and beat for 2 minutes. Pour into 2 greased and floured loaf pans. Bake at 350 degrees for 1 hour 15 minutes. Top will crack when done. Combine glaze ingredients and brush over hot bread.

Grenda Penhollow Moss (Mrs. Ray)

Funnel Cake
Serves 8

2 cups cooking oil
2 cups flour, sifted
1 teaspoon baking powder
1/2 teaspoon salt

2 eggs, beaten
1 1/2 cups milk
Syrup
Powdered sugar

Preheat cooking oil to 360 degrees. (An electric skillet is nice for this.) Mix the sifted dry ingredients into the eggs and milk. Stir until well mixed. Using a standard funnel, cover the small opening with one finger while filling it with the batter. The funnel is then used to dribble the batter into the hot oil in whatever designs catch the cook's fancy, such as ever widening circles, squares, initials, etc. This is very easy for children to do and wonderful entertainment for slumber party breakfasts. The cakes are cooked in minutes and served with syrup and/or dusted with powdered sugar.

Midge Wasson Lindsey (Mrs. Paul)

Nell's Chocolate Chip Pound Cake
Serves 16

1 package yellow cake mix
1 3 1/2-ounce package instant
vanilla pudding
1 4 1/8-ounce package instant
chocolate pudding

4 eggs
1/2 cup salad oil
1 1/2 cups water
1 cup chocolate chips

Mix all ingredients except chips with beater. Fold in chips. Bake at 350 degrees in a greased and floured bundt pan for 1 hour.

Susie Wells Blinn (Mrs. Robert)

Cinnamon Roll Coffee Cake
Serves 8

¼ cup butter, melted
½ cup brown sugar
¼ cup chopped pecans
1 cup sugar

1 teaspoon cinnamon
¼ teaspoon ground cloves
½ cup butter, melted
1 package frozen yeast rolls

Grease bundt pan. Mix first 3 ingredients and spread in the bottom of the pan. Mix sugar and spices together. Dip each frozen roll in butter, roll in sugar and spice mixture and place in bundt pan on top of the first mixture. Pour any remaining butter or sugar mixture over rolls. Let rise overnight. Bake at 325 degrees for 30 minutes. Invert immediately on a warm platter and serve.

Mary Kay Polley Bullard (Mrs. John)

Overnight Cinnamon Rolls
Yields 24

¼ cup butter
½ cup brown sugar
¼ cup chopped pecans
1 package frozen Rhodes
    dinner rolls

½ cup butter
1 cup sugar
1 tablespoon cinnamon
1 3⅝-ounce box instant
    butterscotch pudding

Melt ¼ cup of butter and brown sugar. Put in the bottom of a bundt pan and sprinkle with nuts. Melt ½ cup butter, sugar and cinnamon. Coat frozen rolls with this mixture. Arrange rolls in pan. Sprinkle with instant pudding, cover with damp cloth, and let rise overnight. Bake at 325 degrees for 30 minutes. Let cool 10 to 15 minutes and turn out.

Mary Washington Reneau (Mrs. J. Robert)

German Funny Pancakes
Yields 1 large pancake or serves 2 people

2 eggs
1/2 cup flour
1/2 cup milk
Nutmeg
Cinnamon

4 tablespoons butter
Lemon wedges
Powdered sugar
Maple syrup

Beat eggs with blender. Add flour and slowly stir in milk. Melt butter in a 10-inch ovenproof skillet. Pour in egg mixture and sprinkle with cinnamon and nutmeg. Bake at 450 degrees for 15 minutes. Serve with lemon wedges and powdered sugar or with maple syrup.

Ann Whiting Hargis
(Mrs. V. Burns)

Marty Rhodes Kavanaugh
(Mrs. Daniel P.)

Peaches and Cream French Toast
Yields 6

3 eggs
3 tablespoons peach preserves
3/4 cup half and half

6 slices French bread or
Texas Toast cut 1/2-inch thick

Topping
1/3 cup peach preserves
1/2 cup butter, softened

2 peaches, peeled and sliced

Beat eggs and 3 tablespoons peach preserves with a fork. Beat in half and half. Place a single layer of bread slices in an 8 x 11-inch baking dish. Pour egg mixture over bread. Cover and refrigerate overnight. To prepare topping, beat 1/3 cup peach preserves and 1/2 cup softened butter with a beater or whisk. Mix in fresh sliced peaches. Heat a pancake griddle to medium hot, place toast on griddle and cook until brown, turning once. Serve with preserves and butter on top. Can serve with syrup and/or powdered sugar also.

Marcia Hopping Powell (Mrs. John L.)

Penny's Mock Sourdough Pancakes
Serves 5

2 eggs, separated
2 cups flour
1½ teaspoons salt
2⅓ cups buttermilk

3 tablespoons butter, melted
2½ teaspoons baking soda
1½ tablespoons warm water
2 tablespoons sugar

Beat egg yolks until thick and lemon colored. Sift flour with salt and add to yolks alternately with buttermilk. Stir in melted butter. Dissolve soda in warm water and add to batter. Beat egg whites until stiff, then beat in sugar. Fold egg whites into the batter. Cook on a lightly greased griddle.

Grenda Penhollow Moss (Mrs. Ray)

Orange Praline Toast
Serves 6

12 thick slices French bread
⅓ cup unsalted butter,
   softened
⅔ cup brown sugar

¼ cup freshly squeezed
   orange juice
2 tablespoons freshly grated
   orange peel
½ cup finely chopped pecans

Toast bread on both sides in oven until golden. Spread with softened butter. Combine other 4 ingredients. Spread about one tablespoon of orange mixture on each piece of toast. Place toast on cookie sheet and bake at 350 degrees for 5 to 8 minutes. Watch carefully or sugar will burn.

Carol Sue Jennerjahn Taylor (Mrs. Jerry A.)

Grand Lake Style Squaw Bread
Serves 10

2 cups self-rising flour
4 heaping tablespoons sugar

⅔ to 1 cup hot water
¼ cup butter, melted

Mix first 3 ingredients to form a cake-like dough. Drizzle melted butter on top and around sides of batter. Drop by teaspoonful into hot fat, about 350 degrees until dough rises and turns golden brown. Serve at once with honey butter.

Barbara Workman Vose (Mrs. Charles, Jr.)

Desserts
Candies

Six Egg Pound Cake
Yields 1 loaf

6 eggs
2 cups sugar
2 cups flour

1 cup margarine
2 teaspoons lemon juice or
vanilla extract (lemon
is best)

Beat eggs together until well blended. Add remaining ingredients. Beat together with mixer for 10 minutes. The mixing is the secret to the recipe. Pour into large greased and floured loaf pan. Bake at 350 degrees for 1 hour. Test for doneness. This may be served with fresh peach slices and whipped cream atop warm cake.
Barbara Henderson Nichols (Mrs. John M.)

Italian Cream Cake
Serves 12 to 15

½ cup butter
½ cup shortening
2 cups sugar
5 egg yolks, slightly beaten
1 teaspoon baking soda
1 cup buttermilk

1½ teaspoons vanilla extract
2 cups flour
5 egg whites, beaten
1 cup coconut
1 cup nuts

Frosting
¼ cup butter
1 8-ounce package cream
cheese

1 1-pound box powdered
sugar
1 teaspoon vanilla extract

Cream butter, shortening and sugar until fluffy. Add slightly beaten egg yolks. Dissolve baking soda in buttermilk. Stir in vanilla. Alternate flour and buttermilk mixture to creamed butter and sugar. Fold in beaten egg whites and add coconut and nuts. Bake in 3 9-inch cake pans at 350 degrees for approximately 30 minutes. Test for doneness. To prepare frosting, allow butter to reach room temperature. Cream butter and cream cheese together. Add sugar and vanilla and beat until right consistency to spread.
Hazel Maxey Emery (Mrs. Don)

Rum Cake De Maison
Serves 16

Cake

2 cups sifted cake flour
2 teaspoons baking powder
1/4 teaspoon salt
1/4 teaspoon baking soda
1/2 cup butter
3/4 cup sugar

2 eggs, separated
1 teaspoon grated orange peel
1/2 cup orange juice
White rum
1/4 teaspoon almond extract
1/4 teaspoon vanilla

Filling

2 teaspoons gelatin
2 tablespoons cold water

2 cups heavy cream
1/2 cup powdered sugar

Frosting

4 1-ounce squares
   unsweetened chocolate
1 cup powdered sugar
2 tablespoons hot water

2 eggs
6 tablespoons butter
Chopped pecans

Sift flour, baking powder, salt and soda. Beat butter until soft and creamy; gradually beat in 3/4 cup sugar. Beat until light and fluffy. Beat in egg yolks, one at a time, then orange peel. Combine juice with 3 tablespoons rum, almond extract and vanilla; add alternately with flour mixture to creamed mixture at low speed. Beat whites to soft peaks in a separate bowl. Fold batter into whites. Pour into 2 greased and floured 9-inch round pans. Bake at 350 degrees for 25 minutes. Let cool in pans 10 minutes. Cut each layer in half to make 2 layers or a total of 4 layers. When completely cooled, sprinkle each with 2 tablespoons rum. Prepare filling while baking cake. Heat gelatin and water until dissolved. Cool slightly. Beat cream with sugar until thick. Beat in 1/3 cup rum, then gelatin and refrigerate. After cake has cooled, prepare frosting by melting the chocolate. Gradually beat in sugar and water. Beat in eggs, one at a time, then butter, 2 tablespoons at a time. Beat until lighter in color. Between each layer put the filling and then frost the entire cake with the frosting. Press chopped pecans all around the sides. Then refrigerate at least 18 hours for flavors to blend.

Note: A yellow package cake mix can be used, substituting orange juice for the water and adding orange peel.

Barbara Pannage Stanfield (Mrs. Neil)

Pineapple Shortcake
Serves 8

1 cup butter
2 cups powdered sugar
2 eggs, well-beaten

1 20-ounce can crushed
    pineapple
1/2 cup pecans
1/2 box vanilla wafers

Cream butter and powdered sugar. Add eggs. Drain crushed pineapple very well. Put butter and sugar mixture in a double boiler and allow it to melt. Stir occasionally. Remove from heat and add pineapple and pecans. Alternate layers of vanilla wafers and pineapple mixture in a 9 x 12-inch pan. Start and end with wafers. Refrigerate overnight.
Beverly Buscanics Willey (Mrs. Benjamin, Jr.)

Fresh Coconut Cake and 7 Minute Frosting
Serves 12

1/2 cup shortening
1 cup sugar
2 eggs
2 1/2 cups sifted cake flour

1/2 teaspoon salt
3 tablespoons baking powder
3/4 cup coconut milk
1 1/2 teaspoons vanilla extract

Frosting
2 egg whites, unbeaten
5 tablespoons cold water
1/2 teaspoon cream of tartar
1/8 teaspoon salt

1 1/2 cups sugar
1 teaspoon vanilla extract
3 cups shredded fresh coconut

Cream shortening and sugar. Add eggs one at a time. Beat well after each addition. Measure dry ingredients and mix into batter alternately with coconut milk and vanilla. Beat until thoroughly mixed. Pour into 2 greased and floured 9-inch cake pans. Bake at 350 degrees for 30 to 35 minutes. Cool on wire rack. To prepare frosting mix egg whites, water, cream of tartar and salt in a double boiler. Beat until blended. Increase beater speed and continue beating while cooking until mixture peaks, about 7 minutes. Remove from heat and slowly add sugar and vanilla. Continue to beat until well blended. Add 1 cup of fresh coconut. Spread frosting between layers and on top of cake. Sprinkle remaining coconut on frosting.
Eva Metz Dudley (Mrs. Carter G.)

Squash Cake
Serves 20

3 cups sugar
3 cups flour
1½ teaspoons cinnamon
1½ teaspoons baking powder
1 teaspoon baking soda
½ teaspoon salt

Frosting
2 cups powdered sugar
½ cup margarine

3 cups chopped yellow squash
  or zucchini
4 eggs
1½ cups vegetable oil
1 cup chopped nuts
1 cup raisins

1 3-ounce package cream
  cheese
1 teaspoon vanilla extract

Sift together first 6 ingredients. Mix squash, eggs and oil together. Combine dry ingredients with squash mixture. Add nuts and raisins. Pour into a 9 x 13-inch pan and bake at 350 degrees for 1 hour. Cake is done when toothpick inserted in center comes out clean. To prepare frosting, combine ingredients. Mix well and spread on cooled cake. Good as a breakfast cake!
Jane Clark Crain (Mrs. John S.)

Chocolate Mousse Icebox Cake
Serves 12

4 3-ounce packages
  ladyfingers
1 18-ounce package chocolate
  chips
1 cup sugar

⅓ cup water
1 teaspoon vanilla extract
8 eggs, separated
Whipping cream
Chocolate curls or raspberries

Line side and bottom of springform pan with ladyfingers, split side in. Mix chocolate chips, sugar and water in saucepan over low heat. Remove from heat when melted. Add vanilla. Beat egg yolks slightly. Gradually add chocolate mixture, beating constantly. Beat egg whites. Fold into chocolate mixture until combined. Spread half of mixture into pan. Cover with ladyfingers. Spread with remaining mixture. Refrigerate 4 hours. Just before serving, whip cream. Top cake with whipped cream and chocolate curls or raspberries.
Jamie Lewinson Davis

Raspberry 'n Cream Cheese Cake
Serves 8

1 box white cake mix
½ 3-ounce box raspberry
  Jell-O

1 10-ounce package frozen
  raspberries, drained

Frosting
½ cup butter, softened
1 8-ounce package cream
  cheese, softened
1 1-pound box powdered
  sugar

½ 3-ounce box raspberry
  Jell-O
1 teaspoon vanilla extract or
  ½ teaspoon lime juice

Prepare cake according to package directions. Add Jell-O and drained raspberries. Mix well. Bake at 350 degrees for 30 to 35 minutes in 2 8-inch round cake pans. To prepare frosting, cream butter and cream cheese together until completely blended. Add powdered sugar and Jell-O gradually mixing well. Thin with vanilla, if needed. Make sure cake is completely cooled before frosting. Keep cake refrigerated.

Charlene Saffa Wagner (Mrs. Taylor D.)

Pistachio Cake
Serves 12

1 box Duncan Hines Golden
  Cake Mix
1 3¾-ounce Pistachio Instant
  Pudding

4 eggs
½ pint sour cream
½ cup salad oil

Nut Mixture
1 cup chopped pecans
2 tablespoons sugar

2 teaspoons cinnamon

Glaze
1 cup powdered sugar
½ cup butter

¼ cup Amaretto
¼ cup water

Mix first 5 ingredients with mixer. Pour half of cake batter in greased and floured bundt cake pan. Sprinkle with half of nut mixture. Pour remaining batter into pan and sprinkle with remaining nut mixture. Do not preheat oven. Bake at 350 degrees for 1 hour. Test with toothpick. Remove from oven and prick top of cake with fork. To prepare glaze, cook ingredients over low heat until butter is melted and sugar dissolved. Spoon half of glaze over cake. Invert cake on plate and spoon rest of glaze slowly on top. Let cool. This can be frozen for serving later.

Claire Duffner Anderson (Mrs. Carl B., III)

Coca Cola Cake
Serves 12

1 cup butter
2 cups flour
1¾ cups sugar
3 tablespoons cocoa
1 teaspoon baking soda

1 teaspoon vanilla extract
2 eggs
½ cup buttermilk
1 cup Coca Cola
1½ cups small marshmallows

Frosting
½ cup softened butter
3 tablespoons cocoa
⅓ cup Coca Cola

4 cups powdered sugar
1 cup pecans, toasted

Mix first 9 ingredients and beat well. Stir in marshmallows by hand. Bake in a greased 9 x 13-inch pan at 350 degrees for 40 to 45 minutes. Cool 30 minutes before frosting. To prepare frosting, mix together first 4 ingredients and stir in pecans which have been toasted in a 300 degree oven until brown. Spread over cake.
Michele Moore Hughes (Mrs. Jack)

Oatmeal Cake
Serves 12 to 15

1½ cups boiling water
1 cup Quaker Quick Oats
½ cup unsalted butter
1 cup dark brown sugar
1 cup sugar
2 eggs

1½ cups flour
1 teaspoon baking soda
½ teaspoon salt
½ teaspoon nutmeg
1 teaspoon cinnamon

Topping
6 tablespoons butter, melted
1 cup chopped pecans
½ cup sugar

1 cup coconut
¼ cup evaporated milk
1 teaspoon vanilla extract

Pour boiling water over oats and add butter. Let stand 20 minutes. Combine remaining cake ingredients, and mix well. Add oatmeal mixture, and mix well. Pour batter into a greased and floured 9 x 13-inch pan and bake at 350 degrees for 35 to 40 minutes. Remove cake from oven. To prepare topping, combine ingredients and spread on warm cake. Place under broiler and brown lightly. Watch carefully. Cool.
Carol Sue Jennerjahn Taylor (Mrs. Jerry A.)   *Susan Barnhart Wade*

Pumpkin Cake Roll

Serves 8 to 10

3 eggs
1 cup sugar
2/3 cup canned pumpkin
1 1/2 teaspoons lemon juice
3/4 cup flour
1 teaspoon baking powder

2 teaspoons cinnamon
1 teaspoon ginger
1 teaspoon nutmeg
1/2 teaspoon salt
1 cup finely chopped pecans
1/2 to 3/4 cup powdered sugar

Filling
1 cup powdered sugar
2 3-ounce packages cream
cheese, softened

4 tablespoons butter, softened
1/2 teaspoon vanilla extract

Beat eggs on high in mixer for 5 minutes. Gradually add sugar and continue to beat. Stir in pumpkin and lemon juice. Stir all dry ingredients together except powdered sugar and fold into pumpkin mixture. Spread in well-greased and floured 15 x 10 x 1-inch jelly roll pan or small cookie sheet with sides. Top with nuts and gently pat them in a little. Bake at 375 degrees for 15 minutes. Do not overbake. Sprinkle powdered sugar on a towel that is slightly larger than pan. Do not use terrycloth. Pat out lumps and smooth sugar together over towel. Turn cake out onto powdered sugared towel immediately and roll cake in towel. To prepare filling, mix ingredients and beat in mixer until smooth. Let cake cool and unroll. Spread with filling and roll cake back into roll. Wrap in aluminum foil and chill.

Great gift: Decorate like yule log for Christmas with holly and pine boughs on the tray.

Bette Burke MacKellar
(Mrs. J. P., Jr.)

Beth Sherman Wells
(Mrs. Edward)

Strawberry Ice Box Cake
Serves 8

½ cup butter
1½ cups powdered sugar
2 eggs
1 package vanilla wafers,
  crumbled

1 quart strawberries
½ pint whipping cream
½ teaspoon vanilla extract

Cream butter and powdered sugar. Add eggs 1 at a time. Beat well. Line an 8 x 8-inch pan with vanilla wafer crumbs. Spread mixture over the wafers. Cut berries in half and put on top of mixture. Whip cream, add vanilla and pour over berries. Top cake with crumbled vanilla wafers. Cover and refrigerate overnight or for at least 7 hours.
Connie Collins Givens (Mrs. Charles)

Apple Cake with Hot Caramel Rum Sauce
Serves 8 to 10

1 cup butter
1 cup sugar
2 eggs, beaten
1½ cups flour
1 teaspoon cinnamon
1 teaspoon nutmeg
1 teaspoon baking soda

½ teaspoon salt
3 medium apples, peeled,
  cored and chopped
¾ cup coarsely chopped
  pecans
1½ teaspoons vanilla extract

Sauce
½ cup sugar
½ cup brown sugar
½ cup whipping cream

½ cup butter
¼ cup dark rum

Cream butter and sugar. Add eggs. Sift dry ingredients together and blend into mixture. Add apples, pecans and vanilla. Spread evenly in a greased 10-inch pie plate or square pan. Bake at 350 degrees about 45 minutes or until browned. To prepare sauce, combine the sugars and cream in top of double boiler. Cook over simmering water 1½ hours, stirring occasionally. Add butter and cook another 30 minutes. Mixture may look curdled but will smooth out when beaten. Remove from heat. Add rum. Beat. Serve warm over cake.
Beth Matthews McMullan (Mrs. Harry)

Banana Sheet Cake
Serves 16 to 20

2 cups sugar
1 cup Crisco
4 eggs
4 ripe bananas

2 cups flour
1 teaspoon baking soda
Salt
1 teaspoon vanilla extract

Frosting
1 8-ounce package cream
  cheese, softened

¼ cup margarine, softened
1 1-pound box powdered
  sugar

Cream sugar and Crisco. Add remaining ingredients. Pour batter into a greased 11 x 16-inch jelly roll pan. Bake at 350 degrees for 30 minutes. To prepare frosting, mix all ingredients together in a food processor or mixer and spread on cooled cake. This will freeze either before or after frosting.

Cake and frosting can both be mixed in food processor.

Ranell Bules Brown (Mrs. Steve M.)

Apple Cake
Serves 15

3 cups sifted flour
1 teaspoon cinnamon
1 teaspoon salt
1 teaspoon baking soda
1¼ cups Wesson oil
2 cups sugar

2 eggs
1 teaspoon vanilla
1 cup buttermilk
3 cups diced apples
1 cup chopped nuts

Buttermilk Frosting
½ cup sugar
½ cup margarine
¼ cup buttermilk

½ tablespoon white Karo
  syrup
¼ teaspoon baking soda
½ teaspoon vanilla

Sift together 3 times the flour, cinnamon, salt and soda and set aside. Mix oil and sugar and add eggs and vanilla. Add buttermilk and dry ingredients alternately, ending with the dry. Add the apples and nuts. Grease a bundt pan and dust with sugar. Bake at 350 degrees for 1 hour. To prepare frosting, mix all ingredients. Heat until it comes to a boil, but don't boil. After cake cools a little, puncture it and pour frosting over.

Janie Morrison Stewart (Mrs. Mike)

Rum Cake
Serves 10 to 12

1 cup chopped pecans or
walnuts
1 18½-ounce package yellow
cake mix
1 3¾-ounce package vanilla
instant pudding

4 eggs
½ cup cold water
½ cup vegetable oil
½ cup dark rum

Glaze
½ cup butter
¼ cup water

1 cup sugar
½ cup dark rum

Grease and flour a 10-inch tube or bundt pan. Sprinkle nuts over bottom of pan. Mix all cake ingredients together. Pour batter over nuts. Bake at 325 degrees for 1 hour. Cool. Invert on serving plate. Prick top. To prepare glaze, melt butter in saucepan. Stir in water and sugar. Boil 5 minutes, stirring constantly. Remove from heat. Stir in rum. Drizzle and smooth glaze evenly over top and sides. Allow cake to absorb glaze. Repeat until all glaze is used.

Carol Walton Cordell   *Elizabeth White Hoffman (Mrs. Kent)*

Variation
¾ cup apricot nectar   ½ teaspoon nutmeg

Mix with the above cake ingredients, omitting ½ cup rum and ¼ cup water.

Bette Jo Wantland Hill (Mrs. Frank D.)

Celestial Lemon Cake

2 3-ounce packages
  ladyfingers
2 14-ounce cans sweetened
  condensed milk
8 eggs, separated
2 teaspoons grated lemon peel

½ cup lemon juice
¼ teaspoon cream of tartar
2 tablespoons powdered sugar
Lemon slices or orange slices
Candied violets (optional)
Whipped cream (optional)

Lightly grease a 9 x 3-inch springform pan. Cover bottom of pan with ladyfingers, cutting some to fit. Stand remaining ladyfingers around sides of pan. If necessary, cut ladyfingers level with top of pan. This prevents tips from getting too brown during baking. In a large bowl, mix condensed milk, egg yolks, lemon peel and lemon juice. Beat egg whites with cream of tartar until stiff. Fold into lemon mixture. Pour batter into prepared pan. Bake at 375 degrees for 25 minutes or until top is lightly browned. Cool thoroughly. Cover with aluminum foil and freeze in the springform pan. This will keep frozen for 1 month. Before serving, remove from freezer and remove outside ring of springform pan. Dust top of cake with powdered sugar and decorate with lemon slices or orange slices. Cake can also be decorated with candied violets and whipped cream.

Betsy Alaupovic Hyde (Mrs. Clark)

Cheesecake
Serves 10 to 12

Crust
1¾ cups graham cracker
  crumbs
¼ cup walnuts

½ teaspoon cinnamon
½ cup melted butter

Filling
3 eggs
2 8-ounce packages cream
  cheese

1 cup sugar
2 teaspoons vanilla
3 cups sour cream

To prepare the crust, mix the ingredients together. Press into bottom and sides of a 9-inch springform pan. Reserve 3 tablespoons for top. To prepare filling, combine eggs, cream cheese, sugar and vanilla. Beat until smooth. Blend in sour cream. Pour into crust and top with reserved crumbs. Bake at 375 degrees for 1 hour. Cool. Chill 4 to 5 hours before serving.

Christi McGrew

Heavenly Cheesecake
Serves 30

30 graham crackers, crushed
¾ cup butter, melted
⅜ cup sugar
2 pounds cream cheese
6 eggs
1 cup sugar
4 cups sour cream

2½ cups sugar
2 teaspoons vanilla extract
2 envelopes gelatin
½ cup hot water
Cinnamon
Almonds, sliced

Mix graham crackers with melted butter and ⅜ cup sugar. Press into bottom of a 9 x 13-inch pan. Bake at 350 degrees for 7 minutes. Soften cream cheese. Mix with mixer or food processor until smooth. Add eggs one at a time and 1 cup sugar. Pour on top of crumbs. Bake at 350 degrees for 20 to 25 minutes. Cool until room temperature. Combine sour cream, 2½ cups sugar and vanilla. Dissolve gelatin in hot water. Quickly mix into sour cream mixture. Gently pour over cream cheese layer. Sprinkle cinnamon and sliced almonds on top. Let cool. Chill 24 hours. This can be frozen.
Gennie LeForce Johnson (Mrs. Robert M.)

Petite Cherry Cheesecakes
Serves 12

1 cup vanilla wafer crumbs
3½ tablespoons margarine, melted
1 8-ounce package cream cheese
⅓ cup sugar
1 egg

2 teaspoons lemon juice
½ teaspoon vanilla extract
¼ teaspoon almond extract
¼ teaspoon salt
Cherry pie filling or other fruit pie filling

Mix crumbs and margarine. Press about 1 tablespoon into each muffin liner in muffin tins. Beat cream cheese until fluffy. Beat in the next 6 ingredients until smooth. Spoon about 1 tablespoon into each muffin tin. Bake at 375 degrees for about 15 minutes. Let stand 20 minutes. Remove filled liners from muffin tin. Cool completely. Top with favorite fruit pie filling. Remove paper liners before serving.
Kristen Van der Hoof Freeland (Mrs. Royden R.)

Truly Delicious Cupcakes
Yields 18 to 24

4 1-ounce squares semi-sweet
    chocolate
1 cup margarine
1/4 teaspoon butter flavoring
1 1/2 cups chopped pecans

1 3/4 cups sugar
1 cup flour
4 large eggs
1 teaspoon vanilla extract

Melt chocolate and margarine in heavy pan. Add butter flavoring and nuts. Stir to coat pecans. Remove from heat. Combine sugar, flour, eggs and vanilla with wire whip, but do not beat. Add chocolate and butter mixture. Do not use mixer. Fill muffin cups (foil ones work best) 1/2 to 2/3 full. Bake at 325 degrees for 30 minutes. They may not look done, but do not overcook. They are very moist.

Carol Brown Fisher (Mrs. Ron P.)   *Bette Burke MacKellar (Mrs. J. P., Jr.)*

Apricot Crumble Cake
Serves 12

1 8-ounce package cream
    cheese, softened
1/2 cup butter
1 1/4 cups sugar
2 eggs
1/4 cup milk

1 teaspoon vanilla extract
2 cups sifted cake flour
1 teaspoon baking powder
1/2 teaspoon baking soda
1/4 teaspoon salt
1 12-ounce jar apricot
    preserves

Frosting
2 cups shredded coconut
2/3 cup brown sugar

1 teaspoon cinnamon
1/2 cup butter, melted

Thoroughly blend cream cheese, butter and sugar. Gradually add eggs, milk and vanilla. Add sifted dry ingredients, mixing until well blended. Pour half of batter into greased and floured 9 x 13-inch pan. Cover with apricot preserves. Top with remaining batter. Bake at 350 degrees for 35 to 40 minutes. Cool slightly. To prepare frosting, blend all ingredients well. Spread lightly on warm cake and broil until golden brown. Watch carefully so coconut does not burn.

Jane Bowers McKinney (Mrs. Kenneth N.)

Cherry Tarts
Yields 2 dozen

Sand Tart Shells
1¼ cups butter
¾ cup sugar
1 egg, beaten

1 teaspoon almond extract
½ cup finely chopped pecans
2½ cups flour

Filling
1 1-pound can tart cherries
3 tablespoons flour
¾ cup sugar

Salt
1 teaspoon almond extract

To prepare shells, cream butter and sugar. Add remaining ingredients and chill. Press pieces of dough into small fancy forms or tiny tart tins with fluted sides. Bake at 350 degrees for 12 to 15 minutes until golden or light brown. Invert tins so shells will come out easily when tapped gently. Fill when cool. To prepare filling, drain the can of cherries, reserving the juice. Combine the juice with 3 tablespoons flour, sugar and salt. Stir until smooth with no lumps. Cook over medium heat and add the almond extract. Pour cherries into thickened sauce. Cool slightly and pour into tart shells.
SoRelle Land Fitzgerald (Mrs. Don)

Nancy Chapman's Blueberry Cheese Pie
Yields 2 pies

Crust
2 cups graham cracker crumbs
½ cup finely chopped pecans

½ cup powdered sugar
½ cup butter, not margarine,
    melted

Filling
1 8-ounce package
    Philadelphia cream cheese
1 cup sugar
2 eggs

2 teaspoons lemon juice
3 or 4 bananas
1 can blueberry pie filling
Whipping cream, whipped

To prepare crust, mix together graham cracker crumbs, chopped pecans, powdered sugar and melted butter. Press into 2 9-inch pie pans.
To prepare filling, beat cream cheese, sugar, eggs and lemon juice. Pour into crusts. Bake at 325 to 350 degrees for 15 to 20 minutes. Let cool. Slice bananas on top of each pie. Divide can of blueberry pie filling between the 2 pies and pour over bananas. Refrigerate. Top with whipped cream before serving.
Marilyn Novak Sullivan (Mrs. William H.)

Mexican Plum Pie
Serves 8

1½ to 2 cups sugar
2 pounds fresh red plums, halved and pitted or 1 30-ounce can purple plums, pitted
8 flour tortillas

Butter
4 teaspoons brown sugar
1 teaspoon cinnamon
¼ cup semi-sweet chocolate, grated
1 8-ounce carton sour cream

Sprinkle 1½ to 2 cups sugar over plums in a saucepan. Let stand until sugar dissolves and juice forms. Bring plums and juices to a boil and simmer until tender. While plums are simmering and cooling, butter both sides of tortillas lightly and arrange on a large baking sheet. Combine brown sugar and cinnamon and sprinkle over tortillas. Bake at 350 degrees for 15 minutes. (Tortillas can be turned and sprinkled with sugar and cinnamon mixture after half of the baking time.) To serve, sprinkle chocolate on each tortilla, spoon plums and sauce over chocolate. Top with sour cream and a few more chocolate sprinkles.

Exact measurements are not a must. Adjust sweetness to your taste.
Dee Ingram Harris (Mrs. John H.)

Dutch Apple Pie
Serves 6 to 8

6 tart cooking apples
1 cup sugar
2 tablespoons flour
1 teaspoon ground cinnamon

1 teaspoon grated lemon peel
⅛ teaspoon ground cloves
⅛ teaspoon salt
1 9-inch pie shell

Topping
½ cup flour
¼ cup sugar
⅛ teaspoon salt

½ cup grated Cheddar cheese
¼ cup butter, melted
Sour cream or whipping cream, whipped

Peel, quarter, core, and thinly slice the apples. Mix sugar, flour, cinnamon, lemon peel, cloves and salt. Toss the apples lightly in this mixture. Overlap apple slices in the pie shell.

To prepare topping, combine flour, sugar, salt and cheese. Mix in melted butter. Sprinkle cheese crumb mixture over apples. Bake at 400 degrees for 40 minutes. Serve warm with cream.
Janie Gilbert Axton (Mrs. Jon)

Lemon Chess Pie
Serves 6 to 8

4 eggs, unbeaten
6 tablespoons butter, melted
1/4 cup milk
Peel of 2 lemons, grated
1/4 cup fresh lemon juice

1 3/4 cups sugar
1 tablespoon flour
1 tablespoon cornmeal
1/4 teaspoon salt
1 9-inch pastry shell, unbaked

Put first 9 ingredients in a bowl and beat with a wire whisk until well blended and smooth. Pour into pie shell. Bake at 375 degrees for 30 to 35 minutes until top is golden brown.
Patricia Hadlock Ramsey (Mrs. Christian, Jr.)

Lemon Ice Box Pie
Serves 6 to 8

Crust
1/2 cup margarine, melted

2 1/2 cups crushed graham crackers

Filling
1 14-ounce can Eagle Brand sweetened condensed milk
2 to 3 egg yolks

1/2 cup lemon juice
Lemon peel

Meringue
2 to 3 egg whites, room temperature
1/4 teaspoon cream of tartar

1/2 teaspoon vanilla extract
1/4 cup sugar

To prepare crust, melt margarine in 9-inch pie pan. Add graham cracker crumbs. Mix and press into pie pan bottom and sides. To prepare filling, combine sweetened condensed milk and egg yolks in medium bowl. Gradually add lemon juice and lemon peel to taste. Pour into pie crust. Refrigerate at least 2 hours before serving. To prepare meringue, if desired, beat egg whites in small bowl until almost stiff. Gradually add cream of tartar, vanilla and sugar. When stiff, spoon onto pie. Bake at 325 degrees for 10 minutes. Refrigerate.
Barbara Louise Ketchum

Fruit Pizza
Serves 16

½ cup butter or margarine, softened
½ cup oil
1 egg
1 teaspoon vanilla extract
2½ cups flour
1 teapsoon cream of tartar
1 teaspoon baking soda
¼ teaspoon salt
12 ounces cream cheese
1 teaspoon almond extract

⅓ cup sugar
1 15½-ounce can pineapple chunks
1 cup strawberries, fresh or frozen
1 11-ounce can mandarin oranges
½ to 1 cup blueberries
¾ cup apricot-pineapple preserves
¼ cup or more orange juice

Combine butter, oil, egg and vanilla. Beat well. Add flour, cream of tartar, soda and salt. Beat. Divide in half. Pat each half onto 2 pizza pans. Bake at 350 degrees for 10 minutes, or until light golden brown. Cool. Blend cream cheese, almond extract and sugar until smooth. Spread over crust like pizza sauce. Just prior to serving, top with fruit. Mix preserves and orange juice. Pour over top as glaze. Slice like a pizza and serve.
Jan Rohrer Robinson (Mrs. William J.)

Strawberry Lover's Pie
Serves 6 to 8

1 9-inch pie shell, baked and set aside
2 pints fresh strawberries, washed and stemmed
3 tablespoons cornstarch
1 cup sugar

7 ounces 7-Up
2 to 3 drops red food coloring
1 pint whipping cream
1 teaspoon vanilla extract
1 tablespoon powdered sugar

Heap strawberries into cooled pie shell. Set aside. Mix cornstarch and sugar. Add 7-Up. Cook over medium heat until it boils. Continue boiling until thickened. Add red food coloring. Cool. Pour evenly over strawberries. Whip cream with vanilla and powdered sugar. Top pie with whipped cream. Best when served the day it is made.
Marty Clay Conkle (Mrs. Cliff)

Southern Peanut Butter Pie
Serves 8

1 cup powdered sugar
1/2 cup creamy peanut butter
3 eggs, separated
2/3 cup sugar
1/8 teaspoon salt
1/4 cup cornstarch
2 cups milk, scalded

2 tablespoons butter or
    margarine
1/2 teaspoon vanilla extract
1 9-inch pie shell, baked and
    cooled
1/4 teaspoon cream of tartar

Mix together powdered sugar and peanut butter until it is a coarse, crumbled mixture. Set aside. Beat egg yolks until fluffy. Combine sugar, salt and cornstarch. Beat into egg yolks. Beat in hot milk, gradually. Cook in a double boiler until smooth and thick, stirring constantly. Remove from heat. Add butter and vanilla. Cover bottom of pie shell with 2/3 of the peanut butter mixture. Pour in the hot custard. Beat egg whites and cream of tartar until stiff. Spread on top of filling, then sprinkle the remaining 1/3 of the peanut butter mixture over the top. Bake at 350 degrees for 12 to 15 minutes or until brown. Cool well before serving.
Sally Morrison Stringer (Mrs. Edward)

Fudge Pecan Pie
Serves 6

1/2 cup butter or margarine
2 ounces unsweetened
    chocolate
1 cup sugar
1/4 cup flour
Salt

2 eggs, beaten
1 teaspoon vanilla extract
1/2 cup chopped pecans
1 8-inch pie shell
Vanilla ice cream or whipping
    cream, whipped

Melt butter or margarine and chocolate in top of double boiler or over very low heat. Cool slightly. Mix sugar, flour and pinch of salt. Blend in eggs and vanilla. Fold in chocolate mixture and nuts. Pour filling into pie shell and bake at 325 degrees for 30 to 40 minutes. Serve topped with vanilla ice cream or whipped cream.
Janie McDonald Kimball

Peerless Pecan Pie
Serves 6 to 8

1 cup brown sugar
½ cup sugar
3 eggs, beaten
Pinch of salt

2 tablespoons butter, melted
1 teaspoon vanilla extract
1 cup pecans
1 pie shell, unbaked

Combine first 7 ingredients and place in unbaked pie shell. Bake at 325 degrees for 40 minutes or until thick.

Dixie Goebel Buchwald (Mrs. Charles E.)

Tiny Pecan Pies
Yields 24

Crust
½ cup margarine
1 3-ounce package cream
  cheese, softened

1 cup flour

Filling
⅔ cup brown sugar
1 egg, beaten
1 teaspoon vanilla extract

⅔ cup chopped pecans
1 tablespoon margarine

To prepare crust, mix together the first 3 ingredients. Chill. Then form into 24 small balls. Grease 2 miniature muffin tins and press 1 ball into each tin.

To prepare filling, mix ingredients together. Use a teaspoon to fill tins. Bake at 350 degrees for 30 minutes.

Madelyn Street Bartley (Mrs. Gary)   *Ranell Bules Brown (Mrs. Steve M.)*

Triple Crown Pie
Serves 8

6 tablespoons butter, melted
¾ cup sugar
¾ cup white corn syrup
3 eggs
1 teaspoon vanilla extract

¾ cup chopped pecans
½ heaping cup miniature
   chocolate chips
1 9-inch pie shell, unbaked

Cream butter and sugar together with electric mixer. Mix in corn syrup, eggs and vanilla. Stir in pecans and chocolate chips and pour into pie shell. Bake at 350 degrees for 45 minutes, until set and lightly browned.

Traditional dessert at Kentucky Derby gatherings.

Cokie Anderson Smith (Mrs. Michael C.)

Chocolate Peppermint Pie
Serves 10 to 12

Crust
1 package Famous chocolate
   wafers, crushed

¼ cup sugar
½ cup butter, melted

Filling
1 quart peppermint ice cream
¼ cup crushed peppermints

¼ cup milk

Toppings
Fudge sauce
Whipping cream, whipped

Crushed peppermints

To prepare crust, mix crushed wafers with sugar and add melted butter. Pat into pie pan. To prepare filling, add milk and crushed peppermints to peppermint ice cream. Pour into pie pan. Freeze until hard. To serve, add heated fudge sauce, whipped cream and crushed peppermints to each piece of pie. Coffee ice cream can be substituted for peppermint ice cream and use almonds instead of peppermints.

Lisa Elder

Cream Cheese Pie
Yields 2 pies

1 quart strawberries
1½ cups sugar
1 8-ounce package cream
   cheese

½ pint whipping cream,
   whipped
4 bananas
2 pie shells, baked or Cookie
   Pie Crust (see below)

Cookie Pie Crust
½ cup butter
1 cup flour
¼ teaspoon salt

2 tablespoons sugar
½ cup finely chopped pecans

Slice strawberries and sweeten with approximately ½ cup sugar. Let stand. Blend cream cheese with 1 cup sugar. Fold in whipped cream.

To prepare Cookie Pie Crust, mix ingredients together. Roll in ball, pat into well greased pie plate and bake at 350 degrees for 15 to 20 minutes. Slice bananas into baked pie shells, pour cream cheese mixture over bananas. Chill thoroughly. Top with strawberries just before serving. Garnish with more whipped cream.

Sandy Simon Childress (Mrs. Bob)

Pielsticker's Rum Cream Pie
Serves 6 to 8

6 egg yolks
1 scant cup sugar
1 envelope gelatin
½ cup cold water
1 pint whipping cream,
   whipped

½ cup dark rum
1 graham cracker pie shell
Shaved bittersweet chocolate
   curls

Beat egg yolks until light and add sugar. Soak gelatin in water and place mixture over low heat, bringing it to a boil. Pour over the sugar and egg mixture, stirring briskly. Whip whipping cream until stiff. Fold into egg mixture. Flavor with rum. Cool mixture until it begins to set and pour into graham cracker pie shell. Chill until firm. Sprinkle the top generously with shaved chocolate curls and serve cold.

Great to do ahead – freezes for months!

Marjory Pielsticker Feighny (Mrs. James)

Coffee Creme Pie

Yields 1 10-inch pie

Meringue Pie Shell
2 egg whites
1/2 cup sugar

1/4 teaspoon salt
1/2 cup finely chopped pecans

Filling
2 tablespoons instant coffee
1/2 cup boiling water
1/2 pound marshmallows, cut
in half
2 egg yolks, beaten

2 cups whipping cream,
whipped
1/2 teaspoon almond extract
Shaved chocolate
Whipping cream (optional)
Almonds, sliced and toasted

To prepare meringue pie shell, beat egg whites until stiff. Gradually add sugar and salt to the egg whites, beating as added. Fold in pecans. Press into 10-inch pie pan. Prick with fork. Bake at 250 degrees for 1 hour. Cool.

To prepare filling, mix coffee, water and marshmallows. Add beaten egg yolks. Cook 3 minutes, stirring constantly. Cool. Fold in whipped cream and almond extract. Reserve 1 cup of mixture and pour rest into pie shell. As filling congeals, add reserved mixture to center, to make the center of the pie higher. Refrigerate overnight. Cover with shaved chocolate or more whipped cream and toasted, sliced almonds. The filling can also be poured into a lightly buttered 1 1/2-quart mold and used as a mousse.

Victoria Caudill Moran (Mrs. Henry Thomas)

Heath Pie

Serves 8

5 Heath candy bars
1 9-ounce container frozen
whipped topping

1 cup instant powdered
cocoa mix
1 8-inch graham cracker
pie crust

Crush 4 of the candy bars. Fold crushed candy, whipped topping and cocoa mix together. Spread in pie crust. Crush remaining candy bar and sprinkle on top of pie. Cover and refrigerate.

Becky Brown Johnston (Mrs. Brad)   *Diane Blinn Kenney (Mrs. Herbert)*

Date Crunch Delight
Yields 6 to 12

1 cup dates, chopped
1 cup water
1/2 cup sugar
3/4 cup chopped pecans
1/2 cup butter
1 cup brown sugar
1 cup flour, sifted

1 teaspoon baking powder
1/4 teaspoon salt
1 cup quick cooking oats
Whipped cream or frozen
  whipped topping
1/2 teaspoon vanilla extract
Cinnamon

Combine dates, water and sugar. Cook over medium heat until thick, about 8 minutes. Cool and add nuts. Set aside. Cream butter until soft. Add brown sugar and continue to beat well. Sift dry ingredients and fold into creamed mixture. Add oats and mix until crumbly. Pat half of the crumb mixture in bottom of 8 x 8-inch pan. Spread with date mixture and top with remaining crumbs. Pat in gently. Bake at 325 degrees for 45 minutes. Cool and cut into 2½-inch squares for dessert or 1-inch squares for cookies. For dessert, mix whipped cream or topping with vanilla and dash of cinnamon. Spoon over dessert squares.
Beth Sherman Wells (Mrs. Edward)

Best Ever Blond Brownies
Yields 2 dozen

5⅓ tablespoons butter or
  margarine
1 cup brown sugar
1 egg

3/4 cup self-rising flour
1 teaspoon vanilla extract
1/2 cup pecans

In a saucepan, melt butter. Remove from heat and add brown sugar. Stir. Add egg and stir by hand. Add self-rising flour. Stir until blended. Add vanilla and nuts. Pour into a greased 8 x 8-inch pan. Bake at 325 degrees for 30 minutes. Brownies are done when they shrink from the sides of the pan. Let brownies cool in pan.
Patsy King Hosman
(Mrs. Thomas D.)

Patsy Eskridge King
(Mrs. Arthur E., Jr.)

Tuxedo Treats (Marshmallow Brownies)
Yields 9

Brownies
1/2 cup butter, softened
1 cup sugar
4 tablespoons cocoa
2 eggs
2/3 cup flour

1 teaspoon vanilla extract
1 cup pecans, coarsely
   chopped
16 marshmallows

Frosting
2 cups powdered sugar, sifted
2 tablespoons butter, softened
1/4 cup cocoa

3 tablespoons milk
1 teaspoon vanilla extract

Mix all the brownie ingredients except the marshmallows. Bake in a greased 9-inch pan at 350 degrees for 20 minutes. About 2 or 3 minutes before done, put marshmallows spaced evenly apart on top of brownies and let them get puffy. Then remove from oven and pat marshmallows down flat. While brownies are cooking, prepare frosting by mixing all ingredients in orders listed. Cool brownies on rack. Spread with frosting while still warm.

Joanie McLauchlin Thompson (Mrs. Tom D.)

Butterscotch Brickle Bars
Yields 2 dozen

1 1/2 cups flour, sifted
3/4 cup brown sugar
1/2 cup butter, softened
1/4 teaspoon salt
1 6-ounce package
   butterscotch chips

1/4 cup white Karo syrup
2 tablespoons butter
1 tablespoon water
1/4 teaspoon salt
2 cups pecans, walnuts, or
   almonds, chopped

Combine flour, brown sugar, butter and 1/4 teaspoon salt. Mix until crumbly. Press into a 9 x 13-inch pan. Bake at 375 degrees for 10 minutes or until golden. Over low heat melt chips, syrup, butter, water and 1/4 teaspoon salt. Stir until smooth. Remove from heat and stir in nuts. Spoon over top of baked cookie layer, which does not need to be cooled, and spread evenly. Bake at 375 degrees for 5 to 8 minutes longer. Cut into bars while still warm.

Janie Gilbert Axton (Mrs. Jon)

German Chocolate Brownies

Yields 2 to 3 dozen

1 14-ounce package Kraft
caramels
1 5⅓-ounce can evaporated
milk
1 cup pecans, chopped

¾ cup margarine, melted
1 box German chocolate
cake mix
1 12-ounce package chocolate
chips

Melt caramels in ⅓ cup evaporated milk in double boiler, or micro-wave. Mix by hand remaining evaporated milk, pecans, margarine and cake mix. Mixture will be very thick. Pat half of mixture into a 9 x 13-inch greased pan. Bake at 350 degrees for 6 minutes. Remove from oven. Pour chocolate chips over. Then spread on caramel mixture. Crumble remaining cake mixture on top of caramel mixture. Bake 18 to 20 minutes. Let set and cool before cutting. Freezes well.
Cookbook Committee

German Chocolate Brownie Drops

Yields 4 dozen

2 4-ounce bars German sweet
chocolate
1 tablespoon butter
2 eggs
¾ cup sugar
¼ cup flour

¼ teaspoon baking powder
¼ teaspoon cinnamon
⅛ teaspoon salt
1 teaspoon vanilla extract
¾ cup chopped pecans

Melt chocolate and butter in double boiler. Beat eggs until foamy. Add sugar, two tablespoons at a time. Beat until thickened, about 5 minutes. Blend in chocolate. Add flour, baking powder, cinnamon, salt and blend. Stir in vanilla and nuts. Drop by teaspoons onto greased baking sheet. Bake at 350 degrees for 8 to 10 minutes.
Olive Kees Austin (Mrs. Gerald G.)

German Cream Cheese Brownies
Yields 20

1 4-ounce package German
  sweet chocolate
5 tablespoons butter
1 3-ounce package cream
  cheese
1 cup sugar
3 eggs

1/2 cup plus 1 tablespoon flour,
  unsifted
1 1/2 teaspoons vanilla extract
1/2 teaspoon baking powder
1/4 teaspoon salt
1/2 cup nuts, coarsely chopped
1/4 teaspoon almond extract

Melt chocolate and 3 tablespoons butter over very low heat, stirring constantly. Cool. Cream remaining butter with cream cheese until softened. Gradually add 1/4 cup sugar, creaming until light and fluffy. Stir in 1 egg, 1 tablespoon flour and 1/2 teaspoon vanilla until blended. Set aside. In a separate bowl, beat remaining eggs until fluffy. Gradually add remaining 3/4 cup sugar, beating until thickened. Fold in baking powder, salt and remaining 1/2 cup flour. Blend into cooled chocolate mixture. Stir in nuts, almond extract and remaining vanilla. Measure 1 cup chocolate mixture and set aside. Spread remaining mixture in a greased 9-inch square pan. Pour cheese mixture over the top. Drop measured chocolate mixture by tablespoons onto cheese mixture. Swirl to marble. Bake at 350 degrees for 35 to 40 minutes.

Marion Louise Joullian

Chinese Chews
Yields 20 to 24

3/4 cup butter
3 tablespoons sugar
1 1/2 cups flour
3 egg yolks
2 1/4 cups light brown sugar

3/4 cup shredded coconut
1/2 to 3/4 cup chopped pecans
3 egg whites
Powdered sugar

Cream butter and sugar. Add flour. Spread in a greased 9 x 14-inch pan. Bake at 350 degrees for 15 minutes until light brown. Beat 3 egg yolks. Add brown sugar, coconut and nuts. Mix thoroughly with spoon. Beat 3 egg whites until stiff. Fold into brown sugar mixture. Spread on top of crust. Bake at 350 degrees for 25 minutes. While warm sprinkle with powdered sugar and cut.

Linda Meining Zahn (Mrs. Richard L.)

Carol's Peanut Butter Squares

Yields 100 1-inch squares

1 cup butter, melted
2 cups powdered sugar
1¾ cups graham cracker
  crumbs

1 cup peanut butter
1 12-ounce package chocolate
  chips, melted

Mix melted butter, powdered sugar and graham cracker crumbs by hand. Press mixture into a greased 9 x 13-inch pan. Spread peanut butter over graham cracker mixture. Spread melted chocolate chips on top. Chill 2 hours. Warm to room temperature and cut into small squares.

Franci King Hart (Mrs. William H.)   *Eve Edwards Patterson (Mrs. William)*

Apricot Bars

Yields 2 to 3 dozen

1 6-ounce package dried
  apricots
1 15¼-ounce can crushed
  pineapple in its own juice
1½ cups sugar
½ cup plus 2 tablespoons
  unsalted butter

2 cups flour
½ teaspoon salt
½ teaspoon baking soda
½ cup finely chopped pecans
1½ cups Baker's angel flake
  coconut

Finely chop apricots in food processor. Transfer to a 1-quart saucepan and add canned pineapple with juice. Cover and simmer 20 minutes, checking several times to be sure liquid has not evaporated. Add ½ cup sugar and simmer 2 to 3 minutes more. Remove from heat and cool. With an electric mixer, cream butter and 1 cup sugar until blended. Add flour, salt and soda. Mix well. Add nuts and coconut. Press ⅔ of dry mixture into a lightly greased 9 x 13-inch pan. Bake at 400 degrees for 10 minutes. Remove from oven and cool for 10 minutes. Spread pineapple and apricot filling over crust. Sprinkle remaining crumbs over entire filling pressing down gently. Return to oven and bake 17 to 20 minutes longer. Cool and cut into bars.

Carol Sue Jennerjahn Taylor (Mrs. Jerry A.)

Homemade Gingerbread
Serves 10 to 14

2 cups flour
1 cup sugar
2 teaspoons ground ginger
4 teaspoons cinnamon
1 teaspoon nutmeg
1 teaspoon baking soda

1 teaspoon salt
1 cup salad oil
1 cup molasses
1 cup buttermilk
2 eggs
1 teaspoon vanilla

Frosting
1 1-pound box powdered
  sugar

6 tablespoons milk
8 tablespoons butter

To prepare the gingerbread, mix together the dry ingredients. Next combine the liquid ingredients and mix the two together. Pour into a greased 9 x 13-inch cake pan. Bake at 325 degrees for 45 minutes to 1 hour. To prepare the frosting, melt the butter. Add the powdered sugar and milk and mix well. Pour over the cooled gingerbread.
Connie Collins Givens (Mrs. Charles)

Linda's Sensational Sherry Bars
Yields 4 dozen

First Layer
4 ounces unsweetened
  chocolate
1 cup butter

2 cups sugar
4 eggs
1 cup flour

Second Layer
1 teaspoon vanilla extract
½ cup butter
4 cups powdered sugar

¼ cup half and half
¼ cup sherry
1 cup finely chopped English
  walnuts

Third Layer
1 6-ounce package chocolate
  chips

3 tablespoons water
4 tablespoons butter

To prepare first layer, melt chocolate and butter in double boiler. Cool slightly, then beat in sugar, eggs and flour. Pour into greased and floured 11 x 16-inch pan and bake at 350 degrees for 25 minutes. Cool. To prepare second layer, beat all ingredients together and spread onto cooled first layer. Chill for at least 2 hours. To prepare third layer, melt ingredients in double boiler. Cool slightly. Dribble over first 2 layers and spread with back of spoon. Cut into small bars.
Mary Slattery Price (Mrs. William S.)

Oh-So-Good Oatmeal Cookies
Yields 5 dozen

1 cup shortening
1 cup brown sugar
1 cup white sugar
2 eggs, beaten
1 teaspoon vanilla
1½ cups flour

1 teaspoon soda
1 teaspoon salt
3 cups rolled oats, uncooked
½ cup chopped nuts
  (optional)
½ cup raisins (optional)

Cream shortening and sugars. Add beaten eggs and vanilla. Sift together dry ingredients and add. Mix in oatmeal, nuts and raisins. Shape into rolls and wrap in waxed paper. Chill. Slice cookies ¼-inch thick. Bake at 350 degrees for 10 minutes on ungreased cookie sheet.
Patsy King Hosman (Mrs. Thomas D.)

Applesauce Bars
Yields 25 bars

1 cup cooking oil
1 cup sugar
1 teaspoon baking soda
1 cup applesauce
2 cups flour, sifted

½ teaspoon salt
½ teaspoon cinnamon
¾ cup raisins
1 cup chopped pecans
1 teaspoon vanilla extract

Frosting
2 tablespoons butter or
  margarine
2 tablespoons milk, heated

1½ cups powdered sugar
½ teaspoon vanilla extract
½ teaspoon lemon flavoring

In a large bowl, mix oil with sugar. Add baking soda to applesauce. Combine with sugar mixture. Add flour, salt, cinnamon, raisins, nuts and vanilla. Blend thoroughly. Turn into a greased 8 x 12 x 2-inch pan. Bake at 350 degrees for 30 minutes.

To prepare frosting mix all ingredients together and spread on warm bars before cutting.
Suzanne Peterson Pardue (Mrs. W. Dave)

Monster Cookies
Yields 4 dozen large cookies

1 cup butter or margarine
1 pound brown sugar
2 cups sugar
6 eggs
1 1/2 teaspoons vanilla extract
1 1/2 teaspoons syrup

4 teaspoons baking soda
1 1/2 pounds peanut butter
9 cups rolled oats, uncooked
1 pound M&M candies
1 6-ounce package chocolate chips

Mix ingredients in order given. Drop by tablespoons or ice cream scoop on greased cookie sheet. Mash down some. Bake at 350 degrees for 12 minutes. Let cool slightly before removing from pan.
Cookbook Committee

Macadamia Rum Bars
Yields 32 or 48 bars

Cookie Crust
1/2 cup butter, softened
1/4 cup sugar

1 cup flour

Filling
2 eggs, slightly beaten
1 1/4 cups brown sugar, packed
2 tablespoons flour
1/2 teaspoon salt
1/4 teaspoon baking powder

1 cup flaked coconut
1 cup macadamia nuts, chopped
1 teaspoon vanilla extract
1 tablespoon rum

Frosting
2 tablespoons butter, softened
1 1/4 cups powdered sugar, sifted

1 tablespoon whipping cream
1/2 teaspoon vanilla extract
1 teaspoon rum

To prepare crust mix all ingredients together at medium speed until thoroughly blended. Press mixture evenly into greased 9 x 13-inch or 8 x 10-inch pan. Bake at 350 degrees for 15 to 20 minutes, until just beginning to brown. Remove from oven.

To prepare filling, stir together ingredients until well blended and spread evenly over crust. Bake at 350 degrees for 15 to 20 minutes until firm and golden brown.

To prepare frosting, beat ingredients together until smooth. Add more cream or rum, or both if necessary, to make a good spreading consistency. Spread over cooled bars. May be cut into 32 or 48 bars.

This is a popular Hawaiian dessert served with ice cream or fresh fruit.
Dorthlynn Dent Gaddis (Mrs. Preston)

219

Rich and Famous Theta Bars
Yields 2 dozen

1 box yellow cake mix
3 eggs
1 cup shredded or flake coconut (optional)
1½ cups chopped pecans

1 1-pound box powdered sugar
1 teaspoon vanilla extract
1 8-ounce package cream cheese

Mix together cake mix, 2 eggs, coconut and pecans. When mix is thoroughly moistened, pat it into a greased 9 x 13-inch pan. With an electric mixer or food processor beat powdered sugar, vanilla, 1 egg and cream cheese until smooth and light. Pour over the cake layer and bake at 350 degrees for 30 minutes. Cool completely before cutting into squares.

Nita Forrest Folger (Mrs. Doug)

Cream Cheese Ice Box Cookies
Yields 5 dozen

1 cup butter
1 3-ounce package cream cheese
1 cup sugar

1½ teaspoons vanilla extract
2 cups flour, unsifted
1 cup chopped pecans

Cream butter, cream cheese and sugar. Add vanilla. Stir in flour and nuts. Roll dough into 2 long cylinders. Wrap in waxed paper. Chill well. Slice ⅛-inch thick and bake on cookie sheet at 350 degrees for 8 to 10 minutes. Cookies are done when light brown on edges.

Mary Hart Reeves (Mrs. William George)

Janet's Cutter Cookies
Yields 2 dozen

1 cup butter, softened
½ cup powdered sugar
1 teaspoon vanilla extract

2¼ cups flour
¼ teaspoon salt

Frosting
1 cup powdered sugar
1 teaspoon vanilla extract
1¼ to 2 tablespoons water

Food coloring (optional)
Decorating candies (optional)

Mix butter, sugar and vanilla. Stir in flour and salt. Roll out ¼-inch thick and cut with floured cookie cutters. Bake at 375 degrees on ungreased baking sheet for about 10 minutes or until light brown around edges. Cool and frost. To prepare frosting, combine first 3 ingredients to a spreadable consistency.
Janet Belt Dunlevy (Mrs. F. W., Jr.)

Bewitching Banana Bites
Yields 6 dozen

⅔ cup butter or margarine
1 cup sugar
2 eggs
2 ripe bananas
1 teaspoon vanilla extract
2¼ cups flour, sifted
2 teaspoons baking powder

Salt
¼ teaspoon baking soda
½ to 1 cup chopped pecans
   (optional)
Cinnamon
Sugar

Cream butter and sugar. Add eggs. When thoroughly mixed, add bananas and vanilla. Beat mixture until batter is smooth. Add flour, 1 cup at a time, beating after each addition. Add baking powder, salt and baking soda. Add pecans if desired. Drop by teaspoons onto greased cookie sheet. Sprinkle with a mixture of cinnamon and sugar. Bake at 325 degrees for 10 minutes.
Christi McGrew

Forgotten Cookies (Candy Kisses)
Yields 3 dozen

2 egg whites
1 cup sugar
1 teaspoon vanilla extract

1 6-ounce package chocolate chips
1 cup chopped pecans

Heat oven to 350 degrees. Beat egg whites until stiff. Slowly add 1 cup sugar and beat well. Add vanilla, chocolate chips and pecans. Drop by teaspoons onto greased cookie sheet. Place in oven. Turn off oven and leave overnight or approximately 12 hours.
Linda Polk Klos (Mrs. Tom)

Chocolate Chip Peppermint Cookies
Yields 3 dozen

2 egg whites
1/8 teaspoon cream of tartar
1/2 cup sugar

1 cup chocolate chips
1/4 teaspoon peppermint extract

Beat egg whites until foamy. Add cream of tartar. Beat eggs until stiff peaks form, but not dry. Add sugar, 2 tablespoons at a time, beating thoroughly after each addition. Fold in chocolate chips and peppermint extract. Drop by teaspoons onto heavy paper or paper bag and bake at 300 degrees for 25 minutes. Remove from paper while slightly warm.
Judy Monroe Pitts (Mrs. H. Craig)

Graham Cracker Cookies
Yields 24

24 squares graham crackers
1/2 pound butter or margarine

1 cup firmly packed dark brown sugar
1 cup finely chopped pecans

Arrange graham crackers on a buttered cookie sheet that has sides. Bring butter and sugar to a boil and boil 2 minutes. Add nuts and pour over crackers. Bake at 350 degrees for 10 minutes. Cool slightly. Cut between each square and remove. (Don't use flat cookie sheet as it may run over in your oven!)
Ranell Bules Brown (Mrs. Steve M.)

Phenomenal Peanut Butter Cups
Yields 3 dozen

1 roll Pillsbury slice 'n bake peanut butter cookies

1 package Reese's miniature peanut butter cups

Cut cookie dough into 9 equal slices, then quarter each slice. Place dough into miniature muffin tins. Bake at 375 degrees for 8 minutes. As soon as you remove cookies from oven, press miniature peanut butter cup into center of each. Refrigerate about 5 minutes.

Carol Sue Jennerjahn Taylor (Mrs. Jerry A.)

Melting Moments
Yields 5 dozen

Cookie

2/3 cup cornstarch
1 cup flour

1 cup butter
1/3 cup powdered sugar

Frosting

1/4 cup butter, softened
2 cups powdered sugar

2 tablespoons lemon juice
Rind of 1 lemon, grated

Sift together cornstarch and flour. Cream butter and sugar. Add sifted dry ingredients. Drop by teaspoons on ungreased cookie sheet and bake at 325 degrees for 15 to 20 minutes. Cool and frost. To prepare frosting, cream butter and add sugar alternately with lemon juice and rind.

Barbara Pannage Stanfield (Mrs. Neil)

Doe's Russian Tea Cakes
Yields 4 to 6 dozen

1 cup butter
1/2 cup powdered sugar
1 teaspoon vanilla extract

2 1/4 cups flour
1 cup chopped nuts
Powdered sugar

Mix butter and powdered sugar thoroughly. Add vanilla. Beat in flour on low speed of mixer. Add nuts. Roll into small finger-shaped cookies. Bake at 375 degrees for 12 to 15 minutes. Roll in powdered sugar while hot. Cool on cake rack. Then roll in powdered sugar again. Store in metal cookie tin containers. Keeps for several days.

Barbara Butcher Beeler (Mrs. Claude E., Jr.)

Snickerdoodles
Yields 8 dozen

2 cups butter
3 cups sugar
3 eggs
1/4 cup milk
1 tablespoon vanilla extract
6 cups flour

1 teaspoon salt
1 1/2 teaspoons baking soda
2 teaspoons cream of tartar
1/4 cup sugar
1 tablespoon cinnamon

Cream butter and sugar. Add eggs, milk and vanilla. Blend well. Sift next 4 ingredients together. Gradually add to cream mixture. Shape into balls and roll in mixture of 1/4 cup sugar and 1 tablespoon cinnamon. Bake on ungreased cookie sheet at 350 degrees for 12 to 15 minutes.
Lynn Eskridge File (Mrs. Steve P.)

Choosy Mothers' Peanut Butter Cookies
Yields 8 to 9 dozen

1 cup butter
1 cup brown sugar
1 cup white sugar
2 eggs
1 cup creamy peanut butter
3 cups flour

2 teaspoons baking soda
2 teaspoons vanilla extract
1/4 teaspoon salt
1 12-ounce package Reese's peanut butter flavored chips

Cream butter, sugars, eggs and peanut butter. Add dry ingredients and vanilla. Mix well. Add peanut butter chips. Shape into teaspoon-size balls. Place on cookie sheets and criss-cross lightly with fork. Bake at 375 degrees for 8 to 10 minutes.
Susan Barnhart Wade

Big Daddies Chocolate Chip Cookies
Yields 12 to 14

1/2 cup butter
1/2 cup shortening
1 cup brown sugar
1/2 cup sugar
2 eggs
2 teaspoons vanilla extract

2 1/2 cups flour
1 teaspoon baking soda
1/2 teaspoon salt
1 12-ounce package chocolate chips

Mix all ingredients together. For each cookie, spread about 1/4 cup mixture onto ungreased cookie sheet and flatten with back of spoon. Cookies should be about 2 inches apart. Bake at 375 degrees for about 10 to 12 minutes, depending on size of cookies.
Becky Brown Johnston (Mrs. Brad)

Food Processor Lemon Wafers
Yields 2 dozen

2 tablespoons shortening
1/2 cup sugar
1 egg
1 teaspoon lemon extract

3/4 cup flour
1/8 teaspoon salt
1 teaspoon baking powder
3 tablespoons milk

Place steel blade in processor bowl. Add shortening and sugar and process until creamy, about 10 seconds. With processor running, add egg and lemon extract. Process until blended well, about 5 seconds. Sift together flour, salt and baking powder. Turn on processor and add the dry ingredients alternately with the milk. Process until smooth, scraping the sides if necessary. The batter will be very soft. Drop by 1/2 teaspoons onto a greased cookie sheet, leaving 2 inches between cookies. Bake at 350 degrees for 12 to 15 minutes and only until the edges brown.
Mary Carter Robideaux (Mrs. Vance)

Coeur a la Creme (Heart of Cream)
Serves 6

1 8-ounce package cream
cheese, softened
1 cup plus 3 tablespoons
whipping cream

1 cup powdered sugar
Salt
1 tablespoon lemon juice
1/2 teaspoon vanilla extract

Blend cream cheese, 3 tablespoons cream and sugar until smooth. Add pinch of salt, lemon juice and vanilla and blend. Lightly whip remaining cream and fold into mixture. Pour into individual pots and chill. Or it can be served in chocolate shells with strawberries or blueberries on top.
Sandra Wilkins Lekas (Mrs. Thomas A.)

Red Raspberry Russian Cream
Serves 6

1/2 pint whipping cream
3/4 cup sugar
1 envelope unflavored gelatin
3/4 cup cold water

1 cup sour cream
1 teaspoon vanilla extract
1 10-ounce package frozen
raspberries with juice,
thawed

Warm whipping cream and sugar in double boiler until lukewarm. Soak gelatin in cold water 5 minutes. Add to cream and continue to heat. When gelatin and sugar have completely dissolved, about 2 to 3 minutes, remove from heat and cool. When mixture begins to thicken, stir in sour cream and vanilla. Beat mixture with electric mixer until smooth. Add juice from berries and pour into mold or decorative individual dishes. Set at least 4 hours in refrigerator. Top with thawed berries.
Kay Pappan Musser (Mrs. R. Clark)

Praline Cream
Serves 6 to 8

2 eggs
2 cups brown sugar
¾ cup flour
1 teaspoon baking soda

1 cup chopped pecans
4 cups whipped cream (can be fresh or prepared, but must yield 4 cups when whipped)

Beat eggs well. Add sugar, flour, baking soda and nuts. Spread in lightly greased 15½ x 10½-inch jelly roll pan. Bake at 325 degrees for 20 minutes. When cool, crumble into very small chunks. Fold crumbled mixture into whipped topping. Put in 9-inch pie plate and freeze. Cut into wedges to serve. This may also be frozen in individual paper baking cups.

Great finale for a Mexican dinner!

Kaye Vernon Adams (Mrs. John Edward)

Lemon Parfaits
Serves 8

½ cup fresh lemon juice
1 tablespoon grated lemon peel
3 eggs, separated
1 cup sugar

Cream of tartar
Salt
1 cup whipping cream
3 tablespoons powdered sugar

In a medium saucepan, combine lemon juice, lemon peel, egg yolks and ½ cup sugar. Beat mixture and stir over moderate heat until thickened. Put in a large bowl to cool. In a separate bowl beat egg whites, pinch of cream of tartar and of salt until soft peaks form. Add remaining ½ cup sugar, 1 tablespoon at a time, until stiff peaks form. Fold meringue into lemon custard mixture. Beat whipping cream until stiff peaks form. Add powdered sugar. Fold into lemon custard and meringue mixture. Divide into 8 8-ounce stemmed glasses. Chill in freezer for at least 2 hours before serving.

Stephanie Irwin Neville (Mrs. Drew)

Sinful Chocolate Mousse
Serves 4

6 ounces semi-sweet chocolate
2 tablespoons Kahlua
3 tablespoons orange juice
2 egg yolks
2 eggs
1 teaspoon vanilla extract

¼ cup sugar
1 cup whipping cream
Approximately ½ cup
 whipping cream for topping
Chocolate shavings

Melt chocolate, Kahlua and orange juice over low heat and set aside. Blend egg yolks and eggs with vanilla and sugar in blender for 2 minutes at high speed. Add 1 cup whipping cream and blend 30 seconds. Add melted chocolate and blend until smooth. Pour into a bowl or individual glasses. Refrigerate 2 hours or until jelled. Whip ½ cup whipping cream and spread on top of chocolate before serving. Top with chocolate shavings.

Katie Shoemaker Bates (Mrs. Richard B.)

Blender Chocolate Mousse
Serves 6

1 6-ounce package Nestle
 semi-sweet chocolate
 morsels
5 tablespoons water, boiling
3 eggs, separated

2 tablespoons dark rum
1 pint whipping cream
Powdered sugar to taste, up to
 1 tablespoon

Put chocolate chips in blender and blend on high for 10 to 15 seconds. Add boiling water and blend for an additional 10 to 15 seconds or more. Beat egg whites until stiff and set aside. Add 3 egg yolks to chocolate mixture. Blend for 10 to 15 seconds. Add rum and blend all ingredients until smooth. Fold egg whites and chocolate mixture together by hand and chill overnight. Remove mixture from refrigerator 20 minutes prior to serving. Using mixer, whip cream until stiff and add powdered sugar. Serve as topping with mousse.

Janice Crandall Hickman (Mrs. French)

Aunt Lorena's Strawberry Mousse
Serves 4

2 cups whipping cream   2 cups mashed strawberries
1 cup powdered sugar

Whip cream until stiff, add sugar and berries. Turn into a mold and cover with waxed paper. Chill for 3 hours.
Evalie Hawes Horner (Mrs. David L.)

1800 Club Baked Fudge
Serves 12

4 eggs, well beaten   1/4 teaspoon salt
2 cups sugar   1 cup butter, melted
1/2 cup flour   1 cup chopped pecans
1/2 cup cocoa   2 teaspoons vanilla extract

Beat eggs, sugar, flour, cocoa and salt until well blended. Mix in butter. Stir in pecans and vanilla. Pour into a 3-quart ovenproof dish. Set into a larger pan half full of hot water. Bake at 300 degrees for 40 to 60 minutes, or until set like custard. Do not overbake. Remove from oven and cool. Cut into squares and serve with whipping cream or ice cream.

It is imperative that water bath be hot before pudding is set in it!
Cookbook Committee

Quick Chocolate Souffles
Serves 4

4 eggs   8-ounce package cream
1/3 cup milk   cheese, cubed
1/4 cup sugar   1/2 cup chocolate syrup
                                  Whipping cream

In a blender or food processor combine eggs, milk and sugar. Blend until smooth. Add cheese while machine is running. Blend until smooth. Add chocolate syrup. Cover and blend 10 seconds. Pour into 4 1-cup souffle dishes. Bake at 375 degrees for 30 to 45 minutes. Serve hot with whipped cream on top.
Alison Evans Taylor (Mrs. Zach D., Jr.)

Chocolate Devil Dessert
Serves 16

Crust
1 cup flour
1/2 cup margarine, softened

1/2 cup chopped pecans

First Layer
1 8-ounce package cream
  cheese
1/2 cup powdered sugar

1 cup prepared whipped
  topping

Second Layer
2 4 1/2-ounce boxes instant
  chocolate pudding

3 cups milk
3 teaspoons vanilla extract

Topping
Whipped topping

Chopped nuts

To prepare crust, cut margarine into flour, as for pie crust. Mix in pecans. Press into 9 x 13-inch cake pan. Bake at 325 degrees for 15 minutes. Cool completely. To prepare first layer, mix sugar into cream cheese and fold into whipped topping. Spread on cooled crust. Mix ingredients for second layer together and spread onto first layer. Cover with whipped topping and sprinkle with chopped nuts. Refrigerate several hours.
Claire Duffner Anderson (Mrs. Carl, III)

Sherry-Honey Poached Apples
Serves 4

4 cooking apples, peeled
  and cored
3/4 cup dry or medium dry
  sherry
3/4 cup honey

2 tablespoons fresh lemon
  juice
Salt
Whipping cream or sour
  cream

Cut apples into eighths. Heat sherry, honey, lemon juice and dash of salt almost to boiling. Add apple slices and simmer gently 10 to 15 minutes or just until tender, basting frequently. Cool in liquid. Serve plain or topped with whipped cream or sour cream.
Sally Morrison Stringer (Mrs. Edward H., Jr.)

Glaciale
Serves 12

½ cup light brown sugar
2 bananas
12 ounces frozen orange juice
   concentrate
1 quart cranberry juice

2 tablespoons Cointreau
1 tablespoon fresh lemon
   juice
3 egg whites, beaten until soft
   peaks form

In blender mix sugar, bananas and orange juice until smooth. Add cranberry juice, Cointreau and lemon juice. Freeze to slushy stage, about 4½ hours. Add 3 well beaten egg whites and refreeze. Before serving, thaw until mixture is easily spooned. This can be served with a chocolate sauce or almost any sauce for a richer dessert.
Annett Lowrey Chesnut

After Dinner Dips
Yields 2 cups per dip

Peanut Butter Dip
2 cups frozen whipped
   topping, thawed
¼ cup peanut butter

¼ cup sugar
2 tablespoons water

Mint Dip
2 cups frozen whipped
   topping, thawed
3 tablespoons creme de
   menthe

1 drop red or green food
   coloring

Chocolate Chip Dip
2 cups frozen whipped
   topping, thawed

½ cup mini chocolate chips

Angel food cake, cubed or
   chunks of apples, bananas,
   oranges and strawberries

To prepare dips combine ingredients and stir well. Serve with cake cubes or fruit for dipping.
Adonna Morgan Meyer (Mrs. Stewart N.)

Cherry Crepes Jubilee
Serves 8

Crepes

1 egg
1 cup milk
1 tablespoon butter, melted

1 cup flour, sifted
2 tablespoons butter, melted
3 to 4 tablespoons brandy

Almond Cream Filling

1 cup sugar
¼ cup flour
1 cup milk
2 eggs
2 egg yolks

½ cup finely chopped
  almonds, toasted
3 tablespoons butter
2 teaspoons vanilla extract
¼ teaspoon almond extract

Brandied Cherry Sauce

1 21-ounce can cherry pie
  filling
2 to 4 tablespoons brandy

2 tablespoons butter
½ teaspoon grated lemon peel
1 tablespoon lemon juice

To prepare crepes, beat eggs just enough to blend. Add milk, 1 table-spoon melted butter and flour. Beat until smooth. Heat crepe pan or 6 to 8-inch skillet. Remove from heat and pour in 3 tablespoons batter. Quickly tilt pan from side to side until batter covers bottom. Return to heat. Brown crepes on one side only. Turn out onto paper towels. Repeat with remaining batter to make 8 crepes. Stack crepes with 2 sheets of waxed paper between for easy separation later. To prepare almond cream filling, combine sugar and flour in medium saucepan. Add milk. Cook and stir until thick and bubbly. Cook and stir 2 minutes more. Beat eggs and egg yolks together. Stir small amount of hot mixture into eggs. Return all to hot mixture. Cook and stir just to boiling. Remove from heat. Beat smooth. Stir in remaining ingredients. Cover with waxed paper and cool. Spread about ¼ cup almond cream filling on unbrowned side of each crepe. Roll up and place in 8 x 12-inch baking dish. Brush with 2 table-spoons melted butter. Bake at 350 degrees for 20 to 25 minutes or until hot. To prepare brandied cherry sauce, heat together all ingredients. To serve, spoon brandied cherry sauce over warm crepes. Heat 3 to 4 table-spoons brandy. Pour over sauce and flame.

Joyce Wilson Carson (Mrs. Robert W.)

Almond Tart
Serves 6 to 8

Crust
1 cup flour
½ cup unsalted butter, at room
  temperature
1 tablespoon sugar

Salt
1½ teaspoons water
1 tablespoon vanilla extract

Filling
¾ cup sugar
¾ cup whipping cream
1 teaspoon Grand Marnier
  or brandy

Almond extract
Salt
1 cup sliced almonds

To prepare crust, combine flour, butter, sugar and salt in electric mixer or food processor. Beat on low speed until mixture is the consistency of coarse meal. Mix vanilla with water. With mixer running, gradually add to flour, blending lightly. Do not overmix. Gather dough into a ball. Press into a 9-inch tart pan. Position oven rack to lower third of oven. Bake at 400 degrees until set, about 10 to 15 minutes. Remove from oven. Reduce temperature to 350 degrees for tart filling. To prepare filling, combine sugar, cream, liqueur, a few drops of almond extract and salt in small bowl. Beat until slightly thickened. Stir in almonds, mixing well. Pour into tart crust and bake at 350 degrees for 40 to 45 minutes or until golden brown. Let cool completely and cut into wedges.
Susan Jennings Robertson (Mrs. Mark A.)

Apple Crunch
Serves 4 to 6

3 pounds tart apples
Lemon juice
1 cup brown sugar or 1 cup
  white sugar or half of each
  to make 1 cup

1 cup flour
Cinnamon
½ cup unsalted butter
Vanilla ice cream or whipping
  cream, whipped (optional)

Butter a 1½-quart souffle dish or a 2-quart baking dish. Peel and core apples and slice them into dish. Sprinkle with a little lemon juice. Mix together sugar and flour. Add cinnamon to taste. Sprinkle on top of apples. Cut butter into small pieces and distribute over the topping. Bake at 350 degrees for 1 hour. Serve warm plain or topped with vanilla ice cream or whipped cream.
Janita Guffey Ruth (Mrs. Charles)

Cinnamon Apples
Serves 4 to 6

2 cups water
4 cups sugar
1 cup cinnamon red hots
Red food coloring
4 to 6 Jonathan apples, peeled
 and partially cored

Raisins
Nuts, chopped
Small marshmallows, cut
 in half

Bring water, sugar, red hots and food coloring to boil. Reduce heat to low. Put in apples. Cook until tender, turning gently now and then with wooden spoon to color evenly. Plump raisins by soaking in boiling water. Drain. Add raisins, chopped nuts and small marshmallows to center of apples. Chill. Before serving, tuck small green leaf in top. Pretty on big platter or served in individual dishes.
Marty Johnson Margo (Mrs. Robert C.)

Blue Ribbon Banana Pudding
Serves 15

2 3¾-ounce boxes instant
 French vanilla pudding
4 cups milk
1 8-ounce carton sour cream
1 8-ounce container frozen
 whipped topping, thawed

1 14-ounce can sweetened
 condensed milk (optional)
Vanilla wafers
Ripe bananas

In a large bowl mix pudding and milk. Beat until pudding sets. Add sour cream. Blend well. Add whipped topping. Blend well. Add sweetened condensed milk, if desired, and blend well. Line a 9 x 13-inch pan with vanilla wafers. Slice bananas over wafers. Pour pudding over bananas and wafers. Chill for at least 1 hour before serving.
Suzanne Peterson Pardue (Mrs. W. Dave)

English Plum Pudding
Serves 12

3 cups finely ground bread
  crumbs
1 pound choice kidney suet,
  finely ground (order from
  butcher)
1 cup flour
1 cup sugar
1 box Muscat raisins

1 box currants
1/4 pound candied orange peel
1/4 pound candied lemon peel
1 teaspoon cinnamon
1 teaspoon nutmeg
2 eggs
Milk to moisten

Pudding Sauce
1 egg
1 tablespoon flour
1/2 cup sugar

Approximately 2 cups hot milk
1 tablespoon butter
1 tablespoon vanilla

Mix pudding ingredients very well with hands in large mixing bowl. Butter well 2. 1½-quart earthenware bowls. Pack mixture hard into bowls. Seal the top tightly with a piece of cheesecloth tied with string. On top of that, tie a piece of butcher paper. Put bowls on rack in bottom of large pan with boiling water. (Do not let water cover or come to the rim of the lid of the bowl.) Boil for 5 hours. Store in cool place for up to 2 to 3 months. On day to be served, boil again for 5 hours. Shake gently onto holiday plate. Serve with pudding sauce. To prepare pudding sauce beat egg until fluffy. Add flour and sugar. Scald milk. Add a small amount of milk to above mixture. Add egg mixture to scalded milk. Stir constantly until thick. Add butter and vanilla when ready to serve.

This recipe came from my great grandmother who brought it with her on her honeymoon from England in 1880.
Libby Sadler Steakley (Mrs. Steven R.)

French Mints
Yields 18

1/2 pound butter
2 cups powdered sugar
4 eggs
4 1-ounce squares
  unsweetened chocolate

2 teaspoons vanilla extract
1/2 teaspoon peppermint
  extract
1 1/2 cups vanilla wafer crumbs
Maraschino cherries, cut
  in half

Cream butter and sugar well. Add eggs one at a time, beating 5 minutes after each addition. Melt and add chocolate. Blend in vanilla and peppermint extracts. Place 18 fluted paper liners in muffin tins and place 1 teaspoon of vanilla wafer crumbs in bottom of each. Fill each cup 2/3 full with chocolate mixture. Sprinkle top with crumbs and top each with 1/2 maraschino cherry. Freeze.
Sarah Powell Newcomb (Mrs. Ralph S.)

Lady Finger Delight
Serves 12 to 14

24 lady fingers (sponge cakes)
1 4-ounce bar Sweet German
  Chocolate
1/2 cup sugar
1/4 cup water

Chocolate
4 eggs, separated
1 cup butter, creamed
1 cup powdered sugar

Line bottom and sides of casserole with 2/3 of ladyfingers. Cook German chocolate, granulated sugar and water in double boiler until melted and blended. Separate 4 eggs and add beaten yolks slowly. Cool this mixture quickly. Cream butter and add powdered sugar and beaten egg whites to chocolate mixture. Pour half of chocolate mixture into bowl, add remaining ladyfingers, cover with rest of chocolate. Refrigerate at least 24 hours.
Sandy Bryan Trudgeon (Mrs. Jon H.)

Strawberry Chocolate Cheese Tarts
Serves 8

8 tart shells, purchased or
made with favorite pie
crust recipe
2 1-ounce squares semi-sweet
chocolate, melted
1 8-ounce package cream
cheese, room temperature
1 cup powdered sugar

½ cup whipping cream
¼ cup orange liqueur
½ teaspoon vanilla extract
1 pint strawberries, hulled and
cut in half lengthwise
½ cup raspberry jam, melted
and strained (optional)

Bake tart shells at 400 degrees for 10 minutes or until golden. Spread a very thin layer of chocolate over bottoms of baked, cooled tart shells. Allow chocolate to set by placing it into the refrigerator while you prepare the rest of the recipe. Beat cream cheese and sugar together until fluffy and completely smooth. Add cream, liqueur and vanilla. Spoon cheese mixture over the chocolate-covered shells. Arrange sliced berries over the top of cheese mixture in a pretty pattern. A simple one is to place wide end of berries against rim of tarts, with small ends pointing in to form a pinwheel. A single whole berry can be placed in the center of the pinwheel. Allow tarts to become firm in the refrigerator and then spread a thin coat of jam over each, if desired. Keep refrigerated and serve the same day. Strawberries can be dipped in melted chocolate first to add more chocolate to dessert, or 1 or 2 chocolate dipped berries can be served on the side.
Beth Matthews McMullan (Mrs. Harry)

Oreo Sundae
Serves 20

1 16-ounce package
Oreo cookies
½ cup butter, softened
½ gallon vanilla ice cream

8 ounces Hershey's
chocolate syrup
Chopped nuts

Crush Oreo cookies into crumbs. Mix Oreos with softened butter, reserving ¼ of crumbs for topping. Spread in a 9 x 13-inch pan to form bottom layer. Spread ice cream over Oreo layer. Then pour Hershey syrup over ice cream. Sprinkle nuts and last ¼ of crushed Oreos on top. Put in freezer until ready to serve.
Margaret Patzer Holdridge (Mrs. Curtis)

Chocolate Mint Freeze
Serves 8 to 10

Crust
1¼ cups finely crushed
  vanilla wafers

4 tablespoons butter, melted

Filling
1 quart peppermint ice cream,
  softened
½ cup butter
2 1-ounce squares
  unsweetened chocolate

3 egg yolks, well beaten
1½ cups powdered sugar
1 teaspoon vanilla extract
½ cup chopped pecans
3 egg whites, beaten stiff

To prepare crust, toss 1 cup crushed wafers with 4 tablespoons melted butter. Press into a 9 x 9-inch pan. Spread with softened peppermint ice cream. Freeze. Melt ½ cup butter over low heat. Add chocolate. Gradually stir in egg yolks, powdered sugar, vanilla and nuts. Mix until smooth. Cool thoroughly. Beat egg whites until stiff. Fold chocolate mixture into egg whites. Spread over frozen ice cream. Top with remaining ¼ cup crumbs. Freeze. When ready to serve, let thaw a few minutes.
Christa Schwab Chain (Mrs. John W.)

Pink Arctic Freeze
Serves 8 to 10

2 3-ounce packages cream
  cheese
2 tablespoons Miracle Whip
  salad dressing
2 tablespoons sugar
1 16-ounce can cranberry
  sauce

1 cup crushed pineapple,
  drained
½ cup chopped walnuts
½ pint whipping cream,
  whipped

Soften cream cheese, blend in salad dressing and sugar. Add cranberry sauce, crushed pineapple and nuts. Fold in whipped cream. Pour into 8½ x 4½ x 2½-inch loaf pan. Freeze firm for 6 hours or overnight. To serve, let stand at room temperature about 15 minutes, slice and serve.
Carla Anderson Faulkner (Mrs. R. Barrett)

Dolce Torinese (Chilled Chocolate Loaf)
Serves 8 to 12

Vegetable oil
8 ounces semi-sweet
   chocolate chips
¼ cup Meyers dark rum
½ pound unsalted butter,
   softened
2 tablespoons sugar
2 egg yolks
1½ cups ground blanched
   almonds

2 egg whites
Salt
12 Lorna Doone butter cookies
   broken into 5 or 6 pieces
   each
Powdered sugar
Sweetened whipped cream
   (optional)

Lightly grease the bottom and sides of a 1½-quart loaf pan with vegetable oil. Place a piece of plastic wrap on bottom of the pan to ease the loaf out when chilled. In the top of a double boiler over hot water, melt chocolate chips with rum. Cool slightly. In a food processor or mixer, cream butter until light and fluffy. Beat in sugar and egg yolks, one at a time. Stir in chocolate mixture and add ground almonds. In a separate small bowl, beat egg whites and pinch of salt until soft peaks form. With a rubber spatula fold into chocoalte mixture. Gently fold in the butter cookie bits. Spoon the mixture into loaf pan and smooth the top to spread evenly. Cover the top with plastic wrap directly on it. Refrigerate for at least 4 hours or until the loaf is firm. Unmold 1 hour before serving. Smooth top and sides and return to refrigerator. Just before serving, sieve powdered sugar over top. Serve with whipped cream.
Linda Aguilar Wegener (Mrs. Dick R.)

Myrtle's Slush
Serves 12 to 15

1 6-ounce can frozen
   lemonade concentrate
1 6-ounce can frozen orange
   juice concentrate
1 20-ounce can pineapple
   chunks with juice

1 16-ounce package frozen
   strawberries, sliced
3 bananas, diced
1 cup sugar (optional)

Mix juices with water as directed on can. Mix in remaining ingredients and stir. This may be frozen in individual cups or served as is. Garnish with fruit.
Carole Jo Kerley Evans (Mrs. J. Patrick)

Ice Cream Topping
Serves 4 to 6

12 ounces raspberries, fresh
or frozen
1/2 cup sugar

3 tablespoons Grand Marnier
1 pint fresh strawberries,
washed and hulled

Puree first 3 ingredients in food processor or blender. Fold in fresh strawberries. Chill at least 1 hour. Serve over vanilla ice cream.
Candy Hickman Ainsworth (Mrs. Charles)

The Work, Rest and Play Topping
Serves 2

2 Mars bars
Drop of water
2 jiggers brandy

2 tablespoons whipping
cream
2 scoops vanilla ice cream

Chop Mars bars into 1-inch cubes. Melt the pieces in a small saucepan over low heat with a drop of water added. Remove from heat when completely melted. Flame brandy and pour into melted Mars bars mixture. Stir in whipping cream and pour mixture over each scoop of ice cream. Wait a moment for the toffee in the Mars mixture to become gooey and serve.
Susan Esco Crain (Mrs. R. Dean)

Apple Sorbet
Yields 1 quart

3/4 cup sugar
3/4 cup water
3 large Granny Smith apples
2 tablespoons lemon juice

2 tablespoons applejack
or brandy
Cinnamon
Nutmeg

Combine sugar and water in a small heavy saucepan over medium heat and simmer until sugar is completely dissolved. Chill well. Peel, core and puree the apples. Combine apple puree with sugar syrup and other ingredients. Freeze in an ice cream freezer. You may also freeze in ice cube trays and then process in food processor or blender and refreeze.

A good "palate cleanser" between courses or a light summer dessert.
Beth Matthews McMullan (Mrs. Harry)

Honey Ice Cream
Yields 2 quarts

3 eggs
2 cups milk
¾ cup honey

1 tablespoon vanilla extract
1 quart whipping cream

Mix eggs, milk, honey and vanilla in a saucepan. Cook over medium heat until thick, stirring constantly. Let cool. Add cream. Fill ice cream freezer about ¾ full and freeze according to freezer directions or about 14 minutes. In the summer top with fresh raspberries, peaches or strawberries.

Joan Warren Yoakam (Mrs. Coler, Jr.)

Peppermint Ice Cream
Yields 1 gallon

1 16-ounce bag marshmallows
1 quart milk
1 pound peppermint candy

1 pint half and half
1 15-ounce can evaporated
    milk
Milk

In a large heavy pan melt together marshmallows, milk and candy over low heat. Cool. This part may be done ahead. When ready to make ice cream, add half and half and evaporated milk to marshmallow mixture. Pour into a 1-gallon freezer container. Fill the container to within 1 inch of the top with additional milk. Freeze according to freezer directions.

Janita Guffey Ruth (Mrs. Charles)

Mimi's Apricot Ice Cream
Yields 1 gallon

2 large cans apricots with juice
    or peaches
Juice of 1 lemon
Grated lemon rind

1 cup sugar
1 quart half and half
½ pint whipping cream
⅛ teaspoon salt

Blend 2 large cans apricots in blender or food processor until smooth. Add remaining ingredients and pour into ice cream freezer. Freeze according to freezer directions. After freezer stops, let ice cream ripen for 1 hour.

Catherine Coburn Langford (Mrs. Dennis)

Heavenly Chocolate Ice Cream
Yields 1 gallon

21 ounces Milky Way or
Snickers candy bars
1 14-ounce can Eagle Brand
sweetened condensed milk

Approximately 3 quarts milk
1 5½-ounce can chocolate
syrup

Combine candy and sweetened condensed milk in a large saucepan. Cook over low heat, stirring constantly, until candy melts. Cool, stirring occasionally. Add 1 quart milk to candy mixture. Beat until well blended. Pour mixture into 1-gallon ice cream freezer. Stir in chocolate syrup. Add enough milk to fill freezer container to within 4 inches from the top. Freeze according to freezer directions.

Carole Jo Kerley Evans (Mrs. J. Patrick)   *Janita Guffey Ruth (Mrs. Charles)*

Rich Lemon Ice Cream
Yields 1 gallon

4 lemons, sliced very thin
1½ cups fresh lemon juice,
about 6 lemons
4 cups sugar

1 quart whipping cream
1 quart half and half
Milk

Soak lemon slices, lemon juice and sugar overnight. Stir occasionally to form a syrup. Remove half of the rinds. Chop very fine the remaining rinds and return to the syrup. Combine creams and syrup in ice cream freezer container. Add enough milk to fill to line on freezer. Freeze according to freezer directions. Divine!

Ginger Parker Johnson (Mrs. William J.)

Peanut Butter Chocolate Chip Ice Cream
Yields 1 gallon

6 eggs, separated
2 cups sugar
1 tablespoon vanilla extract
1 pint whipping cream

1 pint half and half
12 ounces peanut butter
1 12-ounce package
mini-chocolate chips
Milk

Beat egg whites and yolks separately and then fold together. Add sugar, vanilla, cream and half and half. Add peanut butter. Pour into ice cream freezer. Put in paddle. Add chocolate chips and milk as needed. Freeze according to freezer directions.

Ranell Bules Brown (Mrs. Steve M.)

Chocolate Covered Marshmallows
Yields 50 to 40

1 18-ounce package chocolate
   chips
1 14-ounce can Eagle Brand
   sweetened condensed milk
1 7-ounce jar or 2 cups
   marshmallow cream

Salt
1 teaspoon vanilla extract
1 cup chopped pecans
1 package large marshmallows

Melt chocolate chips over low heat. Mix Eagle Brand milk and marsh-mallow cream together. Add dash of salt and vanilla. Add to chocolate. Place pecans and marshmallows in a large bowl. Pour chocolate mixture over. Stir until all are coated. Use your hands to accomplish this properly. Place each individually coated marshmallow on waxed paper. Allow to dry overnight. Wrap individually in foil squares and store in covered container or plastic bags in refrigerator.
Susan Esco Crain (Mrs. R. Dean)

Popcorn Balls
Yields 24

1 cup brown sugar
1 cup white sugar
1 cup white Karo syrup
1/2 cup sweet butter or
   margarine

2 1/2 gallons popped popcorn
1 1/4 teaspoons salt
1 1/2 cups pecans, sliced
1 1/2 cups Brazil nuts, sliced

Mix sugars and add syrup. Add butter and cook over low heat until butter melts. Do not overcook or syrup will be too hard. Shake popcorn with salt in paper bag. Put popcorn into dry dish pan. When syrup spins a thread, pour a small amount over popcorn. Stir well to get popcorn well coated. Add nuts and remaining syrup. Continue to stir well. When all the syrup is mixed, butter hands lightly with margarine and form into balls. If they don't stick well at first, let cool a little. Don't press too hard or balls will be hard to eat.
Bobbie Durand Rucks (Mrs. Joseph G.)

Amaretto Truffles
Yields 1 dozen

8 1-ounce squares semi-sweet
baking chocolate
1/4 cup amaretto
2 tablespoons strong coffee
8 tablespoons unsalted butter

1 tablespoon vanilla extract
3/4 cup pulverized vanilla
wafers or butter cookies
1/2 cup powdered cocoa
1/2 cup powdered sugar

Melt baking chocolate, amaretto and coffee in a double boiler for 5 minutes or until perfectly smooth. Remove from the heat and add butter, vanilla and cookies. Set pan in cold water and ice and beat until firm. When firm, form into small balls. Combine cocoa and powdered sugar in a blender or food processor. Next roll the truffles in the mixture and put in small individual paper cups. Cover and keep refrigerated until served.

Laurie Kennedy McCann (Mrs. James K.)

Chocolate Peanut Butter Balls
Yields 5 dozen

2 cups chunky peanut butter
1/2 cup margarine
1 1-pound box powdered
sugar
3 cups Rice Krispies

1 stick paraffin
1 6-ounce package chocolate
chips
1 8-ounce Hershey bar

Melt peanut butter and margarine in a saucepan. Add powdered sugar and mix well. Add Rice Krispies and mix. Shape into 1-inch balls. Melt paraffin, chocolate chips and Hershey bar together. Dip each ball in chocolate mixture and cool on waxed paper.

Linda Tresenwriter Cheatham
(Mrs. James, Jr.)

Mary Frances Hart Reeves
(Mrs. William George)

Candied Beer Nuts
Yields 4 cups

4 cups raw peanuts
2 cups sugar

1 cup water
Salt

Mix together first 3 ingredients and boil until liquid is gone. Spread on cookie sheet and salt to taste. Bake at 300 degrees for 15 minutes. Turn, salt and bake for an additional 15 minutes.

Linda Tresenwriter Cheatham (Mrs. James E., Jr.)

Sugared Pecans
Yields 4 cups

1 cup sugar
½ cup half and half
½ teaspoon salt

1½ teaspoons vanilla
2½ cups pecan halves

Combine sugar and half and half in a large heavy saucepan. Gently boil to soft ball stage or 236 degrees on candy thermometer. Remove pan from heat and add remaining ingredients. Stir until sugar coating turns milky white. Pour mixture out onto foil. Let cool and then separate into pieces. Candy will harden as it cools.

Janita Guffey Ruth (Mrs. Charles)

White Fudge
Yields 64 squares

1½ cups whole pecans
1 tablespoon butter
2 teaspoons salt

2 3-ounce packages cream cheese
1 1-pound box powdered sugar

Toast pecans in butter and salt. Drain on paper towels, if necessary, and cool. Warm cream cheese in large saucepan until soft, but not melted. Remove from heat. Add powdered sugar and beat in pan until smooth. Batter will be thick. Stir in pecans and spread in a buttered 8-inch square pan. Refrigerate until ready to serve.

Janie Gilbert Axton (Mrs. Jon)

Sweetpea's Fudge
Yields 24 pieces

2 cups sugar
10 marshmallows
1 5⅓-ounce can evaporated milk

1 16-ounce package chocolate chips
6 tablespoons margarine
1 cup pecan pieces

Stir sugar, marshmallows and milk in a pan over medium heat. Bring to a boil and cook 5 minutes. Remove from heat and stir in chocolate chips and margarine. Stir until melted. Add pecans. Pour into greased 9 x 9-inch pan. Let set and cut into squares.

Marty Johnson Margo (Mrs. Robert)

Almond Toffee

²/₃ cup butter
½ cup sugar
⅓ cup water
½ teaspoon salt

²/₃ cup slivered almonds,
  blanched
¼ teaspoon baking soda
½ cup chocolate chips
½ cup chopped pecans

Combine butter, sugar, water and salt in saucepan. Cook over low heat, stirring constantly until it boils. Cook without stirring to 236 degrees on candy thermometer or soft ball stage. Add blanched almonds. Continue cooking to 275 degrees or soft crack stage, stirring constantly. Remove from heat. Stir in baking soda. Turn out onto greased baking sheet and spread to ¼-inch thickness. Immediately spread with chocolate chips then sprinkle with pecans. Cool and break into pieces.
Debbi Davidson Dale (Mrs. Mark)

Lillian's Pralines
Yields 35 pieces

1 cup buttermilk
2 cups sugar
1 teaspoon baking soda
½ cup butter

2½ cups pecan halves
Salt
1 teaspoon vanilla

Place buttermilk, sugar and soda in large, heavy saucepan. Bring to a boil on medium low heat, stirring constantly. Boil for 7 minutes, then add butter, pecan halves and dash of salt. Cook to soft ball stage or 236 degrees on candy thermometer. Take off heat and add vanilla. Beat with spoon until creamy. Quickly drop by teaspoons on waxed paper.
Andrea Samara Jones (Mrs. Johnny H., Jr.)

Etcetera

Equivalents
Substitutions
Index

Glossary

GLOSSARY: Collection of specialized terms with accompanying definitions. Measures, equivalents, metric, substitutions, cooking for a crowd, and more extra things you might find helpful when cooking.

Liquid Measure
Ounces to milliliters: multiply ounces by 29.57
Milliliters to ounces: multiply milliliters by 0.034
Quarts to liters: multiply quarts by 0.95
Liters to quarts: multiply liters by 1.057

Weighing
Ounces to grams: multiply ounces by 28.35
Grams to ounces: multiply grams by 0.035

In the metric system, solids are weighed and liquids are measured. This enables one to determine the amount to produce amount one needs to cook.

Measurement By Length
Inches to centimeters: multiply inches by 28.35
Centimeters to inches: multiply centimeters by 0.39

Oven Settings or Temperature
Centigrade to Fahrenheit: multiply by 9, divide by 5, add 32
Fahrenheit to Centigrade: subtract 32, multiply by 5, divide by 9

Terms

A few grains or a dash	Less than 1/8 teaspoon
Pinch	As much as can be taken between tip of finger and thumb
Speck	Less than 1/8 teaspoon
1 jigger	1½ to 2 ounces
1 minim	1 drop
10 drops	Dash
6 dashes	1 teaspoon

Can Sizes

Can Size	Weight	Approximate Cups
8 ounces	8 ounces	1
Picnic	10½ to 12 ounces	1¼
12 ounces	12 ounces	1½
No. 300	14 to 16 ounces	1¾
No. 303	16 to 17 ounces	2
No. 2	20 ounces	2½
No. 2½	1 pound 13 ounces or 27 to 29 ounces	3½
No. 3	32 ounces	4
No. 3 can or 46 ounces	3 pounds 3 ounces or 1 quart 14 fluid ounces	5¾
No. 10	6½ pounds to 7 pounds 5 ounces	12⅓
Sweetened condensed milk	14 ounces	1⅓
Evaporated milk	5.33 ounces or 13 ounces	⅔ 1⅔

Baking Pan Sizes

Rectangular Cake Pans

8 x 8 x 2-inch	8 cups
9 x 9 x 1¾-inch	8 cups
9 x 9 x 2-inch	10 cups
11 x 7 x 1½-inch	8 cups
13 x 9 x 2-inch	14 cups
15 x 10 x 1-inch	10 cups

Rectangular Glass Cake Pans/Casseroles

10 x 6 x 1¾-inch	7½ cups
11¾ x 7½ x ¾-inch	10 cups
13½ x 8¾ x 1¾-inch	13 cups

Pie Plates

8 x 1¼-inch	3 cups level with top; 4 to 4½ cups mounded
9 x 1½-inch	4 cups level with top; 5 to 6 cups mounded
10 x 1½-inch	6 cups level with top; 7 to 8 cups mounded

Loaf Pans

7⅜ x 3⅝ x 2¼-inch	4 cups
8½ x 4½ x ½-inch	6 cups
9 x 5 x 3-inch	8 cups

Tube Pans

7½ x 3-inch bundt pan	6 cups
9 x 3½-inch fancy tube or bundt pan	9 cups
9 x 3½-inch angel cake pan	12 cups
10 x 3¾-inch bundt pan	12 cups
10 by 4-inch kugelhupf pan	16 cups
10 x 4-inch angel cake pan	18 cups

Springform Pans

8 x 3-inch	12 cups
9 x 3-inch	16 cups

Ring Molds

8½ x 2¼-inch	4½ cups
9¼ x 2¾-inch	8 cups

Charlotte Mold

6 x 4¼-inch	7½ cups

Brioche Pan

9½ x 3¼-inch	8 cups

TIP: Use these measurements to determine if a pan can be used for a casserole. Example: If a recipe calls for a 4-cup baking dish, an 8-inch cake pan or 9-inch pie plate could be used.

Estimating Quantities for Cocktail Buffets, Teas and Parties

Allow 10 bites per person for canapes, sandwiches, etc.
Allow 2 buns per person when using miniature buns for sandwiches.
Allow 2½ bar cookies per person.
Allow 2 gallons of punch for 50 people.

Bar Checklist for Cocktail Party for 25

1 quart bourbon
1 fifth Dubonnet, red or white
1 quart gin
1 quart light rum
1 fifth rye or Canadian whiskey
2 quarts Scotch
1 fifth dry sherry
1 fifth dry vermouth
2 quarts vodka
6 large bottles white wine (refrigerated overnight)
4 quarts club soda
2 quarts diet soda
2 quarts ginger ale
4 large bottles mineral water (example: Perrier)
4 quarts tonic
35 pounds ice, this includes enough to chill the wine
2 glasses per person
Cut lemons and limes
Soft drinks and bottled water served in wine glasses make the non-drinker feel less conspicuous

Cooking in Quantities

Quantities for Approximately 50 People

Food

Bread	6 1-pound loaves 100 miniature rolls for a cocktail buffet
Chicken salad	2½ gallons
Lettuce	2½ to 3 heads for sandwiches 10 to 12 heads for salad
Meats	A minimum of 4 ounces per person 2 18- to 20-pound turkeys 1 16- to 18-pound ham 18 pounds hamburger meat 16 to 18 pounds roast beef 13 pounds of frankfurters 15 pounds fish, fillets or steaks 30 pounds chicken for baking
Potato Salad	2¼ gallons
Tomatoes	10 pounds
Vegetables	About 6 quarts of cooked vegetables (fresh or canned)

Beverages

Coffee	1 to 1¼ pounds (add to 3 gallons water)
Iced Tea	3 gallons (⅙ pound tea and 3 gallons water)
Punch	2 gallons (5-ounce servings)

Accompaniments

Butter	1 pound
Cream	1½ pints
Lemons	6 lemons, cut into 8 wedges

Mayonnaise	2 quarts
Sugar	¾ pound granulated

Desserts

Cake	3 layer cakes or 3 angel food cakes (18 to 20 slices per cake) or 1 12- by 20-inch sheet cake, cut in 2-inch squares
Cookies	11 dozen (allow about 2½ per person)
Ice cream	2 gallons
Watermelon	75 pounds

Whipping cream 1 quart, whipped (if needed for topping)

NOTE: These amounts are approximate. Divide or multiply quantities as needed for serving different amounts of people.

Dry Measure Volume Equivalents

United States	Equivalents	Metric
1 pint	2 cups	.551 liters
1 quart	2 pints	1.1 liters
1 peck	8 quarts	8.81 liters
1 bushel	4 pecks	35.24 liters

Weight Equivalents

United States	Equivalents	Metric
1 ounce	16 drams	30 grams
1 pound	16 ounces	454 grams
2.20 pounds	35.2 ounces	1 kilo (1,000 grams)

Measurements and Equivalents in the United States and Metric

In the United States it is customary to measure ingredients such as flour, sugar and shortening in the same manner as liquid measure. Be careful not to confuse dry measure pints and quarts with liquid measure pints and quarts. Dry measure is used for measuring raw fruits and vegetables when dealing with fairly large quantities.

Liquid Measure and Volume Equivalents

United States	Equivalents	Metric
60 drops	1 teaspoon (1/6 ounce)	5 milliliters
1 teaspoon	1/3 tablespoon (1/6 ounce)	5 milliliters
1 1/2 teaspoons	1/2 tablespoon (1/4 ounce)	7.5 milliliters
3 teaspoons	1 tablespoon (1/2 ounce)	15 milliliters
1 tablespoon	3 teaspoons (1/2 ounce)	15 milliliters
2 tablespoons	1/8 cup (1 ounce)	30 milliliters
4 tablespoons	1/4 cup (2 ounces)	60 milliliters
5 1/3 tablespoons	1/3 cup (2.6 ounces)	80 milliliters
8 tablespoons	1/2 cup (4 ounces)	120 milliliters
10 2/3 tablespoons	2/3 cup (5.3 ounces)	160 milliliters
12 tablespoons	3/4 cup (6 ounces)	180 milliliters
16 tablespoons	1 cup (8 ounces)	240 milliliters
1/3 cup	5 tablespoons plus 1 teaspoon (2.65 ounces)	89 milliliters
1/6 cup	2 tablespoons plus 2 teaspoons (1.3 ounces)	55 milliliters

United States	Equivalents	Metric
¼ cup	4 tablespoons (2 ounces)	60 milliliters
⅜ cup	6 tablespoons (or ¼ cup plus 2 tablespoons) (3 ounces)	90 milliliters
½ cup	8 tablespoons (4 ounces)	120 milliliters
⅝ cup	10 tablespoons (or ½ cup plus 2 tablespoons) (5 ounces)	150 milliliters
⅔ cup	10 tablespoons plus 2 teaspoons (5.3 ounces)	177 milliliters
¾ cup	12 tablespoons (6 ounces)	180 milliliters
⅞ cup	¾ cup plus 2 tablespoons (7 ounces)	210 milliliters
1 cup	16 tablespoons (½ pint) (8 ounces)	240 milliliters
2 cups	1 pint (16 ounces)	480 milliliters or .473 liters
1 quart	2 pints, or 4 cups (32 ounces)	960 milliliters or .95 liters
1.06 quarts	33.8 ounces	1 liter
1 gallon	4 quarts (128 ounces)	3.8 liters

Food Yields—Equivalents

	This Much	Equals This Much
Apples	1 pound (3 medium)	3 cups sliced
Bacon	1 pound, thin sliced	24 slices
Bananas	1 pound (3 medium)	2½ cups sliced, 2 cups mashed
Beans		
Dried	1 pound (2½ cups)	6 to 7 cups cooked
Green	1 pound	2 cups cut
Bread	1 slice from sandwich loaf	1 ounce
Bread Crumbs		
Dry	1 slice bread	⅓ cup
Soft	1 slice bread	¾ cup
Butter	1 pound (4 sticks)	2 cups
or Margarine	2 sticks	1 cup
	1 stick	½ cup
	½ stick	¼ cup
Cabbage	1 head (about 1 pound)	4 cups shredded
Carrots	1 pound	3½ cups shredded
Celery	1 medium rib	½ cup sliced
Cheese	1 pound American or Cheddar	4 cups grated
	4 ounces American or Cheddar	1 cup grated
	1 pound cottage cheese	2 cups
	½ pound cottage cheese	1 cup (8 ounces)
	½ pound cream cheese	1 cup (8 ounces)
	6 ounces cream cheese	12 tablespoons (¾ cup)
Chicken	3½ pound fryer, cooked	4 cups chopped
Chocolate	1 ounce	1 square or 4 tablespoons, grated
Cocoa	1 pound	4 cups

	This Much	**Equals This Much**
Coconut	1 pound 1 3½-ounce can flaked	5 cups, shredded 1⅓ cups
Coffee	1 pound	80 tablespoons (makes 40 to 45 cups perked)
Cookie crumbs		
Vanilla wafers	22 wafers	1 cup fine crumbs
Chocolate wafers	19 wafers	1 cup fine crumbs
Corn	4 medium ears	1 cup, when cut from cob
Cornmeal	1 pound	3 cups
Cornstarch	1 pound	3 cups
Cracker crumbs		
Saltine	24 crackers	1 cup fine crumbs
Graham	14 crackers	1 cup fine crumbs
Eggs	5 large, 6 medium or 7 small whole eggs White of 6 to 7 large eggs Yolks of 11 to 12 large eggs	1 cup yolks and whites 1 cup egg whites 1 cup egg yolks
Flour		
All purpose	1 pound	4 cups sifted
Cake	1 pound	4¾ cups sifted
Whole wheat	1 pound	3½ cups unsifted
Green Pepper	1 large	1 cup diced
Honey	1 pound	1⅓ cups
Lemon	1 medium	2 to 3 tablespoons juice 2 to 3 teaspoons grated rind

257

Superlatives

	This Much	Equals This Much
Lime	1 medium	1½ to 2 tablespoons juice
Marshmallows	¼ pound	16 regular size or 160 miniature size
Milk Products		
Evaporated	5.33-ounce can	⅔ cup
	14.5-ounce can	1⅔ cups
Sweetened condensed	14-ounce can	1⅓ cups
Cream, heavy or whipping	1 cup	2 cups whipped
Mushrooms	1 pound	5 cups sliced
Onion	1 medium	½ cup chopped
	1 pound	3 to 3½ cups diced
Orange	1 medium	⅓ to ½ cup juice or 1½ to 2 tablespoons grated
Nuts, shelled		
Almonds	1 pound	3¼ cups
Peanuts	1 pound	3¼ cups
Pecans	1 pound	4½ cups or 3¾ cups chopped
Walnuts	1 pound	4½ cups or 3⅔ cups chopped
Pasta		
Macaroni	8 ounces (2 cups, uncooked)	4 cups cooked
Noodles	8 ounces (3 cups, uncooked)	6 cups cooked
Spaghetti	8 ounces (2 cups, uncooked)	4 cups cooked

	This Much	**Equals This Much**
Potatoes	1 medium	1/2 cup diced
	1 pound	4 medium potatoes
	1 pound	3 1/2 to 4 cups diced
	1 pound	about 2 cups mashed
Raisins	1 pound	3 cups
Rice	1 pound	2 1/2 cups uncooked
	1 cup	3 1/2 cups cooked
Strawberries	1 pint	2 cups sliced
Sugar		
Brown	1 pound	2 1/4 cups packed
Granulated	1 pound	2 cups
Powdered	1 pound	3 3/4 cups unsifted
Tomatoes	1 pound	3 to 4 medium
	1 pound	2 1/2 cups cooked

Equivalents are only estimates to help the cook have some idea of amounts to purchase. An accurate kitchen scale is a very useful item in assuring the success of a recipe by measuring accurately. Weighing of ingredients is one of the real values of the metric system.

Substitutions

SUBSTITUTION: One that takes the place of another; a replacement –
when you don't have ingredient recipe calls for.

Ingredient Called For:	Substitution:
Dry Ingredients	
1 teaspoon baking powder	1/2 teaspoon cream of tartar plus 1/4 teaspoon soda
1 square baking chocolate (1 ounce)	3 tablespoons cocoa plus 1 tablespoon butter or margarine
1 tablespoon cornstarch	3 tablespoons flour
1 cup cake flour	1 cup all-purpose flour minus 2 tablespoons
1 cup self-rising flour	1 cup all-purpose flour plus 1 teaspoon baking powder and 1/2 teaspoon salt
1 tablespoon tapioca	11/2 tablespoons all-purpose flour
1 package active dry yeast	1 cake compressed yeast
Sugars	
1 cup corn syrup	1 cup sugar plus 1/4 cup liquid
1 cup honey	11/4 cups sugar plus 1/4 cup liquid
1 tablespoon maple sugar	1 teaspoon white granulated sugar
1 cup maple sugar	1 cup brown sugar
1 cup molasses	1 cup honey
1 cup sugar	1 cup molasses plus 1/2 teaspoon soda*
1 cup sugar	1 cup honey plus 1/2 teaspoon soda*
1 cup sugar	1 cup maple syrup plus 1/4 cup corn syrup*

*Reduce liquid in recipe by 1/3 cup

Eggs

1 whole egg	2 egg yolks plus 1 tablespoon water
2 large eggs	3 small eggs

Dairy Products

1 cup butter	1 cup margarine
1 cup butter (in baking)	1 cup solid vegetable shortening plus 2 dashes salt
1 cup buttermilk	1 cup fresh milk plus 1 tablespoon vinegar or lemon juice
1 cup coffee cream	$7/8$ cup milk plus 3 tablespoons butter
1 cup commercial sour cream	1 cup evaporated milk plus 1 tablespoon lemon juice
1 cup half and half	$7/8$ cup milk plus $1\frac{1}{2}$ tablespoons butter
1 cup milk	1 cup buttermilk plus $1/2$ teaspoon soda
1 cup milk	$1/2$ cup evaporated milk plus $1/2$ cup water
1 cup milk	4 tablespoons dry whole milk plus 1 cup water
1 cup milk	1 cup skim milk plus 2 tablespoons butter or margarine
1 cup whipping cream	$1/3$ cup butter or margarine plus $3/4$ cup milk
1 cup yogurt	1 cup sour milk or buttermilk

Superlatives

Herbs, Spices and Condiments

1 tablespoon finely chopped fresh chives	1 teaspoon freeze dried chives
1 clove garlic	1 teaspoon garlic salt or ½ teaspoon garlic powder
1 tablespoon fresh herbs	1 teaspoon dried herbs
1 tablespoon fresh horseradish	2 tablespoons bottled horseradish
1 tablespoon prepared mustard	1 teaspoon dry mustard
2 tablespoons minced onion	1 teaspoon onion powder
1 small fresh onion or ¼ cup minced raw onion	1 tablespoon instant minced onion
2 sprigs fresh parsley	1 teaspoon dehydrated parsley flakes

Vegetables

1 pound fresh mushrooms	6 ounces canned mushrooms
1 cup fresh chopped tomato	½ cup tomato puree
1 15-ounce can tomato sauce	6-ounce can tomato paste plus 1 cup water
1 cup canned tomatoes	1⅓ cups fresh tomatoes, cut up and simmered 10 minutes
1 cup tomato juice	½ cup tomato sauce plus ½ cup water
1 cup tomato sauce	3 ounces tomato paste plus ½ cup water

Liquids

1 cup barbecue sauce	1 cup ketchup plus 2 tablespoons Worcestershire sauce
1 cup beef or chicken broth	1 beef or chicken bouillon cube plus 1 cup water
Juice of 1 lemon	3 tablespoons bottled lemon juice

1 teaspoon lemon juice	½ teaspoon vinegar (for cooking only, do not use for lemonade)
Juice of 1 orange	⅓ to ½ cup canned orange juice
1 tablespoon dry sherry	1 tablespoon dry vermouth

Baking Ingredients

1 6-ounce package or 1 cup semi-sweet chocolate pieces, or 6 1-ounce squares semi-sweet chocolate	6 tablespoons unsweetened cocoa plus 7 tablespoons sugar and ¼ cup shortening, butter or margarine
1 4-ounce bar sweet cooking chocolate	3 tablespoons unsweetened cocoa plus ¼ cup plus 1½ teaspoons sugar, and 2 tablespoons plus 2 teaspoons shortening, butter or margarine

Temperature Conversion

Fahrenheit to Celsius

Fahrenheit in degrees	Celsius in degrees
200	93
225	106
250	121
275	135
300	149
325	163
350	176
375	191
400	205
425	218
450	231
475	246
500	260
525	270
550	288

Superlatives

Reducing Recipes
Use exactly half the amount of each ingredient.

If the divided recipe calls for less than 1 egg, beat a whole egg. One tablespoon equals about ⅓ egg, 1½ tablespoons equals about ½ egg. (Leftover egg can be used later for sauces, scrambled eggs, etc.)

Baking pans used for half recipes of cakes, pies, etc. should measure about half the area of those for the whole recipe. Approximate baking time and oven temperature are the same.

Increasing Recipes
To double a recipe use exactly twice the amount of each ingredient. Add extra minute of beating for cakes.

If the increased recipe calls for uneven amounts of ingredients, it is a help to remember:

⅔ cup   equals   ½ cup plus 2⅔ tablespoons
⅝ cup   equals   ½ cup plus 2 tablespoons
⅞ cup   equals   ¾ cup plus 2 tablespoons

In baking, use twice as many pans of the same size indicated for the original recipe or a pan double in area. The batter will be the same depth in the pan and the same baking time and temperature may be maintained.

Tips
Coffee cannot be stretched, so use a standard coffee measure (2 level tablespoons equals a standard coffee measure). As a basis for a good cup of coffee, use 1 coffee measure of coffee to ¾ measuring cup of water. Use fresh water to make coffee or tea and serve as soon as possible.

Margarine may be substituted for butter in recipes but usually a bit of salt needs to be added to the margarine.

Use equal parts of creamed cottage cheese and buttermilk to make mock sour cream. Add small amount of lemon juice and whirl in blender.

To make canned vegetables such as green beans or peas taste better, drain the liquid into a saucepan and cook liquid until it is reduced by about half. Put vegetables in pan with liquid and heat. Add seasonings and butter.

INDEX

269

278

Superlatives
Junior League of Oklahoma City
P.O. Box 21418
Oklahoma City, OK 73156

Please send me _____ copies of **Superlatives** at the $17.50 mail order price, which includes all charges for postage, handling, and applicable sales taxes.

Enclosed is my check or money order in the amount of $_____

☐ Check here for free gift wrap.

Name_____

Address_____

City_____State_____Zip_____

Please make checks payable to Superlatives.

Superlatives
Junior League of Oklahoma City
P.O. Box 21418
Oklahoma City, OK 73156

Please send me _____ copies of **Superlatives** at the $17.50 mail order price, which includes all charges for postage, handling, and applicable sales taxes.

Enclosed is my check or money order in the amount of $_____

☐ Check here for free gift wrap.

Name_____

Address_____

City_____State_____Zip_____

Please make checks payable to Superlatives.

Superlatives
Junior League of Oklahoma City
P.O. Box 21418
Oklahoma City, OK 73156

Please send me _____ copies of **Superlatives** at the $17.50 mail order price, which includes all charges for postage, handling, and applicable sales taxes.

Enclosed is my check or money order in the amount of $_____

☐ Check here for free gift wrap.

Name_____

Address_____

City_____State_____Zip_____

Please make checks payable to Superlatives.

any stores in your area where you would like to have copies
atives available to you:

_____

_____

_____

_____

_____

_____

- -

Please list any stores in your area where you would like to have copies
of **Superlatives** available to you:

_____

_____

_____

_____

_____

_____

- -

Please list any stores in your area where you would like to have copies
of **Superlatives** available to you:

_____

_____

_____

_____

_____

_____

Superlatives
Junior League of Oklahoma City
P.O. Box 21418
Oklahoma City, OK 73156

Please send me _____ copies of **Superlatives** at the $17.50 mail order price, which includes all charges for postage, handling, and applicable sales taxes.

Enclosed is my check or money order in the amount of $_____

☐ Check here for free gift wrap.

Name_____

Address_____

City_____State_____Zip_____

Please make checks payable to Superlatives.

- -

Superlatives
Junior League of Oklahoma City
P.O. Box 21418
Oklahoma City, OK 73156

Please send me _____ copies of **Superlatives** at the $17.50 mail order price, which includes all charges for postage, handling, and applicable sales taxes.

Enclosed is my check or money order in the amount of $_____

☐ Check here for free gift wrap.

Name_____

Address_____

City_____State_____Zip_____

Please make checks payable to Superlatives.

- -

Superlatives
Junior League of Oklahoma City
P.O. Box 21418
Oklahoma City, OK 73156

Please send me _____ copies of **Superlatives** at the $17.50 mail order price, which includes all charges for postage, handling, and applicable sales taxes.

Enclosed is my check or money order in the amount of $_____

☐ Check here for free gift wrap.

Name_____

Address_____

City_____State_____Zip_____

Please make checks payable to Superlatives.

Please list any stores in your area where you would like to have copies
of **Superlatives** available to you:

_____

_____

_____

_____

_____

_____

- -

Please list any stores in your area where you would like to have copies
of **Superlatives** available to you:

_____

_____

_____

_____

_____

_____

- -

Please list any stores in your area where you would like to have copies
of **Superlatives** available to you:

_____

_____

_____

_____

_____

_____